WHAT
THEY
THINK
OF US

❑ ❑ ❑

International Perceptions of the United States since 9/11

Edited by David Farber

PRINCETON UNIVERSITY PRESS

PRINCETON AND OXFORD

Copyright © 2007 by Princeton University Press

Published by Princeton University Press, 41 William Street, Princeton, New Jersey 08540

In the United Kingdom: Princeton University Press, 3 Market Place,

Woodstock, Oxfordshire OX20 1SY

Requests for permission to reproduce material from this work should be sent to Permissions,

Princeton University Press.

Library of Congress Cataloging-in-Publication Data

What they think of us : international perceptions of the United States since 9/11 / edited by

David Farber.

p. cm.

Includes bibliographical references and index.

ISBN-13: 978-0-691-13025-5 (cloth : alk. paper)

ISBN-10: 0-691-13025-6 (cloth : alk. paper)

1. United States—Foreign relations—2001– 2. United States—Foreign public opinion. 3.

Anti-Americanism. 4. September 11 Terrorist Attacks, 2001—Influence. 5. War on Terrorism,

2001– I. Farber, David R.

E902.W475 2007

303.3'80973090511—dc22   2006025453

British Library Cataloging-in-Publication Data is available

This book has been composed in Minion Typeface

Printed on acid-free paper. ∞

pup.princeton.edu

Printed in the United States of America

1   3   5   7   9   10   8   6   4   2

CONTENTS

❑

CONTRIBUTORS

❏

Melani Budianta teaches literature and cultural studies in the Faculty of Humanities, University of Indonesia. She has spoken throughout Asia on her role as a women's activist and advocate of democracy. She writes on gender, culture, globalization, and postcolonial issues. She received her M.A. in American Studies at the University of Southern California and her Ph.D. in English at Cornell University.

Nur Bilge Criss is Professor of International Relations at Bilkent University, Ankara, Turkey. She received her Ph.D. at George Washington University. She has published extensively on Turkish foreign policy; her current scholarship focuses on Turkish-U.S. relations.

Fernando Escalante-Gonzalbo is Professor of International Relations at El Colegio de México. A prolific scholar, his books include La mirada de Dios: Estudios sobre la cultura del sufrimiento, published in translation in the United States as *In the Eyes of God: A Study on the Culture of Suffering.*

David Farber is Professor of History at Temple University. He specializes in recent U.S. history and has published several books including *Taken Hostage: The Iran Hostage Crisis and America's First Encounter with Radical Islam.* He was a senior Fulbright lecturer at the University of Indonesia, Jakarta, and Visiting Scholar at Keio University, Tokyo.

Yufan Hao is Professor of Political Science and the Robert Ho Professor of Chinese Studies at Colgate University. He received his B.A. at Heilongjiang University and his M.A. and Ph.D. at the Johns Hopkins University School of Advanced International Studies. His publications in China include *Power of the Moment: America and the World after 9/11, White House China Decision,* and *Constrained Engagement: Possible Trend of Bush's China Policy.*

Abdul Hadi al-Khalili is the founder of the Iraqi Cultural and Development Society, a NGO in Baghdad. He served as Professor and Head of the Department of Neurosurgery in the College of Medicine in Baghdad as well as a member of the National Research Committee of the Iraqi Ministry of Higher Education. He was a founding member of Arab Translation Council and served as an advisor to the World Health Organization, Eastern Mediterranean Region.

Olga Makhovskaya is a senior research scientist, specializing in cross-cultural psychology at the Institute of Psychology, Russian Academy of Sciences, Moscow, where she received her Ph.D. She is a well-known writer, speaker, policy analyst, and media personality in Russia, commenting frequently on Russian emigration to Europe and the United States. A recipient of major international grants and fellowships, she has, herself, worked extensively in the United States and Europe.

Ibrahim Al-Marashi is a faculty member at Koç University in Istanbul, Turkey. He completed his doctoral dissertation on the Iraqi invasion of Kuwait at the University of Oxford. His most infamous publication, "Iraq's Security and Intelligence Network: A Guide and Analysis," in the fall 2002 issue of the *Middle East Review of International Affairs,* was plagiarized by the British government prior to the 2003 Iraq war.

Federico Romero is Professor of North American Studies in the Department of History and Geography at the University of Florence. He received his Ph.D. from the University of Turin. He has been a National Research Council Visiting Fellow at Yale University and a Fulbright research scholar. His publications include *The United States and European Labor,* published in Italy and the United States, and dozens of articles published in Europe and the United States on the history of the Cold War, cross-border population movements, international labor politics, European perceptions of the United States, and American national politics.

Eric Shiraev is currently affiliated with George Mason University and is a research associate at the Institute for Russian, European, and Eurasian Studies at George Washington University. He received his Ph.D. at St. Petersburg University. He is a prolific writer on cross-cultural perceptions, political psychology and ethnic prejudice. His English-language books include *Anti-Americanism in Russia: From Stalin to Putin* (with Vlad Zubok); *Fears in Post-Communist Societies: A Comparative Perspective* (coedited with Vladimir Shlapentokh); and *Cross-Cultural Psychology* (with David Levy).

Lin Su is Associate Professor of Political Science in the Department of International Relations, School of International Studies, Renmin University of China, and is the Deputy Director for European Studies at Renmin. She was a Visiting Fellow at the School of English and American Studies, University of Sussex in 1994–95, and within the EU-China Higher Education Cooperation Programme visited the Centre for Applied Policy Research, Ludwig-Maximilians-University in April 1998. She is the coauthor of *Global Political Economy.*

Mauricio Tenorio-Trillo is Professor in the Department of History, University of Chicago, and an affiliate professor at the División de Historia, Centro de Investigación y Docencia Económicas (CIDE), Mexico City. He received his Ph.D. at Stanford University. He is a cultural historian who has written extensively about the formation of Mexican nationalism; currently, he is working on a history of American perceptions of Mexico.

PREFACE

❑

David Farber

AT ANDALAS University, Padang, Sumatra, the students were not overly impressed with MTV, KFC, or any of the other pleasures American culture served up in Indonesia. Nor were they particularly interested in the lecture topic offered by the American Fulbright lecturer (me) on the U.S. presidential election process. They wanted answers to harder questions. Several displayed a detailed knowledge of American policy toward Israel and wanted someone to explain why the American government hated Palestinians. The wording of many of the questions—often in English—made measured responses both necessary and difficult to formulate. The bad news, as I saw it, was that the students had little faith that the American government intended to do right by Islamic people. The good news was that they very much still wanted to talk about what they perceived to be the problematic relationship between the United States and themselves.

That conversation took place before the war in Iraq. I don't know if students in heavily Islamic Sumatra would be so patient and generous with an American Fulbright scholar today. Probably they would be; at the time I was struck by how overwhelmingly polite and friendly the students were even as they fiercely challenged American foreign policy. In so many parts of the world in which large majorities are appalled by American policy, people remain remarkably friendly to individual Americans. They find much about the United States—and the American people—appealing, entertaining, and even worthy of emulation. But as the essays in this book demonstrate, that goodwill is at risk.

During the Cold War, especially in the 1950s and early 1960s, American policymakers carefully registered international opinion and aimed to win it over to the American side. American jazz bands, writers, artists, and movie stars were sent hither and yon. America's struggles with racial injustice were officially and carefully—if by no means fully—explained to people in Africa, Asia, and Latin America. The aforementioned Fulbright program began in 1946; it was intended to demonstrate America's new commitment to international exchange, interaction, and communication. The premise behind all these efforts was remarkably optimistic: if you get to know us, you'll like us for who we are and for what we stand. It was an excellent gamble.

Still, such outreach was far from universally successful. Anti-Americanism in the targeted reaches of the world was rife during the early years of the Cold War. While few people could resist American jazz, a large number thought far less well of our economic and political impact on their nations. Richard Nixon recorded that dissatisfaction in 1958 when his boss, President Eisenhower, made him a sacrificial lamb, sending him on a "goodwill" tour of Latin America, where the catchy phrase "Yankee Go Home" was quite popular. Nixon was spat on and stoned in Peru and had to fight off mobs in Venezuela. The problem of anti-Americanism is not new, and neither is the need to address it.

The writers herein, a remarkable group of scholars and intellectuals from Iraq, Turkey, Russia, China, Indonesia, Mexico, and Italy, aim to show that international attitudes towards the United States are far from one-dimensional. A large reserve of goodwill exists, though by no means everywhere. Some people, and not always those one might first think, do surely hate (or at least disrespect) America for what it is and not only for what it does. Many more are agitated or even infuriated by American policies and what they consider insulting behavior by the American government.

The essays that follow were written to describe the historic and contemporary contexts that explain international perceptions of the United States and its role in the world. All are authored by intellectuals from nations whose good opinion should be of interest to Americans. The people writing these essays are not polemicists. They do not represent a raging tide of ill will. They are scholars who for different reasons wish there to be strong relations based on mutual respect between their societies and the United States.

Assembling writers for this book was not easy, but it was almost always fun. Of course, scholars have an unusual idea of what is fun. In finding the right people, I received help from colleagues all over the world, and I spoke or corresponded with numerous marvelously charming and brilliant people. Talking with friends and colleagues in Europe and Japan, I observed people whose work and home lives, whose daily routines were much like my own. But I also talked with people who soldiered on in countries where academic freedom is only a dream, who despite extraordinary talent and productivity were struggling to maintain their economic dignity, and who faced political challenges I could barely imagine. For some of them, to write an essay about their perceptions of the United States in a book to be published in the United States took great courage. At least two potential contributors decided, if I understood their carefully phrased expressions, that the risks were too high.

At first, I thought I would only ask men and women "from" other nations to contribute essays. But I was not always sure how to draw the line between "them" and "us." People's life histories often do not fit into simple definitions of a singular national identity. For example, Ibrahim Al-Marashi, coauthor of the essay on Iraq, is an American-born son of Iraqi immigrants to the United States who received his Ph.D. in England and then began teaching in Turkey. Al-Marashi's coauthor, Abdul Hadi al-Khalili, is an Iraqi citizen who has recently moved (for reasons the Iraq essay makes clear) to North America. Eric Shiraev, coauthor of the essay on Russian perceptions of the United States, was born in the Soviet Union and received his Ph.D. from St. Petersburg University, but is now living and teaching near Washington, D.C.; his coauthor, Olga Makhovskaya, is a Russian, educated and currently living in Russia. Makhovskaya, however, has spent most of her professional career researching the Russian "diaspora" and cross-cultural psychology—which has entailed living for extended periods in the United States and Europe. Yufan Hao, coauthor with Professor Lin Sui of Renmin University in Bejing of the essay on China, came to the United States from China to pursue a Ph.D. at Johns Hopkins University and has become a chaired professor at Colgate University in New York. The bottom line, with respect to national identity, is that at least one author of every essay is a citizen of the nation about which the authors are writing—even if he or she is not, at this moment, living in that nation.

What is certain is that the authors, individually, bring different talents to the task of explaining how their respective societies perceive the contemporary United States. A couple of the writers, social scientists in good standing, deploy survey data to support their analyses. Most engage in more deliberately subjective, even personal, efforts to explore the feelings that move their fellow citizens' views on the United States.

The Indonesian writer Melani Budianta suggests in her essay that communicating across cultures can be like looking through a stained glass window: one sees the other side through a haze of bright colors. The essay by Abdul Hadi al-Khalili and Ibrahim Al-Marashi on Iraqis' perception of the United States makes that painfully clear. American readers may well be taken aback by the picture that emerges. Several times while reading these essays I found myself singing a reworded version of the old Talking Heads song, "This is not my beautiful country, this is not my beautiful home." I can guarantee that the writers herein do not present a version of American culture and society that people in the United States are accustomed to seeing. While it is important to judge whether the critical pictures of the United States given here are valid, I think readers will benefit more from trying to understand how and why these critical images have come to exist.

This exercise in seeing the United States from the outside in will, I hope, improve the possibility of better communication between the United States and the other nations represented here. And improved understandings can produce better relations. In different ways, Nur Bilge Criss's essay on Turkey and the essay on Mexico by Fernando Escalante-Gonzalbo and Mauricio Tenorio-Trillo emphasize this point. Both argue that the blame for widespread misperceptions of the United States must be shared. While the United States often fails to communicate with appropriate sensitivity, transparency, and respect, other nations sometimes lack the public discourse and institutional structures their citizens need to make knowledgeable judgments about the United States. Building such knowledge, all agree (not surprisingly since all of the authors are scholars and intellectuals), should be a priority both for the United States and for other nations.

But on a less cheerful note, these essays reveal that even transparent mutual understanding leaves a great deal of room for animosity and distaste. Many Russians, for example, don't like the United States, Eric Shiraev and Olga Makhovskaya tell us, not because of Russians' misguided understandings of our policies or because of our national "values." Instead, many Russians are angry at the United States because, as

Russians live through hard times in the wake of American "triumph" in the Cold War, the American government has chosen not to spend tens of billions of dollars easing Russia's difficult transition to capitalism. A fuller understanding of American policy on this score is not likely to appease Russian frustration—though knowing how angry Russians are about it might lead, at least, to a few rhetorical bouquets by American policymakers that could brighten up an ugly room. Similarly, Federico Romero argues that the Atlantic divide may well be particularly and even artificially deep right now because of the distrust generated on both sides by the Iraq War but that long-term cultural and political trends may well make it difficult for Europeans and Americans to ever again rebuild the strong bonds that unified the "West" during the coldest of the Cold War years.

Finally, these essays are meant to be more than mere instruments of applied knowledge. These writers offer us voices we almost never hear. Lin Su and Yufan Hao, for example, in their groundbreaking work on Chinese public opinion, de-emphasize the usual official voices that are made to stand in for Chinese views and instead reveal what younger Chinese men and women feel about the United States. They ask us to listen and to ponder the future relationship of two of the world's great powers. In their stories, as in most of the essays written for this book, we see the United States made strange, alluring, and frightening. America, in almost all of these portraits, emerges as a place of uncanny power that can change the world—and often not for the better. These writers remind us that, contrary to the popular images of American-led globalization or of the world made flat, we live in a world of fiercely contested realities.

WHAT
THEY
THINK
OF US

❑ ❑ ❑

IRAQIS'

BLEAK VIEWS

OF THE

UNITED STATES

❏ ❏ ❏

Ibrahim Al-Marashi and Abdul Hadi al-Khalili

FIRST, I (al-Khalili) was carjacked right in front of my home. That was terrifying enough. But then, on April 28, 2004, I was kidnapped. I was riding in a car owned by a friend. Suddenly, a late-model BMW swerved in front of us, blocking our way. Three armed men jumped out, called me by name, and demanded that I come with them. I was handcuffed and blindfolded. They moved me from one car to another and then I was imprisoned in a small house occupied, strangely enough, by a woman and her three children. The kidnappers demanded that my family pay them $500,000. My family desperately negotiated the ransom down to $30,000. They paid and I lived.

Such was life in Iraq a year after the Americans overthrew Saddam Hussein. Kidnappings, killings, and carjackings were carried out in broad daylight. These acts were perpetrated by well-equipped, professional Iraqi criminals organized into gangs. The Iraqi police were, to put it most generously, not committed to stopping this organized crime. After my ordeal, for example, not a single Iraqi official wished to enquire about the details of my kidnapping in order to catch the criminals or to gather information that might help them prevent future attacks. Many middle-class and professional Iraqis responded to this nearly unfettered criminality by fleeing the country or by greatly curtailing their activities.

Here is the tragic irony. Crimes like carjacking, murder, and kidnapping were nearly unheard of during the years of Saddam's repressive police state. The United States successfully dismantled Saddam's government but completely failed to bring a sense of law and order to the nation of Iraq. This failure was disastrous. Worse, the Americans' failure to insure domestic security for Iraqis was and is not the only problem keeping Iraqis from embracing or even accepting the United States as a true friend. Iraq and the United States (as well as Great Britain and Iraq) have an uncomfortable history that few Americans know but that few Iraqis have forgotten. To understand Americans' difficulties in convincing Iraqis that the United States can and should be their ally, some of that history has to be communicated. This historically conditioned perspective combines with the contemporary predicament to explain a great deal about what must be done if Iraqis are to perceive the United States in a more favorable light.

We aim to highlight four key phases during which Iraqis, generally but not totally, came to share strongly negative or cynical views of the United States. The first phase came right after the 1967 Arab-Israeli war, which was punctuated in Iraq with the Ba'ath Party takeover in 1968. Then, in 1980, Iraqis became focused on the Iran-Iraq War. As a result, the Saddam regime, which had total control of the mass media, toned down its anti-U.S. rhetoric as a means to garner American support for its war against Iran. This stage in Iraqis' perceptions of the United States ended in August 1990 when Saddam, in an attempt to stop the United States from ending the takeover of Kuwait, used his control of the mass media to focus the nation's hatred toward the United States. This era of unrelenting anti-Americanism lasted throughout the 1991 Gulf War and the twelve years of UN-imposed sanctions. The fourth phase began after the American occupation, which resulted in the emergence of an independent Iraqi media and numerous civil society organizations that tended to blast the United States for its mishandling of the occupation or for simply being an aggressive imperialist nation.

These four phases have produced, to put the matter schematically, some common Iraqi perceptions of the United States. Many Iraqis argue, sometime in only inchoate forms, that American policy in Iraq is repeating the same disastrous mistakes British imperialists made in their administration of Iraq after 1920. And a great many people have continued to believe the view of the United States spread so effectively and sometimes quite accurately by the Saddam regime that the United States is a neocolonialist, pro-"Zionist" power that wants to steal Iraq's oil resources.

The Rise of the Ba'ath and Anti-Americanism in Iraq

First, a bit of deep historical context: the modern nation of Iraq since the sixteenth century had comprised three provinces of the Ottoman Turkish Empire. British forces overran these provinces toward the end of World War I, beginning a military occupation that was met with widespread resistance among Iraq's tribes, as well as other segments of the Sunni, Shia, and Kurdish communities. The events culminated in 1920 in what is referred to by the Iraqis as the "Great Revolt." Iraq gained independence in 1932. However, the ruling monarchy had signed an Anglo-Iraqi treaty that allowed Great Britain to intervene in Iraq's domestic affairs. The British interference in Iraqi affairs fiercely alienated many segments of its population. In 1958, Iraqi military officer Abdul Karim Qassim overthrew the monarchy in a military coup and ended its pro-Western stance. Qassim's government was overthrown on February 8, 1963, by elements of the Arab Socialist Ba'ath Party and the military. However, the Ba'ath Party held power for only nine months, until they were purged from the government by factions loyal to General Abdul Salam Arif.[1] Much of the public discourse in Iraqi circles from the 1920s to 1958 expressed hostility toward British control over Iraq's affairs.

This hostility was slowly redirected toward the Americans after the 1967 Six-Day War between Israel and its Arab neighbors.[2] After Israel's lightning victory, the United States began to side far more openly with Israel, in part in an effort to confront Arab states supported by the USSR. As a result of this heavy tilt toward Israel, Iraq broke off diplomatic ties with the United States in 1967.[3] Just a year after this war, on July 30, 1968, a second Ba'ath coup brought General Ahmad Hasan al-Bakr to power. He presided as president of Iraq, and his cousin, Saddam Hussein al-Tikriti served as vice president.[4] The basic principles of the Ba'ath

Party were socialism and pan-Arab unity, and the party officially declared, with justification, that the United States opposed both of these goals.

Ba'athist hostility towards the United States became more pronounced after the 1973 October War, in which Egypt and Syria launched a surprise attack against Israel in an attempt to regain lands they lost in the 1967 war. Many Arabs, including the Iraqis, blamed the United States, which supplied Israel with emergency military supplies, for the Arab defeat in this war. Thereafter, Iraqis perceived Israeli actions throughout the region as part and parcel of American "imperialism."[5]

The official Iraqi discourse in the 1970s emphasized Iraq's policy of nonalignment while condemning U.S. imperialism and U.S. support for the "racist-Zionist entity" (i.e. Israel) or what was euphemistically referred to as the "Washington–Tel Aviv Axis."[6] During this period, Iraqi writers regularly condemned the alleged "Zionist conspiracy" to control American foreign and domestic policy: "Since Presidential candidates in the United States know it is unthinkable to win anything without Zionist support, they have come to the natural conclusion that the more weapons they promise [Israel], the more likely they are to win elections."[7]

In the aftermath of the 1973 October War, Arab oil-producing nations imposed an oil embargo to punish the United States and the West for supporting Israel. The Iraqis believed that the United States, in response, wanted a military base in the Middle East to attack Arab oil countries and gain a ready supply of oil.[8] In the mid-1970s Iraqi government sources stated over and over again that American support for Kurdish rebels was aimed at gaining a military base in northern Iraq. From 1974 to 1975, the government-controlled press and government spokesmen claimed that the United States, Iran, and Israel were colluding to create the Kurdish "separatist insurrection" in Iraq.[9] When President Carter attempted to mediate the Arab-Israeli conflict in the late 1970s, Iraqis claimed that the United States was merely covering up its real intentions, to "further plunder Arab oil."[10] When Egyptian president Anwar Sadat sought a peace treaty with Israel with American help, Iraqi officials labeled him an Arab "defeatist," unlike the Iraqis who were at the forefront of the "Arab patriotic movement."[11]

This anti-Americanism continued after Saddam Hussein officially took power as president in July 1979.[12] Hussein blasted Carter, claming that he was scheming to control Arab oil. Saddam also invoked an analogy that would be used repeatedly during the 1990–91 Gulf crisis: the Vietnam War. He argued that the United States had suffered a devastating setback after the Vietnam War and that the Americans had failed to heed the lesson of this conflict: "These were too well known lessons to be forgotten by the imperialists. However, the contemporary incumbents of the White House, State Department and the Pentagon needed a breather to absorb the shock of the Vietnam debacle. They therefore, decided to lie low for some time."[13] The Vietnam analogy gave the Iraqis the impression that the Americans could not stomach another conflict with high casualties, a theme that would prove significant during the 1991 Gulf crisis.

An Iraqi-U.S. Rapprochement?

After the Iranian government of Shah Riza Pahlavi collapsed and Ayatollah Ruhollah Khomeini made his triumphant return to Tehran on February 1, 1979, Iraq was overjoyed. The Saddam regime perceived the shah as an American puppet in the region and, at first, welcomed the new Iranian government's anti-U.S. position. However, this relationship quickly changed, as Saddam Hussein feared that Iran's Islamic revolution could spread to Iraq.[14]

On September 22, 1980, Iraqi aircraft attacked bases near the Iranian capital of Tehran, marking the first day of the Iran-Iraq War.[15] In a November 1980 interview, Iraqi foreign minister Sadun Hammadi justified the attack by claiming that the United States was trying to establish a long-term friendship with Khomeini's government: "Obviously, the United States does not want the war to come to an end in such a way as to involve the settlement of the dispute in favor of Iraq."[16] Ironically, events seven years later proved the exact opposite, as the United States intervened to end the war on terms favorable to Iraq.

As Iraq found itself on the defensive following the Iranian offensives of June 1982, the government declared that it was willing to negotiate a settlement. At this juncture, official Iraqi rhetoric against the United States was toned down, as the leadership hoped that the American superpower would intervene and end the conflict. In November 1984, the

Iraqis successfully restored diplomatic relations with the United States.[17] The United States enforced an arms embargo on Iran, but not on Iraq. The new relationship even survived the grave difficulties produced by the Reagan administration's secret supplying of arms to the Iranian government (the Iran-Contra affair) and then the Iraqis' accidental missile attack on the USS *Stark* that killed 37 American sailors.[18] President Reagan chose to blame Iran for the attack, stating that it had escalated tensions in the Gulf and thus had created the context in which the tragedy occurred.[19]

Despite occasionally condemning Iraqi military atrocities, throughout the 1982–88 period the United States shared satellite photos of Iranian troop movements with the Iraqi government.[20] The United States, fearing that an Iranian victory would result in the spread of Khomeini's revolution through the oil-rich Gulf states, chose to treat the enemy of their primary regional enemy as its friend. The U.S.-supplied photos led to Iraqi victories on the battlefield, bringing the war to an end on terms favorable to Iraq. This U.S. covert support was known to segments of Iraqi society during the war, and it was widely reported after the 1991 Gulf War in Iraq as an example of American duplicity. Several influential Iraqis have told us in recent conversations that U.S. aid during the Iran-Iraq War convinced them at the time that the United States government supported Saddam's regime and wanted to keep Hussein in power.

Saddam's Hostility toward the United States

Official Iraqi perceptions of the United States quickly deteriorated after the Iran-Iraq War. On February 15, 1990, a U.S. Voice of America commentary broadcast in Iraq, made after Romanian dictator Ceauşescu was overthrown, stated that Saddam Hussein's dictatorship would likely collapse in a similar fashion.[21] This commentary, not surprisingly, made Saddam furious, and he and his inner circle feared that the United States was out to get them. These fears had begun to grow in the immediate aftermath of the Iran-Iraq War. Not without reason, Saddam was convinced that the United States, in collaboration with Israel, wanted to undermine Iraq's emergence as a regional power. He held such conceptions despite the fact that the United States had provided substantial economic and intelligence aid to Iraq during the war itself.

We have unusually detailed insight into Saddam's views of the United States during the key years of 1989–91 because numerous Iraqi documents were left in Kuwait after the retreat of its forces during the Gulf War.[22] These documents reveal that Saddam and high Ba'ath Party officials believed that the Americans intended to assume the role that the British played in the Middle East after the collapse of the Ottoman Empire. The British were perceived as acting against the Arab world, splitting it up by imposing arbitrary borders and exploiting its natural resources. In this vein, the United States was maintaining the colonial legacy of Great Britain. Given that the Soviet Union was collapsing, the Iraqis perceived that no power existed to check American designs on the Middle East.[23]

Saddam's concerns over unchecked American power during this period compounded his profound belief in an American-led conspiracy, supported by Israel and Kuwait, to overthrow his rule. Saddam viewed the Kuwait invasion not as an offensive operation but rather as a preemptive maneuver aimed at stopping the American effort to overthrow him and gain control of Iraqi oil. A document from Saddam, issued to Iraqi military commanders in 1990, reveals his deep suspicions of U.S. aims; it asserts his belief that the United States was conspiring with Israel against Iraq. It states, "The American-Zionist union against our country means to steal the natural resources of the Arab world, under an international umbrella and the approval of the Security Council."[24]

In the face of American belligerency in 1990 and 1991, Saddam and at least some of his loyalists laid their hopes on the "Vietnam syndrome." Saddam seemed to truly believe that the United States would quit the war if his army could inflict enough casualties on the Americans. Saddam was well aware that in 1983 the Reagan administration had withdrawn from Lebanon after incurring relatively few casualties. The following directives were sent by Saddam to the Iraqi military on the eve of Operation Desert Storm: "Try to cause many casualties and have a long war. Wait underground for the end of the air attack."[25] While things did not go quite as Saddam had hoped during Operation Desert Storm, his perception of American resolve in the face of mass casualties was not changed, since Americans chose not to carry the war to Baghdad in order, he believed, to avoid American battlefield deaths. Essentially, Saddam continued to hold on to the Vietnam analogy from the 1970s until his last war in 2003.

In the immediate aftermath of the first United States–Iraq war anti-Saddam Iraqis found their own reasons for not trusting the United States. In 1991, President Bush Sr. publicly asked Iraqis to revolt against Saddam Hussein. When the Shias revolted in the south and the Kurds in the north, Bush withdrew his offer of support, and Saddam's army slaughtered the insurgents. Not only did the United States not support the insurgents, many Iraqis believe that specific American actions led directly to Saddam's maintenance of his power. First, the United States had declared a cease-fire before Iraq's Republican Guards were destroyed. Those very soldiers suppressed the twin uprisings that shook the country in the aftermath of the 1991 war. Numerous Iraqis point out that the United States allowed the Republican Guards to move across territory held by the Americans and that U.S. troops kept the poorly equipped insurgents from acquiring arms at Iraqi arms depots. Many Kurds and Shias also state that the United States allowed Iraqi helicopters to fly after the cease-fire; these gunships helped to slaughter the rebels. Some Iraqis believed that the United States failed to intervene on behalf of the Kurdish and Shia rebels out of fears that their success would lead to collapse of the Iraqi government and the dismemberment of Iraq, creating chaos in the region or a Shia Islamic republic closely allied to Iran. In sum, Iraqis were convinced that the United States, despite rhetoric by the first President Bush, wanted to keep Saddam in power. And anti-Saddam elements in Iraq, including Kurds, learned to be wary in the extreme of American promises.

Post–Gulf War Perceptions

When U.S. forces concluded Operation Desert Storm on April 11, 1991, the war against Iraq did not completely end. Instead, a low-intensity conflict began from that day, with sanctions, UN weapons inspections, covert CIA support for the Iraqi opposition, failed coup attempts, and numerous air raids against Iraqi radar stations, intelligence headquarters, and missile sites.

The United States justified stationing a large military presence in Saudi Arabia to counter the "Iraqi threat" to Kuwait. At the same time, U.S. arms sales to the Gulf countries, especially Saudi Arabia, increased dramatically after the 1991 Gulf War. These military acts deepened Iraqis' suspicions of the United States. First, many Iraqis believed that the U.S. troop presence had nothing to do with the "Iraq threat" but rather was aimed at controlling the world's oil supply. Second, Iraqis were convinced that the United States greatly exaggerated Saddam's threat to other Gulf countries in order to keep the American arms industry alive after the end of the Cold War.

In the immediate aftermath of Operation Desert Storm, the U.S. administration mistakenly predicted that Hussein would be overthrown by his own military. Both American and British intelligence services repeatedly tried to foment a coup within the Ba'ath regime.[26] Their goal was to overthrow Saddam but leave his Sunni-dominated totalitarian state intact. As these attempts failed, many Iraqis were convinced that the coup attempts were not genuine and that the United States wanted Hussein to stay in power. Other well-informed Iraqis argued that the U.S. desire to keep the Ba'athist regime in power sans Saddam Hussein proved America had no desire for democracy to take root in Iraq. These views of U.S. policy contributed to sophisticated Iraqis' suspicion of U.S. motives and goals during and after Operation Iraqi Freedom.

Anti-U.S. feelings in Iraq intensified in the dozen years that followed the first United States–Iraq war. The sanctions regime imposed on Iraq, aimed at pressuring the Saddam government to dismantle its weapons of mass destruction program, grievously hurt the Iraqi people. Saddam blamed the United States for the sanctions and their terrible societal impact. While the sanctions were, of course, placed under a United Nations resolution, most Iraqis blamed the United States for continuing the embargo. And here is an unexpected twist to the story. Even educated Iraqis during this period believed that the sanctions were actually an American ploy aimed at helping Saddam stay in power. As they saw it, the sanctions enabled Saddam to strengthen his grip over the nation because his regime was able to control rations distribution. This control over food, fuel, and the necessities of life gave the regime immense power over individual Iraqis, and it also enabled Saddam and his cronies to gain great wealth, as they took kickbacks by awarding contracts to foreign companies via the UN Oil-for-Food program. This hidden support was inflated, in the minds of Iraqis, to the point where many, even in the most educated strata of society, believed that Saddam had to be a CIA agent.

Post–September 11 Perceptions

While Saddam was ecstatic that he outlived the political career of his rival George Bush Sr., Iraqis opposed to the Hussein regime hoped that Bush's son would complete the job his father failed to finish. The September 11, 2001, terrorist attacks seemed to make that possibility more likely. On September 12, the Iraqi government, via official Baghdad-based Republic of Iraq Television, praised the attacks, the only country in the Middle East to do so. The Iraqi declaration stated, "The American cowboy is reaping the fruits of his crimes against humanity."[27] The term "cowboy" was a common rhetorical tool in the Iraqi media to convey U.S. foreign policy recklessness and to suggest that this "gun-toting" country was determined to dominate the Middle East. The declaration further stated, "It is a black day in the history of America, which is tasting the bitter defeat of its crimes and disregard for peoples' will to lead a free and decent life." The September 12 statement continued: "The collapse of U.S. centers of power is a collapse of U.S. policy, which deviates from human values and stands by world Zionism at all international forums to continue to slaughter of the Palestinian Arab people and implement U.S. plans to dominate the world under the cover of what is called the new world order. These are the fruits of the new US order."[28]

This statement, while obviously propagandistic, hit most of the key points that alienated Iraqis from the United States. First, it connected the United States to Israel, referring to the "American-Zionist alliance." Second, it called on Iraq's overwhelming support for the Palestinian people. Finally, it referred to the first Bush's call for a "new world order," which Iraqis saw as nothing more than U.S. global domination. The September 11 attacks served the Iraqi leadership as vicarious revenge for a war launched against its nation more than a decade earlier.

By 2003, most Iraqis had lived under the Saddam dictatorship for most or all of their lives. That dictatorship controlled the media and education. Through these controls, as well as through simple terror and brutal repression, the Saddam regime had indoctrinated its people to withstand three wars and a decade of sanctions by deflecting Iraq's problems onto an external foe: the United States of America. By the time Saddam's state collapsed, many Iraqis had internalized the anti-American discourse of the Ba'athist regime. Not surprisingly, many anti-Ba'athist Iraqis today who are critical of the United States continue to use the same basic words and themes to attack tit. While Saddam may have not been popular with all segments of Iraqi society, the themes extrapolated in his speeches obviously struck a chord among many Iraqis. The language and tactics used during the current insurgency demonstrate that many discursive remnants from the former regime continue to resonate in Iraq today.

Iraqis Perceptions of the United States in a Post-Saddam Iraq

It is not easy to determine how Iraqis feel about the United States in the aftermath of the 2003 Iraq War. Only a select group of Iraqi political factions command any respect and authority. And since Saddam systemically destroyed Iraqi civil society, the kinds of forums in which free speech, public debate, and serious inquiry occur are few and far between. Combined with the generally upbeat views from U.S. politicians or optimistic predictions from photogenic Iraqi political figures, a true Iraqi voice is absent in the debate on this nation's future, and it is that voice which needs to be examined in order to fully appreciate Iraqi perceptions of the United States.

It is not easy to understand what the "Iraqi street" is saying. Public opinion polls in Iraq are conducted by local partisan institutions, and few international polling organizations have conducted recent studies. On-the-street interviews and call-ins on Iraqi talk shows express views of the general public, but they are usually edited or screened to suit the channel's agenda. Because of these limitations, we have set out to examine how the emerging political and intellectual elites in Iraq perceive America, combined with our own personal experiences of talking with groups of Iraqis to get a sense for the contemporary Iraqi response to the U.S. presence in Iraq. Examining their statements can help gauge sentiments among common Iraqis. While the role of the United States in Iraq and the nature of Iraq's developing state are matters hotly contested, these opinions are rarely examined in an analytical fashion.

One of the questions we tried to answer is the common American one: why didn't Iraqis welcome U.S. troops with open arms after they "liberated" Iraq. When the now deceased Ayatollah al-Hakim, leader of one of Iraq's Shia parties, the Supreme Council for the Islamic Revolution in Iraq (SCIRI), was asked why the Iraqi Shia, long oppressed by the Saddam government, failed to revolt and support the U.S. advances during the 2003 Iraq war, he said, "There are a number of reasons why there has not been an uprising, most important of which is that Iraqis perceive the United States as an occupying rather than a liberating force. The second reason has to do with people's strong sense of nationalism, the painful memories of the war of 1991 and the fear that anyone who rises up against the regime will be crushed."[29] As we underlined earlier, because of past American policy, many Iraqis believed that Saddam was a creation of the United States. Therefore, many Iraqis saw no reason to thank the United States for removing him.[30] While many Iraqis were happy to see Saddam Hussein leave, they did not necessarily believe they had to thank the United States for removing him, and they feared that the American occupation might just well be a new form of subjugation.

Furthermore, many Iraqis were deeply suspicious of how U.S. troops acted in the immediate aftermath of the war. They quickly realized that in the post-Saddam Iraq the United States had clear priorities that were not those of the Iraqi people. While looting of hospitals and museums and general lawlessness terrified and saddened the people, U.S. troops guarded oil facilities and the Oil Ministry, giving the impression Americans cared little about the Iraqi people but a great deal about safeguarding Iraq's oil.[31] Following the looting, the United States chose not to stop the waves of revenge killings and humanitarian crises or to reconstruct devastated infrastructure. The American authorities failed to deal effectively with the power grabs of warlords, independent militias, and tribal leaders, or to stop land grabs or the dangerous meddling of Iran, Syria, and Saudi Arabia. Nor did the U.S. authorities handle wisely the touchy issue of the "de-Ba'thification" of Iraq.

While the Iraqis were critical of the United States for the aforementioned failings, they were most critical of the Americans' inability to restore security in Iraq. Many Iraqi believe that the Americans encouraged chaos to give them a pretext for maintaining an extended force deployment in Iraq.

Ironically, some Iraqis have called for a ruthless dictator to bring security back to Iraq, rejecting the Americans' stated goal of installing a liberal elected leader. Many, many Iraqis wondered: After the eight-year Iran-Iraq War and after the 1991 Gulf War, with no help from anyone, the Iraqi people successfully reconstructed their own country and maintained domestic security. How is it that the most advanced and most wealthy country in the world, the United States, has failed to bring about basic security and economic reconstruction? Iraqis note that despite UN-imposed sanctions, Saddam Hussein rebuilt his country after 1991 more effectively and quicker than has the U.S. Coalition Provisional Authority. Hence, some Iraqis desire the return of a firm and authoritative leader.

The Beginnings of an Insurgency

Several specific blunders on the part of the American occupiers greatly contributed to the rise of armed resistance in Iraq. On April 29, 2003, as many as thirteen Iraqis, protesting the American military presence in Falluja, a town west of Baghdad, were gunned down by American soldiers. On the following day the U.S. army fired on another crowd of one thousand protesters demonstrating over the thirteen civilian deaths.[32] The Iraqis of Falluja were most upset over the fact that American soldiers made no attempts to apologize for the deaths of innocents in the crowds. If the U.S. authorities had made an immediate formal and serious apology for the tragic deaths it had caused, a great deal of trouble may well have been avoided. Instead, the Americans did nothing, which produced a deep-rooted desire for revenge among the Fallujans that continues to this day and has made this small town a focal point of Iraqi discontent with the United States. Similarly, the way the U.S. military conducted searches and military operations in Falluja, and other towns and cities throughout Iraqi, indicated disrespect for Iraqi culture, creating an unhealthy atmosphere between civilians and the Coalition military.

Such "offending" actions included indiscriminate killings of civilian by-standers, oftentimes members of tribes whose fellow tribesmen then felt a mandatory duty according to their code of honor to exact revenge against Coalition forces. Other humiliating offenses included arrests of tribal chiefs, the frisking of Iraqi females by U.S. male soldiers at checkpoints, and using dogs, an animal considered unclean in Islam, to conduct searches. All of these events contributed to what would be later termed the "Iraqi insurgency," centered around Falluja. On May 1, President Bush landed aboard a U.S. aircraft carrier and announced the end of major battle operations in Iraq.[33] Little did he know that the hardest battle had begun: winning the "hearts and minds" of the Iraqis.

The second mistake made by the United States in the mind of the Iraqis was when the Coalition Provisional Authority (CPA), led by Paul Bremer, disbanded the Iraqi army. Not only did Bremer not have enough U.S. troops to keep the peace, but he dissolved the last symbol of Iraqi sovereignty. This action and similar actions—dissolving the intelligence services and all police forces—are widely perceived by Iraqis as a colonial humiliation reminiscent of the British rule. Many Iraqis agree that some of these forces were corrupt and had to be removed. However, Iraqis also argue that many elements of the former military could have been won over to the Coalition side if their salaries were paid. Disbanding the Iraqi army, one of nation's largest employers, sent many disgruntled men with combat training into the ranks of the Iraqi insurgency. Even Saddam Hussein realized he could not disband the Iraqi military after the Iran-Iraq War, for doing so would send bands of restless warriors into the streets and possibly in the direction of the Presidential Palace. In this case, Bremer could have learned a few lessons from the detested dictator. After losing their jobs, many former military and intelligence employees simply had to find ways to get paid; at least some chose, with deadly consequences, to take money offered by terrorist sources.

The United States has blamed the violence in Iraq on "the insurgency," suggesting that one group foments all the internal disturbances. Really, multiple "insurgencies" rage throughout Iraq. Some insurgents are former Saddam Hussein loyalists, while others are Iraqis who loathed Saddam but loathe the Americans even more. Other insurgents are sympathetic to Osama bin Ladin, a man who personally despised Saddam Hussein.[34] However, the label "the insurgency" is a convenient tool, as it simplifies the nature of the threat from this multifaceted guerrilla war. Many Iraqis cite how the U.S. pins the violence in Iraq conveniently on either the fedayeen, Saddam's former militia, or Al Qaeda. However, Iraqis point out that inadequate American forces allowed the terrorists to infiltrate Iraq's borders in the first place. Some Iraqi do not use the label "insurgency" but the more sympathetic term *al-muqawama,* or "the resistance," linking the Iraqi case with the Algerian resistance to the French in the 1960s or the Palestinian intifada against the Israelis. Some Iraqis criticize the U.S. media and government statements that typically claim that violent actions are only occurring in a small swath of territory referred to as the "Sunni Arab Triangle," a geographic area that includes the restive towns of Falluja, Ramadi, and Tikrit, Saddam Hussein's birthplace. Iraqis argue that this label is misleading as it confines the violence to a small area, whereas in fact violence has struck almost every part of the country.

The Sadr Uprising

After major hostilities ended in April 2003, the U.S. administration in Iraq expected to rely on the relative stability of the Arab Shia south, as opposed to the Arab Sunni heartland, where guerrilla attacks occurred on a nearly daily basis. While many Iraqi Shias held critical perspectives on U.S. policy in Iraq, these criticisms had never turned into violence. The conflict between Muqtada al-Sadr and U.S. forces signaled the spread of bitter anti-American perceptions that fueled a violent uprising in the south of Iraq. Sadr is a young cleric who inherited his father's credentials as a prominent critic of the Saddam Hussein government. After years of hiding, Sadr reappeared in Najaf when the American military captured the city. On October 10, 2003, al-Sadr called for the establishment of a rival government to challenge the U.S. Coalition-sponsored Iraqi Governing Council.[35] His declaration was the first organized Shia response from a community that had for the most part acquiesced to the American presence.

The Americans responded angrily to this new challenge. In April 2004, the American authorities hurt their credibility by ordering the closure of the al-Sadr-linked weekly newspaper *Al-Hawza,* stating that it carried articles that "stirred up hatred." Ironically, by shutting the paper down, the Americans incited the violence they had tried to avoid. Afterwards, Coalition soldiers were ambushed by Sadr's militia, the Mahdi Army in the Shia holy cities of Najaf and Karbala and in the neighborhood of Baghdad known as Sadr City, a stronghold of al-Sadr. The pro-Sadr preachers in the mosques of this area proclaimed that this area was an "American-free zone."

Sadr had not always been violently opposed to the United States. The CPA had, for several months, turned a "blind eye" to his militia, and, at first, al-Sadr had stressed that his followers only conduct civil disobedience to challenge the CPA. Still, he was always vehemently opposed to the American presence in Iraq, and he had opposed religious leaders such as the revered Ayatollah al-Sistani, who had begrudgingly acquiesced to the CPA's attempt to establish a post-Saddam leadership.[36] Sadr's uncompromising hatred of the American presence in Iraq was given far greater credibility by another one of the Americans' blunders.

The U.S. military decision to imprison Iraqis in the Abu Ghraib prison was a terrible error in judgment. It greatly angered the Iraqi populace even before the scandalous nature of that imprisonment was well known. The facility was synonymous with the tortures and executions that typified life under Saddam. The United States had promised that such living nightmares were over. Not only did the United States continue to use Abu Ghraib, but Iraqis learned they had continued to torture people within its bloody walls. The pictures released in April 2004 of U.S. military interrogators torturing and humiliating naked Iraqi prisoners will symbolize the failings of the American "liberators" in Iraq for years to come.

Anti-American factions in Iraq were quick to use the infamous photos to their advantage. A spokesman for Muqtada al-Sadr claimed that Iraqis detained in Saddam's prisons were treated better than in the American-run prisons. He concluded: "This is a very good opportunity for the whole world to know that the alleged democracy is a lie and falsehood."[37] American errors of judgment are often seen in Iraq as the true face of American power.

Kurdish Perceptions

The Kurds, generally, are an exception to the general rule of Iraqi discontent with their American occupiers. Though the Kurds were abandoned by the United States during their revolt in the mid-1970s, most have stood by the United States since the overthrow of Saddam. For example, in the Iraqi town of Dohuk, forty-five minutes from the Turkish border, one is greeted by a sign, "God Bless the Coalition." Dohuk is the only town in Iraq where American soldiers can walk around unarmed. In fact, they come to Dohuk for short vacations while on duty in various other parts of Iraq. Another sign in Dohuk reads, "Thank God for Our New Constitution." The Kurds have generally been content with the nature of political change in Iraq, as they have won several major concessions, including the establishment of the Kurdish Regional Government, an autonomous entity in the north that enjoys substantial powers within Iraq.

However, even the Kurds have their concerns. The Kurds worry about perceived American favoritism toward the Shia. The next flash point between the United States and the Kurds will likely emerge over the city of Kirkuk. This city is divided among ethnic Kurds, Arabs, and Turkmens, and Sunnis, Shias, and Christians. Some call it the Iraqi Jerusalem, and like that contested city, Kirkuk has witnessed almost daily armed skirmishes over control of neighborhoods and its long-term demographic fate. The Turkmen minority of Iraq, closely allied with Turkey, accuse the United States of turning a blind eye to what they term a Kurdish-led "ethnic cleansing" of the city.

Kirkuk is more than a symbol; it sits atop one of the largest oil fields in the Middle East. The American government has made it clear that it intends to secure the Kirkuk oil fields, and it has established a military base and airfield literally just outside of the oil fields to protect this asset. In return, Iraqi insurgents angry over American control of this valuable resource have lobbed mortar shells at the base on an almost daily basis. Then, too, the Kurdish political parties want complete control of the oil-rich Kirkuk region and fear that the United States will not give it to them, since doing so could prompt Turkey to intervene to prevent a powerful Kurdish entity from forming in the north of Iraq. So even as the Americans have gained an ally among the Kurdish people of Iraq, the long-term fate of this special relationship remains unclear.

Perceptions of U.S.-Sponsored Democracy

Throughout Iraq, people animatedly discuss the course of their political evolution, the desirability of democracy, and whether or not the Americans truly wish to foster democracy in Iraq. Many are dubious about Americans' commitment to a democratic Iraq, pointing out that since the Arab Shias are a majority in Iraq, an elected post-Saddam leader would most likely be a Shia. These Iraqis believe that the United States would not accept such a leader because he might form an alliance with Shia Iran and then the Shias would come to dominate the Gulf. Instead, they believed the Americans will try to do what the British did: impose a leader on the people from above.

Above all, Iraqis believe that the United States is far less interested in a democratic Iraq than in using permanent American military bases to control the region's oil. Just as the British forced the first Iraqi government to accept British military bases in Iraq, so they believe the United States will coerce the new Iraqi government to accept American bases. Iraqis argue that the instability in Iraq at the moment has actually served that U.S. policy. An unstable Iraq justifies a continued American military presence. Along these lines, some Iraqis argue that the U.S. claim that it invaded Iraq to remove weapons of mass destruction was just smokescreen that allowed the creation of a pro-American state in the heart of the world's oil reserves.

Americans' claim that they only want to help the Iraqi people to establish democracy touches another nerve. Iraqis perceive Americans as suggesting that because they are Arabs and Muslims, they are not capable of establishing their own democracy. The Association of Muslim Scholars seeks to represents the views of the Iraqi Sunni Arabs in political and social affairs. One of its clerics, in an interview with the Arabic satellite channel Al-Jazeera, questioned America's audacity in helping Iraq with drafting its 2005 constitution: "Iraq does not need the help of a state whose age is no more than two and a half centuries. We are an ancient nation in history. We are the first to write the alphabet and enact constitutions."[38] Iraqis believe that too often, indeed almost exclusively, the literature on the prospects of democracy in Iraq is written by academics or think tanks in Washington. Few American authorities have bothered to look at what the Iraqis themselves say about democracy.

Ironically, it is from Shia clerics, whom Americans feared would try to engineer an Iranian-style theocracy in Iraq, that the most strident calls for democracy have emerged. Ayatollah Ali al-Sistani, the country's most influential Shia leader, rejected a U.S. formula to transfer power to the Iraqis via a provisional legislature selected by eighteen regional caucuses. When the Coalition Provisional Authority suggested that Iraq's first referendum be based on this system, Sistani criticized it, since candidates would be handpicked by the Americans. It was Sistani who insisted that a truly democratic system is based on an one-person, one-vote system.

Muhammad Taqi al-Mudarassi, a Shia cleric once on the State Department list of terrorists, has also been an active advocate of democracy in Iraq. He questioned the actions of the United States in an interview: "On one hand, they have decided to transfer sovereignty to the people, and on the other hand, they are beginning to talk about sharing it with them? Or does it mean that they have changed their policy of openness toward the political forces and now believe in the policy of the iron fist, as Saddam did?"[39] Ironically, he adopted the language of the Bush administration to challenge the U.S. occupation authorities: "We advise all those who love peace and security to support the march for genuine democracy in Iraq. It would be the best solution to prevent the spread of terrorism and support what they call political reform in the greater Middle East." He also said, "In our opinion, the question of people's vote and respecting the principle of democracy is an important issue, and the Islamic government is a secondary issue." Two decades ago the same man had argued for an Islamic revolution in Iraq. His statements indicate that he has abandoned the first goal and is ready to work for a democratic Iraq: "The Iraqi people are on the verge of frustration because of the increasing feeling that the Coalition forces have failed in achieving security and democracy."[40]

Even the Iraqi Kurds, whom the United States counted as its staunchest allies in Iraq, have criticized American failures to deliver democracy. The Kurdish paper *Howalati* said that the United States will only depart from Iraq when it can leave a "repressive singular authority, which is dependent on the United States." The editorial concluded: "In the end the United States wants a democracy in Iraq that is more pro-American than pro-people's choice and the outcome of the ballot boxes."[41]

Likewise, the Iraqi Turkmens in their newspaper *Turkomaneli* were very critical of U.S. actions in Falluja and Najaf in April 2004. The paper has repeatedly argued that such actions jeopardized democracy in Iraq: "Under the auspices of supposed democracy in the new Iraq, the blood of many thousands of innocent children, women and old has been spilled, be it in Falluja, Baghdad, Najaf, or any governorate of our beloved country."[42] Questioning American motives for trying to arrest al-Sadr, this editorialist asked, "What equation is being applied today by the Coalition forces? Is this democracy?" He answers, "By God, if the democracy you understand is this, then we do not want it and we will reject it in every possible way." Intriguingly, this Turkmenian newspaper, representing a religiously mixed Turkic, non-Arab, non-Kurdish ethnicity in Iraq, was displaying sympathy for both Arab Shias and Sunnis attacked in Najaf and Falluja. Nationalistically, they are referred to as the "sons of Iraq." Out of such anger with the United States had come a new kind of Iraqi unity.[43]

Discontent with the United States is prevalent along the Iraqi political spectrum. An editorial in *Al-Dustur,* an independent political daily, stated: "Iraq may become an example of a progressive country with a good infrastructure, a model for democracy in the entire region, but it will nevertheless become one of the best new U.S. colonies governed indirectly by the U.S. administration." The editorialist argued that all political and economic decisions made by the future Iraqi governments will be bound to U.S. political and economic interest: "The new model of Iraq is a U.S. national park. The six U.S. military bases that will be established in Iraq are proof of this."[44] In *Al-Furat,* another independent, a writer stated that a democracy cannot be implemented in Iraq under an American occupation: "We were surprised by the many resounding names that had a lot to tell us the day they entered Iraq and talked about democracy, human rights, and the individual freedoms that abound in the paragraphs of the American constitution drafted for the transitional postoccupation period." He argued that while Iraqis were looking forward to a democratic Iraq, promises of democracy have amounted to nothing for the average Iraqi.[45]

While external observers debated the likelihood of democracy taking root in Iraq, Iraqis, while worried about the efficiency of democratic decision-making, seem to be excited about the possibility of creating a liberal democracy. But many worried that such a democracy will only be a shell for American interests. We believe that the twinned desire for an autonomous democracy and suspicion about American interests in Iraq at least temporarily unified Iraq's disparate ethnic and sectarian communities.

Perceptions of the United States in a "Sovereign Iraq"

As the American presence in Iraq evolves, Iraqis are looking at several key issues. They want to be sure that Iraq, not the United States, determines the role of the American military alliance in Iraq and the duration of its stay. Intellectuals in Iraq, at least, remember the widely unpopular Anglo-Iraq treaties in the 1930s, forced on the Iraqi monarchy by the United Kingdom, that allowed British forces to stay in Iraq indefinitely. Iraqis also want to make sure that their oil stays in their hands. While various agreements seem to offer this guarantee, time alone will test such assurances.

Internationally much was made over the January 2005 elections for a transitional assembly. During the run-up to Iraq's elections, most of the emerging Arab Sunni political factions failed to engage in the process after losing control of a state they had dominated for decades. The Shia factions demonstrated a will to take part in the elections, since an elected government would be in a better position to end the U.S. occupation. Even Ayatollah Sistani stressed that successful elections would be the only way to "expel the occupation."[46]

An article in the Shia SCIRI party paper *Al-Adala* stated that while Iraqis looked forward to transparent elections, it feared that "the United States is not ready to lose control over Iraq. Such [losing control] would be the case if a group of people who would never fulfill U.S. interests, or would oppose them, were to win the elections."[47] Nevertheless, the United States did allow SCIRI to dominate the transitional government, the constitution-writing process, the Interior Ministry, and the permanent assembly elected after December 15, 2005. None of this is admitted in the SCIRI media, but the critical remarks against the United States were eventually toned down.

During the run-up to the 2004 American presidential election, Iraqis overwhelmingly came to believe that the American occupation of their nation had more to do with President Bush's political needs and domestic agenda than it did with Iraqis' own desires and needs. This view grew in strength even after the election. In early 2005, an Iraqi wrote of Bush's appearing on American television with "a striking Hollywood smile" to denounce his political detractors and announce the success of his policy in Iraq—even as violence wracked the Iraqi people.[48]

This issue became ever so much more important in the summer of 2005 when the Iraqis began writing their constitution, amid fears of American interference in drafting the charter. Mahmud Othman, a Kurdish politicain who sat on the committee drafting the constitution, stated that U.S. ambassador Zalmay Khalilzad played an impartial role during the process.[49] Tariq Al-Hashimi of the Iraqi Islamic Party, which had been critical of American policy in Iraq, described the United States in a positive manner in an interview, saying, "In this mess over the constitution, for once they have conducted themselves well." Prior to the January elections, his party condemned the United States as heavy-handed "occupiers," but during this interview he said, "Instead, in this impossible birth, the Americans have conducted themselves like impartial midwives." He acknowledged that the United States, for once, intervened on behalf of the Arab Sunnis, who pushed for their inclusion on the drafting committee.[50]

Concerns about America's role are shaped, in part, by Iraqi worries about sectarian conflict. The February 22, 2006, bombing of the Al-Askari Shrine in Samarra had sparked an unprecedented level of sectarian violence in Iraq, raising the specter of civil war. Killings between Kurds and Turkmen, and Arab Sunnis and Shias, were occurring at an alarming level prior to the attack, but failed to make headlines in the United States; there the news highlighted attacks against American forces in Iraq. The fact that the chant "Death for America for bringing terrorism to Iraq" was shouted from the Samarra mosque's speakers indicate that some blamed the United States for the attack, since it was in charge of Iraq's security forces. Other critics argue that a civil war would ultimately benefit American covert plans to divide Iraq into three separate states, undoing what was once one of the most powerful nations in the Arab world.

In 2003 and 2004, Iraqis were skeptical that they would be allowed to control their nation in a democratic fashion. Anger and distrust toward the United States is now being shifted inwards against other Iraqi communities. While differences have always existed between Iraq's Arab Shias, Sunnis, and Kurds, such divisions were never discussed openly and were glaringly absent in the Iraq media that emerged after the fall of the Ba'ath government in 2003. While the United States has proven that it is willing to give control to the Iraqis, the current fear is what type of nation they will inherit if the country collapses into sectarian conflict.

Iraqis are still waiting to see what will come next. And so long as American troops remain in Iraq, numerous factions will fight them. And so long as the Iraqi government depends on American troops for its security, most Iraqis will remain unconvinced of their government's autonomy or its ability to protect them. And as long as everyday Iraqis see American troops patrolling their streets, wait in long lines for gasoline, suffer from a lack of electricity, fail to find work, and witness a deluge of car bombs, with the prospect of civil war on the horizon, they will not trust their government nor lose their anger toward Americans.

Conclusion

Iraqi perceptions of the United States, while historically conditioned and forcefully shaped by the recent war and its deadly and dispiriting aftermath, are by no means fixed. And different factions, groups, and individuals have different perspectives. Iraq's political scene is convoluted and cannot be easily explained just by looking at simple sectarian or ethnic divisions. Still, many Iraqis do share some common perceptions of the role of the United States in shaping their national destiny.

During World War I, the victorious British general Maude entered Baghdad and told its inhabitants that they were "liberated" from years of "Ottoman tyranny." While the Kurds, Turkomans, Sunni Arabs, and Shia Arabs of that time had little in common with each other, they quickly became unified by their common hatred of the British. These communities all saw the British "liberation" as their "occupation." They united to expel the British. The British responded by creating a very pro-British monarchy. By 1958, the Iraqi people again united and overthrew what they perceived as a government too subservient to the British. In the chaos that followed the 1958 revolution, tyranny gained the upper hand in Iraq.

Saddam Hussein did his utmost to implant in the Iraqi psyche an ugly image of the United States: colonizer, Zionist, bully, and greedy oil thief. The United States was the new British imperialist. These images remain alive in Iraqi society today. Just as the British greedily exploited Iraqi oil so, too, Iraqis believe, will the United States. The image of the United States as a brutal, even murderous neocolonial power has already led many Iraqis to become ardent anti-Americanists.

Americans who wish to change these Iraqi perceptions of the United States do not face an easy task. Americans' failure to understand Iraq's history and politics led to terrible miscalculations during Operation Iraqi Freedom. More such miscalculations will likely produce disastrous results. Iraq has had an agonizing history: it was created out of the ravages of the First World War, went through a nationwide revolt in the 1920s, suffered through the Second World War, underwent revolutions in 1958, 1963, and 1968, endured almost continuous Kurdish rebellion, faced a mass uprising in March 1991, and has now recently gone three disastrous wars with foreign powers. Chaos, colonization, dictatorship, brutal repression, and foreign occupation have not left the Iraqis a sentimental people. But Iraqis are a capable people, and if the U.S. government wishes to maintain a viable relationship with Iraq, its representatives must learn to understand Iraq and listen to its people. Otherwise we will all reap the whirlwind.

Notes

1. Kanan Makiya, *Republic of Fear: The Politics of Modern Iraq* (Berkeley and Los Angeles: University of California Press, 1998), 314.

2. Saad E. M. Ibrahim, "Arab Images of the United States and the Soviet Union before and after the June War of 1967," *Journal of Conflict Resolution* 16, no. 2 (1972): 227–40.

3. Bruce W. Jentleson, *With Friends Like These: Reagan, Bush, and Saddam, 1982–1990* (New York: Norton, 1994), 32.

4. Efraim Karsh and Inari Rautsi, *Saddam Hussein: A Political Biography* (New York: Macmillan, 1991), 32.

5. *Iraq Today,* June 16–30, 1976, 6.

6. "Subversion against the Unity of Arab People," *Iraq Today,* September 1–15, 1976, 17.

7. Medhat Magar, "Six Years in Two," *Iraq Today,* June 16–30, 1976, 25.

8. M. Salama, "Diego Garcia," *Iraq Today,* May 16–31, 1977, 14–15.

9. Yakhdan Sadoun al-Amir, "Don't You Think, Mr. President . . . ?" *Iraq Today,* November 16–30, 1980, 20–21.

10. Kamal Butti, "One Way Out," *Iraq Today,* October 1–15, 1976, 25.

11. "Morality vs. Realpolitik," *Iraq Today,* April 16–30, 1977, 31.

12. John Bulloch and Harvey Morris, *The Gulf War: Its Origins, History and Consequences* (London: Methuen, 1989), 27.

13. "Unity—A Strategic Task," *Iraq Today,* June 16–July 31, 1979, 18.

14. Philip Robins, "Iraq in the Gulf War: Objectives, Strategies and Problems," in Hanns W. Maull and Otto Pick, eds., *The Gulf War: Regional and International Dimensions* (London: Pinter, 1989), 6.

15. Chaim Herzog, "A Military-Strategic Overview," in Efraim Karsh, ed., *The Iran-Iraq War: Impact and Implications* (London: Macmillan, 1987), 259.

16. "US Efforts to Salvage Isolated Iranian Regime," *Iraq Today,* November 1–15, 1980.

17. Jentleson, *With Friends Like These,* 47.

18. Amazia Baram, "Iraq: Between East and West," in Karsh, *The Iran-Iraq War,* 86.

19. Thomas L. McNaugher, "Walking the Tightropes in the Gulf," in Karsh, *The Iran-Iraq War,* 175.

20. Avigdor Haselkorn, *The Continuing Storm: Iraq, Poisonous Weapons, and Deterrence* (New Haven: Yale University Press, 1999), 32.

21. Michael J. Mazarr, Don M. Snider, and James A. Blackwell, Jr., eds., *Desert Storm: The Gulf War and What We Learned* (Boulder, Colo.: Westview, 1993), 26.

22. These files from the Iraq Research and Documentation Project's Kuwait Data Set (KDS) can be accessed at www.fas.harvard.edu/~irdp.

23. F. Gregory Gause III, "Iraq's Decisions to Go to War, 1980 and 1990," *Middle East Journal* 56, no. 1 (2002): 56.

24. KDS Folder CD 9, File 104-6-015, p. 6.

25. KDS Folder CD004, File 084-2-002, p. 5, and File 084-2-002a, pp. 2–17.

26. On postwar attempts to oust Saddam Hussein see Kenneth Katzman, "Iraq's Opposition Movements," *Congressional Research Service,* March 26, 1998.

27. Baghdad Republic of Iraq Television, September 12, 2001, 1700 GMT.

28. Baghdad Republic of Iraq Television, September 12, 2001, 1700 GMT.

29. Omayma Abd el-Latif, "Resisting Occupation," *Al-Ahram Weekly,* April 3–9, 2003.

30. "Accepting Extremism and Tyranny," *Al-Ta'akhi,* April 22, 2004.

31. Shibley Telhami, "Arab Public Opinion on the United States and Iraq: Postwar Prospects for Changing Prewar Views," *Brookings Review* 21, no. 3 (2003): 24.

32. Charles Clover, "The Fighters of Falluja," *Financial Times,* April 24, 2004.

33. Liam Anderson and Gareth Stansfield, *The Future of Iraq: Dictatorship, Democracy, or Division?* (New York: Palgrave Macmillan, 2004), 225.

34. "Accepting Extremism and Tyranny," *Al-Ta'akhi,*April 22, 2004.

35. "Muqtada al-Sadr Issues Statement on Bloody Incidents in Karbala," *Al-Safir,* October 18, 2003.

36. "We Reject the Presence of Foreign Forces in Iraq: Interview of Sayyid Mohammad Ridha Sistani, Ayatollah Sistani's Son and Spokesman," *Al-Mostaqbal,* May 28, 2003.

37. Al-Jazeera Satellite Channel, May 1, 2004, 1815 GMT.

38. Al-Jazeera Satellite Channel Television, August 24, 2005, 1100 GMT.

39. Statement of Grand Ayatollah Al-Sayyid Muhammad Taqi al-Din al-Mudarrisi, April 29, 2004, http://www.ebaa.net.

40. Statement of Al-Sayyid Muhammad Taqi al-Din al-Mudarrisi.

41. Kamal Rauf, "The Governing Council between the Pressure of U.S. and the Extremism of Arab Nationalism," *Howalati,* April 28, 2004.

42. Sabir Damirchi, "The Excuse Is Worse Than the Fault," *Turkomaneli,* April 18, 2004.

43. Damirchi, "Excuse."

44. Basim al-Shaykh, "Neocolonialism," *Al-Dustur,* April 22, 2004.

45. Muhammad Hanun, "Those Standing on the Hills!" *Al-Furat,* April 13, 2004.

46. See Ibrahim Al-Marashi, "Boycotts, Coalitions, and the Threat of Violence: The Run-Up to the January 2005, Iraqi Elections," *Middle East Review of International Affairs News,* January 2005, http://meria.idc.ac.il/news/2005/05 news1.html.

47. Al-Marashi, "Boycotts."

48. Quoted in Ibrahim Al-Marashi, "Iraq's Constitutional Debate," *Middle East Review of International Affairs* 9, no. 3 (2005): 160–61.

49. Al-Marashi, "Iraq's Constitutional Debate," 160–61

50. Al-Marashi, "Iraq's Constitutional Debate," 160–61.

BEYOND

THE STAINED

GLASS

WINDOW

❏ ❏ ❏

INDONESIAN PERCEPTIONS OF THE UNITED STATES

AND THE WAR ON TERROR

Melani Budianta

> Attacking terrorism contains a different challenge: how to
> act so that victory is not the same as further strengthening . . .
> imbalance. In other words: being mindful of how great
> the danger is of an awesome power that has no
> self-doubt that it is just and right.
> —GOENAWAN MOHAMAD, "New York Diary,"
> *Manhattan Sonnet*

IN STEPHEN CRANE'S novel *Active Service* (1899), a war correspondent covering the Greco-Turkish War is frustrated by his inability to speak directly to a group of friendly Turkish soldiers. He complains that "talking through an interpreter to the minds of other men was as satisfactory as looking at landscape through a stained glass window."[1] I fear that in my attempts to explain what Indonesians now think of the United States, I, too, am partially separated from American readers by the gaudy translucency of colorful, too resonant words—*Islamic fundamentalists, war on terrorism, President Bush, September 11, democracy, human rights, Israel, Iraq*—that carry little common meaning across the mental boundaries that separate most Americans from the multitudes of people who live in Indonesia, a non-Islamic country with the biggest Muslim population in the world. Apparently, we live in a time in which the common currency of critical concepts and everyday language is nearly bankrupt, making cross-cultural dialogue more complicated than ever.

So, how do Indonesian intellectuals, especially those like me who were educated in the United States, soldier through the cultural wars that distort perceptions across the international realm and that make communication, especially between Islamic nations and the United States, so difficult? By simply trying, I guess. I hope that the years I spent in the United States and the professional commitment I have made to studying the United States provide me a window (streaked with all kinds of biases, for sure) through which I can look in both directions.

The Looking Glass of Terrorism

An Indonesian exclaims: "Who is actually the terrorist, the one who is against human rights? The answer is the U.S., because they attacked Iraq; they are leaders of terrorists, the initiators of war."[2] We might hope that these are the words of an ill-informed, easily excited taxi driver in Jakarta. No such luck. Hamzah Haz, then vice president of Indonesia, who was also head of the Islamic coalition party, the United Development Party, made this statement at the end of 2003 while addressing the directors of the *pesantren* (Muslim boarding schools) in Brebes, Central Java. Haz made his remarks shortly before George W. Bush was scheduled to visit Indonesia. The Indonesian Ministry of Foreign Affairs was suitably embarrassed by Haz's blunt words, but no one in Indonesia could deny that the vice president had expressed how most Indonesians felt towards America's post–September 11 foreign policy.

The United States and Indonesia have never had an easy relationship. American scholar Paul Gardner argues that the bilateral relationship has amounted to a series of "government created catastrophes." Both countries have been guilty of creating such catastrophes. In 1957, a decade after the United States played a successful mediating role between the fledgling Republic of Indonesia and the ex-colonizer, the Netherlands, the CIA gave military assistance to Indonesian dissident groups in its Cold War strategy to curb the growing leftist orientation of the Indonesian government. In 1963, in turn, the Indonesian government under Sukarno attacked British policies in Malaysia, and then launched a vituperative campaign against capitalism, the West in general, and the United States in specific. Sukarno even banned Indonesia's most popular musical group, Koes Plus, because the band was heavily influenced by the Beatles. When I was a primary school student in these days, I was instructed that wearing the bell-bottom fashion of the sixties was anti-Indonesian. In school we were taught to chant the rhyme *Inggris kita linggis, Amerika kita seterika* (Let's crush the British, Let's iron Americans).

Indonesians' attitudes toward the United States have always been conditioned by Indonesia's own internal political-economic dynamic. Government-sponsored anti-Western sentiment, thus, ended when Sukarno stepped down from power after a bloody anti-Communist purge led by General Soeharto in 1965. Indonesia's second president, Soeharto, was seen as a Cold War hero by the West; he did not just open Indonesia to American culture, he also warmly welcomed American corporate investment. By the late 1990s more than four hundred American business firms operated in Indonesia. No single political event since, global or local, has stopped Indonesians' growing familiarity with and even affection for American popular culture—nor the powerful presence of American corporations. Because the MTV/McDonald's era and Soeharto's authoritarian and corrupt New Order were so closely interwoven, the rush of American culture and business into Indonesia has been seen by some progressive activists as a pernicious force that blinded the young to the most damaging aspects of unfettered capitalism practiced by giant multinational corporations and numbed them to the antidemocratic aspects of the Indonesian political system under the Soeharto regime.

A marked shift towards democratization occurred in 1998 when the people's movement popularly called the Reformation forced Soeharto out of power in the aftermath of the economic crisis that swept Southeast Asia in 1997. The post-Reformation era witnessed the growth of democratic processes and institutions championed by the United States, the flowering of a free press, peaceful general elections, decentralization, and the political participation of minority groups. This transformation was not without difficulties, instability, and uncertainty. In the eight years after the Reformation, Indonesia elected four different presidents. With the weakening of the central government, a chaotic, conflict-ridden democratic space has emerged, and while such freedom is welcome, the free press in Indonesia has given voice to a small, but growing, militantly anti-Western, right-wing political faction.

The course taken by U.S. foreign policy after September 11 has intensified this openly expressed anti-Americanism. When Bush's antiterrorist policy took on an aggressively militaristic form, widespread popular sympathy for American victims of the September 11 attack rapidly turned to concern over Muslim casualties of the American military. Many Indonesians recoiled when they read that certain American politicians and pundits were suggesting that terrorism was a central aspect of Muslim fundamentalism or that a "clash of civilizations" was inevitable between Muslims and Christians. These presumed attacks against fundamentalism incited pan-Islamic solidarity among the Muslim majority of Indonesia's population even as the U.S. policy towards Iraq caused a great majority of Indonesians across the political spectrum to view the U.S. government as an aggressive, militaristic danger to the world.

Even before the Bush administration launched its preemptive war on Iraq, Indonesians began public protests against the American war on terrorism. Protestors burning American flags, and effigies of President Bush were common in 2002, especially outside McDonald's restaurants, which, in Indonesia, are seen as symbols of the United States.

Sadly, the October 2002 bombing of a popular nightclub in Bali that killed some two hundred people, most of them young Australians, only contributed to anti-American hostility in Indonesia. While few Indonesians approved of the horrific slaughter, many were angry at how the American government responded to it. After Indonesian and international security forces linked the bombing to the Jamaah Islamiah (JI) network, the American government, as well as Australia, began to target Indonesia as a terrorist hot spot. Indonesia was red-flagged as a major recruiting ground and base for terrorists, the only Southeast Asian country so named. Indonesian citizens visiting the United States had to report to the Immigration and Naturalization Service for especially rigorous treatment. In response to this labeling and special treatment, even the editorial page of *Kompas,* Indonesia's major national daily newspaper founded by Catholic intellectuals, angrily protested, declaring American treatment of Indonesia "discriminative and insulting."[3]

Muslim fundamentalists within Indonesia responded most vehemently against America's post–September 11 policies and statements that broadly linked terrorism to Islam. The conservative Islamist journal *Sabilli* went so far as to declare the Muslim community leader Abubakar Ba'asyir its 2002 man of the year. Ba'asyir had been detained in connection with the Bali bombing and had been routinely depicted in the U.S. mass media as the spiritual leader of Indonesian terrorists. Conspiracy theories abounded in various e-group discussions: "Many people believe that the false accusation against Ustadz Abubakar Ba'asyir is actually an entry point for a systemic strategy to commit a character assassination on Islam, which at the same time works to repress [the] Islamic movement and which will enable the U.S. led Zionist-Christian hegemony to rob resources from the lands of the Moslem people."[4]

Many Muslims in Indonesia who are neither radicals nor fundamentalists believed that American government policy against fundamentalism was highly biased and unfair. The Council of the Indonesian Ulammas (MUI) responded bitterly to President Bush's demand that Muslims in Indonesia speak out against the fundamentalists and condemn terrorists, stating that it was "arrogant for Bush to ask the Indonesian Moslem to be moderate," as if Islam were the seed of terrorism, when, the council insisted, really "the U.S. is the sponsor of state terrorism."[5] Similarly, Indonesian public intellectual Riza Sihbudi argued, "The U.S. condemns radicalism, which it calls violent. Actually, state violence practiced in the name of democracy . . . should also be considered terrorism."[6] An editorial in the newspaper *Koran Tempo* stated that throughout Indonesia the word *Bush* "symbolizes the new world colonizer and terrorist."[7]

Blurred Shadows: Fundamentalism and Terrorism

From the Indonesian perspective, at least, it appears that since September 11 Americans have been led by their government and the mass media to believe that a direct connection exists between Islamic fundamentalism and terrorism. As a result of this equation, American officials have treated all Islamic groups in Indonesia who oppose U.S. policy in the Islamic world as a unified terrorist threat. This American tendency to lump together all critical voices as Islamic terrorists is, perhaps, an aspect of President Bush's declaration that you are either for the United States and its war on terrorism or you are against the United States and a supporter of terrorism. However, lumping all of these critics into one terrorist camp or organized terrorist network is tremendously misleading and prevents Americans from understanding how pro-Islamic elements and the increasingly powerful fundamentalist movement in Indonesia actually see the United States and prevents the United States from even trying to manage Indonesians' ever-growing mistrust of America.

Islamic fundamentalism in Indonesia is not new. It is, however, growing in popularity and influence, and its evolving status is conditioned by specific political issues and social conditions. When modern Indonesia was founded after World War II, its founding fathers deliberately chose not to make Indonesia an Islamic state. Although 90 percent of the Indonesian population was Muslim, the country was marked by pluralism. Buddhism, Hinduism, and, much more recently, Christianity have left strong cultural marks on this country made up of seven hundred ethnic groups spread over thirteen thousand islands. Despite this pluralist reality, a good many Muslim fundamentalists were disappointed that Indonesia was not created as an Islamic state. That feeling remains strong even today. Contemporary Islamic fundamentalists believe in an Islamic way of life in which their beliefs are the law of the land; in other words, they want Indonesia to be an Islamic nation in which there is no separation of state and religion. Under both the Sukarno and the Soeharto regimes, Islamic citizens who demanded the end of the secular state were repressed, often violently. Several scholars have argued that the Soeharto regime's harsh treatment of pro-Islamic political forces pushed that movement underground, where it became more radical and militant.[8] When Soeharto attempted to save his regime in the late 1990s by embracing political Islam, he unleashed a militant force that his prior policy of repression had radicalized. After Soeharto fell in 1998, the turbulent democratic transition served as a battlefield for various forces—including both fundamentalist and more moderate Islamic groups—each of which sought to negotiate a new place for Islam in Indonesia.

Radical Islamic fundamentalism has become increasingly popular in Indonesia for several interconnected reasons. First, fundamentalist leaders in Indonesia have been outspoken in their demands for greater economic justice. In impoverished Indonesia this call is powerful. Second, the fundamentalists offer Indonesians caught in the riptides of modernization and secularization a straightforward set of moral prescriptions and spiritual practices that a great many people, even young, well-educated Indonesians, find life-saving (This is similar to the growing popularity of Christian fundamentalism among the young generation in the United States.) Third, Islamic fundamentalists have been uncompromising in their support for the Palestinian people, a position of utmost importance to most Indonesians. It is worth adding here that support for the Palestinians and anger over America's extraordinary support for Israel has contributed to the radicalization of many Indonesians and unified an array of factionalized Islamic and non-Islamic groups. Islamic fundamentalists are joined by moderate Islamists, as well as secular intellectuals, in decrying the U.S. government's double standard in its Middle East foreign policy. Even the generally pro-Western, English-language newspaper *Jakarta Post* editorialized:

> How can the U.S. preach to the world about justice when it permits Israel's efforts to subjugate the Palestinians by whatever means it deems fit to continue? Why does the superpower demand that Iran stop its nuclear program while defending Israel's nuclear program at the same time?[9]

In Indonesian universities, the Palestinian issue, more than any other, drives the growing popularity of Islamic study groups. These groups, in turn, use the American government's "pro-Israeli stance" to disseminate a Zionist-Christian anti-Islam conspiracy theory, which was first spread and is still spread most vociferously in Indonesia by Islamic fundamentalist groups.

Given the anger many Indonesians, especially fundamentalists, already felt towards U.S. policies in the Middle East, the U.S. air raids against Afghanistan and the Iraq war were seen by many Indonesians not as wars on terrorism but as further attacks on Islamic people. These attacks have been perceived by substantial numbers in Indonesia as a deliberate campaign by American-commanded Western forces to destroy the Islamic world. In the days right after the invasion of Iraq, some in

Indonesia, as in other Islamic countries, called for a jihad to prevent the destruction of Islam. Immediately, about eleven thousand civilians from Sumatra and Java volunteered for the Defender of Islam Front, which sought to send armed men to defend Iraq.[10] Simultaneously, militant groups threatened to do *sweeping,* meaning that they intended to to identify and drive away Americans and other Westerners in a number of Indonesian cities. Although these threats were not acted upon, the American war on Iraq greatly intensified anti-Western feelings in Indonesia and greatly increased the popularity of Islamic fundamentalist groups, which had long been the most vocal opponents of American foreign policy.

So, by the end of 2004 many Indonesians were furious with the United States. U.S. support of Israel was almost universally deplored, and the invasion of Iraq was widely despised. Fundamentalists led the anti-American charge, though many others voiced similar outrage. But—and here is where I wish to be very clear—many, many other Indonesians, including Islamic fundamentalists, while opposed to U.S. policies, did not support armed jihad, did not support terrorism, and did not support violent acts against Americans or other westerners. A random survey of twelve hundred Islamic citizens of Indonesia done by the PPIM, or Pusat Pengkajian Islam dan Masyarakat (Center of Islamic and Social Studies), in 2005 showed that only 1.5 percent of the respondents had been involved in anti-American activities. A high percentage (43.9 percent) of the respondents reported that they were appreciative of American culture and values, but at the same time 32 percent of them admitted to harboring anti-American sentiments, geared especially at U.S. foreign policies.[11]

In Indonesia, Islamic fundamentalism does not equal terrorism. In Indonesia, Islam takes many forms, and within that broad set of differences Islamic fundamentalism, as well, takes many forms. At a basic level, the *dakwah* movement ("religious purification and intensification"), which is at the core of Islamic fundamentalism, is expressed in different ways and flows in different political directions.[12] Some Indonesian fundamentalists argue that democracy is incompatible with Islam. Others, like the proponents of the Partai Keadilan Sejahtera (Prosperous Justice Party), are strong believers in democracy. This party, composed mostly of young urban intellectuals, makes up the benign face of Indonesian Islamic fundamentalism.

Moderate elements in Indonesia fear that American policies that fail to distinguish fundamentalism from terrorism will result in radicalizing all fundamentalists and possibly even all Muslims. They worry, too, that the constant American attacks on fundamentalists will unify Muslims of all beliefs, who will perceive the attack on fundamentalism as an attack on Islamic belief in general. Khamami Zada from the political party Nachdatul Ulama warns that if the United States does not redefine its policy against the Islamic world, it will invite a rising "cultural resistance" from moderate Islamists.[13] Riza Sihbudi further argues that "Fundamentalism and radicalism—at the level of concepts and beliefs—are not threats against democracy. They are [only] against democracy if they resort to violence."[14]

I don't want to soft-pedal the threat some militant groups, like the Forum for Defending Islam (FDI), pose for democratic practice and peaceful coexistence in Indonesia. FDI members do take the law into their own hands by raiding places they believe to be sanctioning immoral acts, and by threatening to oust Americans. But for Indonesians the question is: where does fundamentalism end and violence begin?

The intellectual Rizal Sukma argues that the period of democratization after the fall of Soeharto allowed the fundamentalist movement to grow at the same time that weakened state institutions and law enforcement made Indonesia susceptible to terrorist acts. He believes that "the growth of [violent] radicalism can be checked if Indonesia manages to accelerate economic recovery and to establish a solid democracy, based on the rule of law."[15] Critically, he argues, fundamentalism is not essentially linked to political violence. Political violence in Indonesia practiced by fundamentalists, he believes, was caused by the specific social context of the early twenty-first century, not because of the nature of Islamic fundamentalism. By extension, he argues, at the global level the establishment of democracy, economic and social justice, and the rule of international law—instead of the use of military aggression—are the best means for fighting terrorism.

Whether the U.S. government, which under President Bush preferred a policy of unilateral and militaristic foreign policy, can help to produce those conditions remains to be seen. Americans need to understand that in Indonesia and in many other Islamic nations many people think that the United States does not want to help them, does not want to see justice for Palestinians, does not want to see Islam remain a respected faith because the U.S. government is a global hegemon dedicated to global economic exploitation and the forced conversion of other societies to its cultural and religious verities.

Double Mirrors: Fundamentalism and Globalization

No Indonesian intellectuals want to see their society become a cultural, political, or economic tributary to the American colossus. Almost all argue that Indonesia needs to resist becoming overly depdendent on the United States or any other Western power. Even those of the younger generation who see themselves as secular in orientation and who were educated in Western nations champion an antihegemonic struggle against an ever more aggressive American presence in their complex culture and in their fragile nation.

For the director of CETRO (Center for Electorate Reform), Smita Notosusanto, the threat of American military and economic hegemony is a given fact that must be confronted. Since World War II, she argues, the U.S. government has sold itself to the world as "the benevolent Hegemon."[16] In the United States, this world-shaping ideology is presented as a kind of messianic mission that is self-evidently legitimated by Americans' sense that their ends are pure and their means are always appropriate to the virtuous task at hand. In her columns in the *Tempo* weekly news magazine, Notosusanto points out that American foreign policy, at least in the Islamic world, is rarely benevolent and too often deadly for the people supposedly being so generously helped. In Indonesia, America's preemptive strike against Iraq, its threats against Islamic nations such as Syria and Sudan, and its blatant disregard for the legitimate rights of the Palestinian people are seen as proof positive of American hypocrisy, militaristic bullying, and xenophobia towards the Moslem population. For Smita, Vedi Hadiz, Manneke Budiman, and Reni Winata, the new American campaign against Islamic fundamentalism is a mask for America's quest for empire and domination.[17]

This perspective casts a different light on the American war on Iraq. "Freedom is on the march," Bush says to the American people, assuming that thanks to the Americans, Iraq is now in the process of becoming a democratic nation. Using democracy and human rights as their yardsticks, however, the Indonesian scholars mentioned above question the consistency with which the United States applies these core American values in their foreign policy. According to Hadiz, "The victims of the American imperium are the very principles of democracy and human rights." For Sihbudi, the Iraq war is proof that its unjustifiable fear of Islamic fundamentalism has caused the West to work against democratic principles.[18] These intellectuals have not forgotten Bush's earlier misrepresentation of the arms situation in the prewar Iraq, nor the way Bush insisted on the unilateral decision to launch the war despite UN opposition and global civil society protests. Since Iraq did not in fact present a direct threat to the United States and had not conspired with the September 11 terrorists, they believe that the attack on Iraq was a power grab exercised by the United States to secure Iraq's huge oil reserves. In this way the United States is "capitalizing" the discourse of terrorism in order to strengthen its global economic position, even as it secures its geopolitical domination.[19]

Before the war broke out, few Indonesians were interested in defending Saddam Hussein or his regime. In the weeks leading up to the war, Saddam was commonly referred to in the press as "the Butcher." However, President Bush also was caricatured as the "Cowboy," and in Indonesia, where far more people identify with American Indians, this nickname was not a positive one. Thus, the battle was seen in Indonesia as being between "the Butcher and the Cowboy"—or to play off President Bush's rhetoric regarding the "axis of evil," it was a battle between two evildoers.

Unlike the wild conspiracy theorists in Indonesia's popular press, who argue that President Bush, undoubtedly in league with the Israeli government, was behind the September 11 attacks, Indonesia's public intellectuals recognize a genuine terrorist threat to the United States. Still, most believe that the United States is making full use of that real threat to justify attacks on those in the Islamic world that stand as threats to American need for control of global economic resources, especially oil. Muhammad Fuad, an American Studies scholar and historian at the University of Indonesia, states the issue bluntly: "The U.S. imperium policy has caused too much injustice in the world because the U.S. has grown to be a huge country with huge consumption needs. It is like a giant that needs too much." For Fuad and other Indonesian intellectuals the root of America's current war on terrorism is not the acts of the terrorists but the global economic injustices to which terrorists are responding. Manneke Budiman, a scholar at the Australian Studies Center, explains:

> The root of the problem should be traced to what happens to many third world countries when cultural imperialism and globalization can no longer be checked. . . . What people are fighting is the effect of globalization, when on the one hand globalization brings diversity and chance, but on the other hand causes marginalization and injustice. . . . The first wave of globalization that occurred earlier had this mechanism for pulling a brake, for checking its growth for a while in order to absorb criticism and resistance in order to transform itself to be a new updated model that can accommodate all of the demands in its further growth. This second wave of global capitalism—which America stands for—has lost this ability to accommodate difference.[20]

Many of Indonesia's most sophisticated analysts of post–September 11 American foreign policy see the war on terrorism as merely being a far more aggressive version of pre–September 11 neoconservative foreign policy. This policy in its current form aims to create a unipolar world system in which American-dominated economic investment and resource exploitation opportunities are locked in through military pressure or attack. Budiman, and he is not alone, sees terrorism as a predictable, though not acceptable, response to the coercive and corrosive force of American global intervention on behalf of its own expansive needs. As Muhammad Fuad notes: "With its prosperity and advanced technology, it is easy for the U.S. to produce food, but half of the world population is starving. The U.S. could have led efforts in finding balance."[21] Besides sharing its immense productive capacity with those who are in dire need, such a balance between American capacity and other people's needs should also include a willingness to sign and abide by environmental treaties that the UN has prepared, such as the Kyoto Protocol and the Rio Declaration. Just as Indonesians are highly suspicious of American global policy, they are equally confident—probably unrealistically so—that because the United States has so much productive power and so much wealth, its government could, if it so decided, lead the world to peace and a better future. Americans need to understand that in many parts of the world anger at the United States is caused not only by what policies it does pursue but also by what policies it scorns or disregards.

Even those Indonesians who are most dedicated to developing good relations with the United States feel constantly frustrated by the American government's arrogant insensitivity to conditions on the ground in Indonesia. For example, back in October 2003 Bush jetted into Bali and gave a five-minute speech in which he managed to declare that *pesantren* schools in Indonesia had to revise their curriculum to discourage the growth of Islamic fundamentalism. This casual remark created bitter fallout in Indonesia, where for many years moderates, secularists, and fundamentalists had been working toward recasting aspects of these schools, especially in regard to issues of gender equity.[22] Bush's remarks and those made by right-wing Australian politicians in the aftermath of the Bali bomb tragedy may have played well inside their respective nations, but they showed a destructive lack of understanding about Indonesia and did nothing to help curb the appeal of extremism among radical Islamic factions.

Many Indonesian intellectuals hope that American citizens and America's vibrant civil society can offer them help in fighting the twin swords of radical, violent religious militants and rapacious, armed, government-sponsored capitalists. In a column published by the *Tempo* weekly magazine, Vedi Hadiz described the antiwar civilian protests in America as "the only signs that democratic and universal humanitarian values are still alive in the hearts of some American people."[23] Another *Tempo* columnist, Smita Notosusanto, hoped that such protests might spark "an effective domestic opposition movement [that would] wake up the apolitical mass of American people . . . so that they will be more enlightened in watching the position of the U.S. in international relations, and channel their aspirations through the ballot."[24] While the 2004 American presidential election put an end to that particular hope, many of us do realize that the whole of the American people and the particular policies of the Bush administration are not the same thing and that change is still possible. For Farkha Ciciek, civil society activist and director of the Women's Islamic Center for Reproductive Rights, people-to-people interaction[25] and global civil society are the best hope for changing the global climate of suspicion, aggression, and xenophobia. Such solidarity could be strengthened if the civilians of both countries realize that they all suffer from the blunders of high politics, and from the misleading discourse on terrorism. Civilian solidarities could lead to effective political diplomacy. Even as President Bush's political rhetoric continued to anger many Indonesians, the American people's massive outpouring of concern and help during the Christmastime 2004 tsunami tragedy in the Islamic province of Aceh won the hearts of many Indonesians. Americans' response to Indonesia's disaster has not been forgotten here.

Refractions: The Role of the Intellectuals

I began this essay with a reference to Stephen Crane's metaphor for speaking to foreigners through an interpreter: a stained glass window. This kind of pane seems to allow through the light of meaning, but in fact it produces only misleading images as people on both sides strain to see one another through a too-colorful, translucent barrier. In many of his stories, Crane depicts the fatal consequences of such misperceptions and mistranslations: violent death and even war. For this essay, I spoke with many Indonesian intellectuals, many of them experts on the United States, Europe, or Australia, and almost without exception they shared a common fear, that between Indonesia and the West lies a dangerous barrier of mutual misunderstanding and ignorance.

Those of us in Indonesia who serve professionally as cultural brokers between the West and our own society feel a tremendous need to find a way to communicate both transnationally and internally. It is not easy for us. We find ourselves caught in our own uncertainties about Western nations' motives, our own place in Indonesia, our relationship to Islam, and the American government's policies. Post-Soeharto Indonesia is in the early stages of a difficult reconstruction of its national political system. We are a new democracy, struggling to create majoritarian rule while at the same time protecting minority rights. Prodemocracy activists are struggling to balance the pressure of right-wing extremism domestically, as well as globally. Islamic feminists like Ciciek Farkha, who are fighting hard to guarantee a place for women in a society in which much ambivalence exists about basic issues of gender equity, are often seen as selling out to the West. We cannot help but refract the American war on terror through our own difficult struggle to create a just and vital Indonesia. We want the United States to be our ally in that effort, but we are too aware that the American government thinks little about how its actions in the war on terror affect our struggle.

"How can we explain America after September 11?" Muhammad Fuad asked himself. He finds no simple answer: "Given the nature of the September 11 attack, I understand the anger and the frustrations of American people. Law needs to be enforced, although the criminals cry 'Allahu Akbar.' But whether the enforcement has to be done through war is highly questionable. By attacking Afghanistan and later Iraq . . . America failed to be the world leader that has all the opportunity and capability to create world peace."[26] Tommy Christomy, trained in American pragmatism, feels himself emotionally torn by American foreign policy:

> As a Moslem in Indonesia, I have been observing what happened in Bosnia, Palestine, and Iraq. I find the facts disturbing, although I always wonder, whether the media did not distort this impression that I got about the U.S. I looked at the civilian casualties, and I asked, is this what America wants? I met a Palestinian, who told me that he was a refugee since he was born, and then I notice how supportive the U.S. is towards Israel. I am still collecting my observations, and have reached no conclusive answers yet. But intellectually and emotionally, what I observe is troubling. Every day a child dies in these wars [in the Middle East and in Iraq]. There is an intellectual matter here about how to address the issue of conflict. At the same time, my sense of humanity is hurt.[27]

Those of us who are Western-educated and know that the United States is a complex and fluid society want to speak out and explain the current predicament to our Indonesian countrymen. But finding a critical tone that is rational, fair-minded, and useful is not easy; it is rarely welcome; and it can be risky. Reni Winata, the director of the Indonesian Australian Studies center in Jakarta, wrote a newspaper article right after the Bali bombing that tried to carefully critique the war-on-terror policies pursued by the United States and Australia that had inadvertently, she said, led to the Bali horror. She was censured by Indonesians and Australians alike for not showing sufficient sympathy for the bombing victims, and she was told that her critique could be hijacked by militant terrorists. Hermawan Sulistiyo, a leading Indonesian commentator on the war on terror, sees another problem. In Indonesia few people want to hear a rational analysis of the issues that separate most Islamic people from the United States. He observes: "This 'battle' of West vs. Islam is dominated by one singular perception. The stupidest or weirdest information—

e.g., the discussion of a micro-nuclear bomb—is considered true if the information attacks the West and supports the 'Moslem perspective.'"[28] Then, too, writers who express too critical a stance against violent Islamic groups are readily dismissed by many in Indonesia as turncoats likely under the pay of the American government. Zamira Loebis, an Indonesian who works for *Time* magazine, says that members of the fundamentalist groups she interviews often accuse her of being an agent of the CIA. That she is a Christian woman further complicates the matter. Loebis says that her difficulties run in both directions. The American mass media has its own biases and certainties that get in the way of understanding the situation on the ground in Indonesia: "I have to warn them again and again that JI [Jamaah Islamiyah] is a generic name for many Islamic groups, and that it is very tricky to associate it directly with terrorism."[29]

In spite of these difficulties, all of the Western-educated intellectuals with whom I talked want to play a part in improving relations between Indonesia and the West. Tommy Christomy said it best: we have to find a way to "fight with words, not bullets."[30] Very few Indonesians are fervent supporters of violent jihad. Far more are still eagerly awaiting the next big pop music hit from the United States. Somewhere on the Indonesian mental landscape, in the space between fierce anti-Western anger and complacent pro-Western consumerism, room exists for a critical and informed discourse about the role the United States and other Western nations can and should play in Indonesia, in the Islamic world, and throughout the vast developing regions of the planet. In Indonesia, I believe this balanced discourse must be presented most forcefully in the nation's secular universities. These universities are where Indonesia's professional classes, governing elite, and cultural leaders are educated. Right now, even in these secular universities, fundamentalists groups are growing ever stronger. Those of us who oppose this development are not idle. Moderate Indonesian intellectuals have formed numerous organizations such as the Network of Liberal Islam and the Institute of Civil Society to challenge the fundamentalists' expanding reach.

However, many Indonesians are still in the process of making up their minds about the role the United States should play in their world. How the masses of Indonesians will decide will depend on many internal and external factors, but, simply enough, most will choose based on a simple criterion: does the West help me and my family find some economic and political justice or does it hurt me and my family? Radicalism, whether secular or religious, provides people with a collective mission, self-worth, and a sense of belonging. Religious fundamentalists, as well as secular radicals, are responding to what they perceive to be global injustice; in that struggle some turn to terrorist actions. If Americans want to turn people away from such radicalism, they need to find better alternatives and to find the resources to support such efforts. For Indonesians the hundreds of billions the American government spent on the Iraq war was not money well spent.

Indonesian intellectuals like us, who are educated and critically looking at the West, are struggling to see through the stained glass window of bias and prejudice to better understand what the United States and the West have to offer our nation.[31] "There is no such thing as a neutral position," says my colleague Budiman. As scholars who are at home in both cultures, we know we have to take a stand, as stated by Reni Winata: "Sometimes we have to speak on behalf of our first home, Indonesia, [sometimes on behalf of] our second home [the West]." Striking a balance during a time of extraordinarily heated emotions is never easy. Living in this time of crisis, in between cultures, is like inhabiting what poet Gloria Anzaldúa called the borderlands. She writes, "To live in the Borderlands means you / are . . . caught in the crossfire between camps / . . . not knowing which side to turn to, run from; / . . . People walk through you, the wind steals your voice."[32] To be able to speak for and to opposing sides, and to negotiate a position for oneself is crucial, as Anzaldúa believes: "To survive the Borderlands / you must live *sin fronteras* / be a crossroads."[33]

Paul Gardner wrote in 1997 that the long-term nature of the relationship between the United States and Indonesia would be "determined less by the two governments' reactions to issues of the moment than by gradual change in popular attitudes created by increased contact and shared experiences through trade, educational exchanges, and increased communications."[34] This optimistic hope for the future seems to have been derailed, at least in the short term, by recent events. U.S. foreign policy following September 11—especially the air raids on Afghanistan and the Iraqi war—have unfortunately served, to use Gardner's phrase, as new "government created catastrophes" that have solidified popular hostility in Indonesia towards the U.S. government.

However, Gardner is right when he suggests that many Indonesians, despite the current situation, like aspects of American culture and are growing more familiar with it. This cultural connection is real, from popular culture to the arts and literature. While the young generation is attuned to MTV, many people in their forties and older, Americans will be surprised to know, have become loyal fans of local country music programs. Professionals of all walks of life, from mathematicians to musicians—many of whom have directly experienced the magic of Broadway—founded the Jakarta Broadway Singers, and spend their leisure time putting on their own creative renditions of American smash hits such as of *West Side Story* and *Miss Saigon*. Urban middle-class people of my generation, born in the years just after World War II, spent our childhood reading, in translation, *Tom Sawyer, Huckleberry Finn, Uncle Tom's Cabin, Little House on the Prairie,* and later, *Little Women*. As a result, American literature and culture is not only familiar to many Indonesians, but is a part of ourselves.

American influence on Indonesian arts and culture cannot be overlooked. Indonesia's most renowned author, the late Pramoedya Ananta Toer, translated John Steinbeck's *Of Mice and Men* and acknowledged his literary debt to William Saroyan. The famous playwright W. S. Rendra developed his theatrical aesthetics upon returning from the United States. The Iowa Writing Program has been the home of more than two dozens Indonesian poets, novelists, and short-story writers. American foundations, especially the Rockefeller Foundation, have given Indonesian artists and dancers, such as Bagong Kussudiardja, the opportunity to use America as a training ground for their artistic talents; as a result, American grant-makers have strengthened Indonesia's traditional cultural repertoires.

For several decades, the United States has helped Indonesia develop strong cohorts of intellectuals and professionals who have played a direct role in building a dynamic society. The Fulbright-Hayes scholarship program, for example, has enabled hundreds of top Indonesian students to attend outstanding academic institutions in the United States. American fellowship grantees, almost all of whom returned to Indonesia, further imbued with respect for principles of democratic government and individual rights, have gone on to take leading positions in the Indonesian government, universities, and private sector. Along these same lines, when the people power movement struggled to end Soeharto's militaristic rule, Indonesian prodemocracy forces worked closely with global human rights organizations, many of which were American-based, seeking help and protection. Then, in the aftermath of the political upheaval, international funding agencies, including the Ford Foundation, supported Indonesian publishers as they fought to create a lively, open public sphere. American nongovernmental organizations have continued to play a valuable role in helping Indonesians create a more democratic, free society, and some intellectuals and activists appreciate and acknowledge their assistance.

This due respect was openly displayed in the immediate aftermath of the September 11 attacks when a group of Indonesian writers, as an expression of sympathy for the victims, rushed into press *The Manhattan Sonnets,* an anthology of literary works by Indonesian writers on New York City. This work, as captured in these lines by Sitor Situmorang, reflects the close emotional ties the authors have with the American people and culture:

> When we parted that night
> At the corner of Broadway & Waverly Place
> (we might as well have been in Sanur, Bali!)
> when you vanished
> in the flow of traffic
> I did not feel that we had parted
> For New York is you.

The poem speaks of two lovers, the speaker and the American lover (whose boyfriend was waiting even as they met), both of whom, in the end of their encounter, are changed by their common passion:

> Are you still you,
> am I still I?
> stretched across,
> the old bed,
> in entirety consumed
> by the same flame?

As symbolized by the intimacy that transformed the two lovers, close encounters between Indonesians and Americans have produced enhanced cultural affinity. What is uncanny, since this poem was first published in 1988, is the unintended reference to Bali, which on October 12, 2001, was, like New York City, "in entirety consumed by the same flame" of terrorism. It is tragic that the terrorism that has besieged both of our nations has not resulted in more mutual compassion.

Still, I want to underline that individual Americans have for decades played valued roles in bridging our two nations. Decades ago, George McTurnan Kahin became the first great modern American scholar of Indonesia; he championed Indonesian independence immediately after World War II and created an enduring institutional home for the scholarly study of Indonesia at Cornell University. It is no accident that it was at Cornell that I was able to pursue my doctoral work in literature. Yet the history of our two societies has been governed more by government-created catastrophes than it has been by cultural and humanistic ties woven inch by inch by scholars, artists, activists, and everyday citizens. Even so, we learn from history that public pressure, often inspired by committed individuals can improve nation-states' foreign policies and mend nation-states' broken relations. We expect that the U.S. government, which plays such a powerful role, often unknowingly, in the affairs of other nations, will eventually use its power wisely, not to answer violence with violence but instead to seek alternative solutions. Without compromise on the American side, forces of moderation in Indonesia will find little room in which to champion ideals of fair-mindedness, rational discourse, and fact-based problem-solving. During these dangerous times, Indonesians and Americans alike must see beyond the distortions of the stained glass windows of the present to keep their yet unbalanced love affair alive.

Notes

1. Stephen Crane, "Active Service," in *Tales of Adventure* (Charlotttesville: University Press of Virginia, 1970), 3:183.

2. Suara Karya, "Deplu Berharap Ucapan Wapres Tak Pengaruhi Hubungan RI-AS" (The Indonesian Ministry of Foreign Affairs hopes vice president's remarks do not impact Indonesia-U.S. relations), September 5, 2003.

3. "Perlu Paradigma Baru Politik Luar Negeri AS" (New paradigm of U.S. foreign policy needed), *Kompas,* October 23, 2003.

4. From an e-group discussion, www.iias.nl/host/inis/INL/docs/Selasa0701 .doc.

5. Quoted from the editorial of the leading Moslem newspaper, *Republika,* October 20, 2003, "Ormas Islam Sikapi Kedatangan Bush" (Moslem mass organizations respond to Bush's visit).

6. Riza Sihbudi, "Islam, Radikalisme dan Demokrasi" (Islam, radicalism, and democracy), public oration booklet, Lembaga Ilmu Pengetahuan Indonesia, September 23, 2004, 13. See also his article "Timur Tengah Pasca Saddam" (Middle East Post-Saddam), *Tempo,* April 6, 2003.

7. "Aksi Menolak Kedatangan Bush Meluas" (Anti-Bush demonstrations spreading), *Koran Tempo,* October 22, 2003. See also the harsh criticism of Bush's policy in "Kebijakan Bush Ancam Peradaban" (Bush's policy threatens civilization), *Republika,* October 22, 2003.

8. See the following on the growth of Islamic radicalism: Rizal Sukma, "Militant Islam and Indonesia's Frail Democracy," *Kultur* 3, no. 1 (2003): 115–32; Elizabeth Fuller-Collins, "Islam is the Solution: Dakwah and Democracy in Indonesia," *Kultur* 3, no. 1 (2003): 151–82; and Hasan Noorhaidi, "The Radical Muslim Discourse on Jihad and the Hatred of Christians," paper presented at the International Symposium on Christianity in Indonesia: Perspectives of Power, University of Frankfurt, Germany, December 12–24, 2003, www.Christianity-in-Indonesia.de/pdf/muslim%20%discourse%20jihad.pdf.

9. An article without byline in the *Jakarta Post,* October 23, 2003, "Indonesians like Americans, Spurn U.S."

10. From the cover page report in the weekly news magazine *Tempo,* April 13, 2003, "Ke Irak Menyambung Nyawa" (To Iraq to offer lives), 32–33.

11. See Saiful Mujani, Jajat Burhanudin, Ismatu Ropi, et al., *Benturan Peradaban, Sikap dan Perilaku Islamis Indonesia terhadap Amerika Serikat* (Clash of civilizations: Attitudes and behavior of Islamic Indonesians towards the United States) (Jakarta: Freedom Institute and PPIM-UIN Jakarta, 2005).

12. Fuller-Collins distinguishes at least four streams of the *dakwah* movement, which expresses the nature of Islam fundamentalism in Indonesia. See her discussion of the changing configuration and group dynamics of the fundamentalist movement in "Islam is the Solution."

13. See Khamami Zada, "Bush and Islam Moderat" (Bush and moderate Islam), *Suara Karya,* October 25, 2003.

14. See Sihbudi, "Islam, Radikalisme dan Demokrasi."

15. Sukma, "Militant Islam," 127.

16. See Smita Notosusanto, "Hegemon," *Tempo,* February 2, 2003. See also her article "Gus, Pergilah ke Amerika!" (Go to America, Gus!), *Tempo,* February 2, 2003.

17. Based on interviews with Renny Winata, director of the Australian Studies Center, University of Indonesia, Jakarta, September 22, 2004; and Manneke Budiman, vice director of the Australian Studies Center, September 14, 2004. See Vedi R. Hadiz, "Imperium Amerika" (American imperium), *Tempo*, February 2, 2003.

18. Hadiz, "Imperium Amerika"; and Sihbudi, "Islam, Radikalisme dan Demokrasi."

19. Based on interviews with Winata; Budiman; and Mohammad Fuad, Jakarta, August 20, 2004; and Hadiz, "Imperium Amerika"; Notosusanto, "Hegemon"; Sihbudi, "Islam, Radikalisme dan Demokrasi"; and Sukma, "Militant Islam."

20. Budiman, interview.

21. Fuad, interview.

22. Ciciek Farkha, interview by the author, Jakarta, September 8, 2004.

23. See Hadiz, "Imperium Amerika."

24. Notosusanto, "Hegemon."

25. Farkha (interview) believes that cultural dialogue should occur through individual interaction. Exchange programs should be directed not only to urban intellectuals, but also to local community leaders. Inviting American Moslems to live in Islamic communities in Indonesia is another means for more intense, individualized cultural interaction that can counter negative stereotyping.

26. Fuad, interview.

27. Tommy Christommi, interview by the author, Jakarta, August 14, 2004.

28. Hermawan Sulistyo, *Bom Bali: Buku Putih tidak resmi Investigasi Teror Bom Bali* (Unofficial report on Bali bomb terror investigation) (Jakarta: Pensil-324, 2002), 77. See also his other works: *Beyond Terrorism: Dampak dan Strategi Masa Depan* (Impact and future strategy) (Jakarta: Sinar Harapan, Concern, FES, 2002), and *Saddam Melawan Amerika* (Saddam against the United States) (Jakarta: Pensil-324, 2003).

29. Zamira Loebis, interview, Jakarta, October 1, 2004.

30. Christommi, interview.

31. For an analytical essay on Indonesian perception of the West, see Julia Suryakusuma, "Marriage of Inconvenience: Indonesian Perceptions of the West," in *Sex, Power, and Nation* (Jakarta: Metafor, 2004).

32. Gloria Anzaldúa, *Borderlands/La Frontera: The New Meztiza* (San Fransico: Aunt Lute, 1987), 194.

33. Anzaldúa, *Borderlands*.

34. Paul Gardner, *Shared Hopes, Separate Fears: Fifty Years of US-Indonesian Relations* (Boulder, Colo.: Westview, 1997).

TURKISH

PERCEPTIONS

OF THE

UNITED STATES

❑ ❑ ❑

Nur Bilge Criss

IN TURKEY, when people look at the American government's so-called war of preemption in Iraq and the Bush administration's errant confidence in its right to make the world over in its own image, power management becomes an issue of importance. At some emotional level, some members of the political and intellectual elite can vaguely relate to the temptation, the peril, and the grandiosity of the dream of a vast order crafted in one's own image and controlled by one's own interests. But the long-gone Ottoman imperial reach also reminds that an empire's longevity depends not just on the power of its military but on the quality of its statesmanship and its ability to disseminate among less powerful peoples at least the appearance of justice. Military power has to withstand the test of moral authority to insure that bloody conflict does not turn the complex pleasures and responsibilities of an empire into a nightmare of endless rebellion and resistance.[1]

Turks, today, from across the political spectrum fear that the United States, the contemporary aspirant to world hegemon, has lost its moral authority as it dispenses its own unacceptable brand of vigilante justice. Everyone registers America's military might, its ability to "shock and awe" both its allies and its enemies. People do not, however, trust that the

United States has the moral and political capacity to use that power wisely to safeguard its friends, eliminate its enemies, or manage the complexities of a world in which no nation is simply "with" the United States or "against" the United States. In particular, Turkish policy elites are frustrated by the American government's failures to respect Turkey's own geopolitical concerns and to understand how Turkey seeks to balance its secular raison d'être with its religious cultural needs. And as the war in Iraq drags on and grows more horrific, the people of Turkey turn away in greater numbers from the United States. Distrust of the American government's motives has created a popular, often hyperbolic, if also fashionable anti-Americanism in Turkey.

This essay presents a tour of the horizon of Turkish perspectives on America. First it will provide a historical perspective that explores how culture, politics, and security issues created bonds between Turkey and the United States. Then, it will examine why elites' acceptance of American alliance and a general admiration of American culture have not produced support of current U.S. foreign policies or a more stable basis for a pro-American public opinion in Turkey.

Constructing the American Image in a Receptive Turkey

On April 5, 1946, the USS *Missouri* brought the remains of deceased Turkish ambassador Ahmet Münir Ertegün to Istanbul. The ambassador had died during World War II, and the casket could not be transported until after the war. The timing, however, was auspicious because it immediately followed Stalin's demands from Turkey for territory and bases to be used for the joint defense of the Turkish Straits. The Turks interpreted the visit of the battleship as a gesture that the United States would stand by Ankara against Soviet threats. Turkey was jubilant because the *Missouri* symbolized an end to Ankara's military and diplomatic isolation, a position dreaded in the country's foreign policy tradition. To honor the *Missouri*, the government issued postage stamps, and cigarette manufacturers produced wildly popular special cigarettes. The ship's American officers reciprocated by inviting thousands of admiring Turkish citizens to tour the vessel. At the end of World War II and the onset of the Cold War, America and Turkey were fast becoming allied.

President Truman, famously, would formalize that alliance and make Turkey, along with Greece, a recipient of American Cold War support.

Throughout the 1950s, as Turkey and the United States formed a geopolitical alliance under the auspices of NATO, the kind of symbolic or cultural bonds that the voyage of the *Missouri* produced, multiplied. For example, early in the decade, Turks discovered that Americans were listening to a catchy pop tune titled "Istanbul (Not Constantinople)":

> Every gal in Constantinople
> Lives in Istanbul, not Constantinople
> So if you have a date in Constantinople
> She'll be waiting in Istanbul.

The song became a hit in Turkey and definitely appealed to Turkish linguistic nationalism (though it is highly doubtful that American songwriter Jimmy Kennedy had any such thoughts in mind when he wrote it). [2] Soon thereafter, disc jockeys at Radio Ankara found an even better cultural bridge. The marvelous Eartha Kitt had recorded an old Istanbul/Macedonian song, "Üsküdar'a Gider İken" (On the way to Scutari) in Turkish and made it into an unlikely pop hit in the United States. Kitt had heard the song when she had toured Turkey in 1951 as a member of Katherine Dunham's dance troupe. Radio Ankara gave the song ample airtime, and it became a big hit, as did Ms. Kitt.[3] There is no accessible evidence of exactly why she visited Turkey in 1951, but it is likely that her trip was subsidized by the U.S. government, just as other American entertainers introduced jazz and blues to Turkey as part of the cultural cold war promotion of the United States abroad.[4] Along those lines, a third musical tune, "The Song of Friendship" (*Dostluk Şarkısı*), recorded in 1954 right after the Korean War (1950–53), was perhaps not so mysteriously distributed free of charge throughout Turkey and aired repeatedly. The lyrics said that Turkey would stand by the United States until eternity in fighting for freedom, and that the two peoples had become blood brothers fighting together in Korea.[5]

American novels and other works of fiction, too, became widely available in Turkey in translation during the early years of the Cold War. Even many years later, older Turkish people remember their happy discovery of works by John Steinbeck, Jack London, Tennessee Williams, Arthur Miller, William Faulkner, Ernest Hemingway, O. Henry, William Saroyan, and Mark Twain.[6] By the 1950s, American children's books were also available in Turkey. *The Adventures of Huckleberry Finn* (Twain), *Uncle Tom's Cabin* (Beecher Stowe), *Bambi* (Salten), and *A Tree Grows in Brooklyn* (Smith) gave a glimpse of America to Turkey's middle-class urban children. An entire generation of young Turks grew up on comic books about Tom Mix, Daniel Boone (*Texas*), Wild Bill Hickok (*Pekos Bill),* Calamity Jane (*Kalamiti Ceyn),* Lucky Luke (*Red Kit),* and the Dalton Brothers (*Dalton Biraderler).* These characters were all perceived as good though mischievous and intriguingly rebellious.

Hollywood, naturally, had a distinct imprint abroad, too, buttressing U.S. cultural expansion. American movies played all over Turkey throughout the Cold War years. Some people remember watching *Khartoum* as youngsters in the mid-1960s and not thinking twice about its portrait of British imperialism as seen through the lens of American movie-making. Gordon "Pasha," played by the dreamy Charlton Heston (pre-NRA days!), symbolized the "good," while Ahmad Mahdi's rebellion against British occupation and colonial rule in 1885 symbolized the "barbaric."[7] Across the cultural matrix, American songs, films, and literature showed the people of Turkey a vibrant, dynamic society that seemed heroic, generous, and open-minded.

During the 1950s and 1960s, of course, more than culture linked Turkey and the United States. The Cold War brought the two nations together, and Turkey's political elite looked to the United States for security and for economic leadership. Upon President Dwight Eisenhower's invitation in 1954 (January 28–February 27, 1954), President Celal Bayar of Turkey visited the United States. He was very impressed and was pleased to be received with unusual pomp and circumstance by the American Greek, Armenian, and Jewish communities,[8] former minorities of the Ottoman Empire. In the election campaign of 1957, President Bayar publicly stated that Turkey's role model for progress was the United States; and that in thirty years' time, Turkey would become a little America.[9]

America's direct economic aid to Turkey was widely appreciated as well. Governing elites, no doubt, most appreciated the massive military support. But families, too, were on the receiving end of generous supplies of American surplus food. Although at least one little girl, Nur Bilge, was less than thrilled by the American powdered milk and cheese that she was offered at school, rather oddly, given the fact that I attended an exclusive private elementary school. However, the Turkish Ministry of Education had ordered distribution of these supplies to all schools regardless of need.

In the Cold War years, America was not just an abstract presence or mediated through its cultural products. Thousands of Americans appeared in Turkey. Professor İlber Ortaylı, an Ottoman social historian, maintains that key aspects of westernization were, in fact, introduced to Turkey by the Americans in the post–World War II years.[10] Since the eighteenth century, European-style westernization had been largely confined to Istanbul and Izmir as well as to limited circles, such as the military, medical schools, missionary schools, the Levantines (Europeans who settled in the Near East, indigenous people who belonged to ancient Christian sects and Jews) and some upper-middle-class families. During the 1950s and after, however, Americans—government officials, military personnel, and businessmen—appeared all over Turkey. Many middle-class apartment buildings in Ankara and Izmir had at least one American family resident. And even if the Turkish families could not speak English (though their children were, by the 1950s, studying English in school as a second language), the medium of reciprocal hospitality served as a common language. Similar, though more limited informal contacts took place in Turkish provincial cities where U.S. military bases were located. During this anxious Cold War time, the United States was widely treated as a heroic benefactor, and the Soviet Union was denigrated. Even food names were affected by the Cold War battle; potato salad had been known as Russian salad in Turkey, but in the 1950s it was renamed American salad (the recipe, fortunately, stayed the same). And a popular children's limerick that in the 1940s ended with the line "Germans are swine" became, in the 1950s, "Russians are swine." Americans were a vivid and powerful force in the cultural and political life of Turkey.

Transformations of the American Image

Many scholars have carefully explored the ups and downs of American-Turkish government-to-government relations during the Cold War, and that exercise will not be repeated here.[11] Needless to say, throughout the

Cold War, perceptions of the United States varied, depending on global political and domestic conjunctures, as well as during crises in bilateral relations. These usually stemmed from issues related to Turkey's perceptions of American infringements on its sovereign rights and "out-of-area" activities of the United States that affected Turkey.

A few major turning points in the two nations' generally warm relations, however, should be briefly noted. The first major sour note between the allies occurred when the U.S. Congress applied an embargo on arms transfers to Turkey, between February 1975 and August 1978. The proximate cause of this sanction was Turkey's armed intervention into Cyprus in 1974, to prevent ethnic cleansing of the Turkish Cypriots by the Greek Cypriots. Congressional leaders deemed that since U.S.-supplied arms were used for purposes other than self-defense, Turkey's military action had violated section 620(x) of the Foreign Assistance Act. Though other U.S. allies had employed American arms elsewhere, (and in this case, Greece had done the same), sanctions were imposed on a NATO ally—Turkey—for the first time in the history of the alliance. Turks felt betrayed by their longtime ally, and both the Turkish military and the economy were hit badly by the embargo. As a policy measure aimed at forcing Turkish troop withdrawal from Cyprus, the embargo was a total failure. The Turkish government refused to bow to American pressure, and the Greeks, pleased to see the Turks suffer at others' hands, lost all interest in negotiating. Turkey retaliated by closing down U.S. bases and listening installations at a time when Washington needed those assets to monitor Soviet compliance with arms reduction agreements. The punitive aspect of the sanction fed Turkish anti-Americanism, and instilled feelings of suspicion towards the United States on the part of Turkish decision-makers that still reverberate today.[12]

One of the most interesting points regarding anti-Americanism in Turkey during the late 1970s is that it became a useful rhetorical tool and policy claim for domestic militants on both the radical Left and the ultra Right (including Islamic radicals). Extremists on the left claimed to be fighting for Turkish autonomy from the United States. Their antagonists, the extreme Right and Islamists, were supposedly fighting against atheist Communism. It should be underlined, however, that none of these factions attacked American citizens. Leftist anti-Americanism was aimed at the government of Turkey, while the rightist factions' rage fell upon the leftists. All sides understood that Turkey had voluntarily joined NATO and opted for strong linkages to the United States. No one claimed that Americans had forced themselves on the government.[13] This may be one distinguishing factor of anti-Americanism *à la Turca* as opposed to anti-Americanism elsewhere in the Near East.

In a case of very bad timing, in 1979, shortly after the embargo had been ended, the Carter administration asked Turkey for the use of İncirlik air base in an attempt to obstruct the Islamic revolution in Iran, and then again to try to rescue American hostages from the U.S. embassy in Tehran. Without any public discussion, both requests were promptly turned down. That same year, President Carter asked the Turkish government for permission for U-2 reconnaissance flights to oversee Soviet compliance with the SALT II agreement. Prime Minister Bülent Ecevit insisted that the Soviets had to be informed, which the American interlocutors were not willing to do. Ankara rejected the proposal. Then SALT II became a nonissue, because the U.S. Congress did not ratify the agreement, and that point of contention between the allies, at least, disappeared.

The 1980s were a trying decade for Turkey, both domestically and internationally, but were also a time of improved relations with the United States. On September 12, 1980, a military coup took place, putting an end to fratricide and coalition-government deadlocks. European nations responded to this military coup by threatening to sever their ties with Turkey. The Carter administration reacted far more calmly, an attitude much appreciated in Ankara. As had been true after the two previous military takeovers (1960 and 1971) the military quickly returned to their barracks and handed over the government to the newly formed Motherland Party (Anavatan Partisi, ANAP) after national elections. The rising star of ANAP, Prime Minister Turgut Özal, carried out American-style liberal fiscal and economic reform packages, which had been prepared before the coup. The market economy brought increased wealth, conspicuous consumption patterns, and a nouveau riche class with aspirations towards an American lifestyle, although only in its superficial, material manifestations. An aura of Americanization also pervaded private educational institutions in Turkey, which flourished from the 1980s onward.

From the End of the Cold War to September 11

The end of the Cold War immediately changed the geopolitical relationship between Turkey and the United States. Turkey's political elite feared, at first, that the demise of the Soviet Union might also lead the United States and the NATO nations to lose interest in Turkey. After a short period of introspection, Ankara began to develop Turkey as a regional power,[14] even as it chose to remain a committed NATO member.

According to Duygu Sezer, professor of international relations, Turkey's NATO membership was not only perceived domestically as an expedient way to modernize the military. Turkey was also adopting key ideas about national security from the West, such as collective thinking, collective preparedness, and international solidarity.[15] In line with these concepts of collective security, in 1993, Ankara took a leadership role in urging Washington to take military action, in conjunction with NATO, against Serbian aggression over Bosnia-Herzegovina. European Union and UN declarations had proved ineffective in stopping the massacres of the Bosnians. Although NATO was not activated during this conflict, later in 1993, Turkey not only managed to help broker peace between Bosnia and Croatia, but it also helped to establish the Bosnian-Croat Federation. In 1995, under U.S. auspices, Serbian aggression came to a halt with the Dayton Peace Accord. Turkey's political and military leaders were pleased when the United States supported Turkey's participation in the multilateral peacekeeping operation Implementation Force (IFOR) in Bosnia.

Turkey and the United States continued to cooperate closely in 1998 when conflict between Kosovar Albanians and Serbs turned into armed aggression. When diplomacy failed, Turkey participated in the NATO air campaign against Serbia by sending F-16s and by implementing military-economic sanctions. Later, Turkey took part in the multilateral peace force Kosova Force (KFOR). U.S.-Turkish collaboration continued in 1999 when Ankara initiated a Balkan peacekeeping force. The Southeastern Europe Brigade (SEEBRIG) consisted of Greek, Bulgarian, and Turkish troops. These forces would be deployed in NATO or WEU (Western European Union) operations against future conflict in the Balkans, under the orders of the UN or the Organization for Security and Cooperation in Europe (OSCE).[16] In the late 1990s the United States also supported Turkey's approach to constructing a massive regional oil pipeline: the Baku-Tbilisi-Ceyhan (BTC) project, which will eventually transport Kazakh and Azerbaijani oil to the Mediterranean port of Ceyhan.

This cozy relationship hit a positive high when President William Clinton visited Turkey on November 14–19, 1999, on the occasion of an OSCE meeting. Clinton was the first and only U.S. president ever invited to speak at the Turkish parliament. When he arrived at parliament, he received a standing ovation. When he told the assembled representatives that he believed in a "strategic partnership with Turkey" he was enthusiastically cheered. Turkish attitudes toward the United States, at least as they were represented in the mass media, had returned to the cheerful, if naive, harmony of the 1950s.

The horrors of September 11 only served to compound Turkish support for the United States. Given its own immediate past history of fighting the separatist Kurdistan Workers' Party (PKK), it is not surprising that Turkey stood by the United States in its fight against terrorism during the Afghan war. This support was cemented by the Bush administration's efforts to create a multilateral effort under the auspices of the UN and NATO. Professor Ali Karaosmanoğlu wrote, "The September 12 (1368) and September 28 (1373) resolutions of the Security Council, affirmed the right of individual and common response of the United States against terrorism. ... Thus NATO included the anti-terrorism struggle [in] the common defense obligations recorded in the 5th Article of the North Atlantic Alliance."[17]

However, when the United States decided to attack Iraq, based on slim evidence and without the explicit approval of the UN Security Council, both the government and the people of Turkey were astonished. People believed that the United States, by acting without strong international support and solidarity, as it had done when Washington attacked Afghanistan in pursuit of the Taliban-supported Al Qaeda during the previous year, had broken faith with the world and was acting, instead, like a bully. Evidence of such a shift in people's attitude is never easy to measure, but not long after the Iraq invasion I worked with a number of my university students to gain a sense for it and to analyze it. They interviewed fifty professional men and women about their views of America. Students spoke to people who were at least fifty-five years old because I wanted to hear from men and women who had a range of experiences with the United States and who could contextualize the shock of the Iraqi invasion. These interviews are far from a scientific sampling and are by no means representative of the general population, but they tell us something useful about how a sophisticated group of older Turks who were predisposed to look favorably upon the United States felt postinvasion.

To put the matter clearly, most felt disappointed if not downright alienated. Many feared that the Iraq invasion revealed the true face of the United States that they had failed to see before. One older man spoke for practically all of those interviewed when he stated that when he was young he used to think of the United States as the defender of democracy and freedom, a model nation. But when he traveled in the United States in 2004, he observed that American democracy failed to generate a meaningful debate on the war. He was disheartened to see that so many Americans regarded themselves and their nation as the epitome of virtuousness and that anyone who opposed the American war effort must be evil. Many of the men and women interviewed spoke similarly of feeling dismayed by the Americans' arrogant use of force. The Cold War era, many said, had made them think that the United States—and few differentiated here between the American people and the American government—was genuinely motivated by noble ideals and even an altruistic impulse to help others. After the Iraq invasion they felt that they had been naive in believing so strongly in the United States. Overwhelmingly, they resented the Bush administration's attempts to force Turkey to cooperate with the American attack, and several argued that the United States used its economic power, in general, and its control over the International Monetary Fund, in particular, to pressure Turkey into acting against its own interests and its cultural precepts. Several argued that the United States wants Turkey to carry out America's dirty work in the Middle East and become a base for American imperial expansion in the region.[18]

Most of the men and women interviewed insisted that the strong, mutually beneficial tactical Turkish-American partnership ended with the Iraqi crisis. Many maintained that America could not force Turkey to do its bidding and that American hegemony in the region could not exist without the acquiescence of the people of Turkey. Thus, Turkey could and should pursue a regional and international path separate from that of the United States. On the other hand, most also feared that Turkey could not afford to confront the United States because Turkey's interests do overlap quite often with those of the Americans; thus, Turkey can only cautiously resist Washington's wayward behavior and ambition.

It was not particularly surprising to see the specific opinions offered by this older, sophisticated generation on the Iraq crisis. The sense of betrayal so many revealed, however, was remarkable. America had long represented an exceptionalist nation in their political imaginations, even through the various ups and downs in bilateral relations they had experienced. The Iraq crisis and their sense that the United States was now aspiring to the role of international bully had qualitatively changed their perspective, but it also made one cognizant that many displayed an old-fashioned "orientalist," if you will, approach to Turkey's relation with the United States. Several seemed to believe that there was little Turkey could really do about the imperialist ambitions of the United States and that it might be best to simply go along, foot-dragging where possible and criticizing on occasion.[19] While it is true that a gross asymmetry in power exists between Turkey and the United States, it was striking how hopeless many of the men and women interviewed were about Turkey's ability to determine its own policy and future. This attitude may also have something to do with their lack of confidence in the current Turkish government. It has been an unfortunate trait of the Eastern peoples (though historically much less so in Turkey) to blame third parties for all ills. Indigenous historiography of the Middle East, at least until very recently, has focused on how Western imperialism kept Persia down (as if their leaders had nothing to do with it); on how Ottoman imperialism had kept the Arabs down (as if they had no will or agency); and on how Western imperialism had reduced the Ottomans economically to a semicolonial position (as if incessant wars of the seventeenth, eighteenth, and nineteenth centuries had not drained the Ottoman treasury). Avoiding the concept of will and agency not only oversimplifies history, but also feeds the psychology of victimization. The result is a vicious cycle, which holds no hope or offers no dignity to the younger generations. Is it any wonder, then, that the young turn to radicalism in extreme cases? This state of affairs does not absolve authorities who have been using religion as an effective opiate. The opiate no longer serves as a sedative, but has rather become a stimulant gone awry towards nihilistic ends, as in the case of September 11. Listening to the comments of many of the older generation interviewed compels one to think that one of Turkey's foremost objectives must be to prevent this type of social psychology and the fierce activist manifestation it produces, that is, political Islam,[20] from entrenching itself seditiously, especially now that there is a majority government in Ankara implicated by an Islamist past.[21]

Challenges, Threat Perceptions, and Prospects in the New Century

After the Iraq invasion, four formidable challenges face Turkey. One is the profile of the current government. Its members, including Prime Minister Recep Tayyip Erdoğan, were until recently proponents of what is, by Turkish standards, a reactionary Islam. Now the leadership claims only to represent a conservative-right, democratic position. And it is true that republican traditions in Turkey have a taming effect on militancy and extremism. Likewise, our democratic institutions, such as the presidency and constitutional court, impede the Justice and Development Party (Adalet ve Kalkınma Partisi, AKP) government's attempts to pass new laws that would promote religiously oriented policies, especially in the realm of education. Still, the political-religious firestorms ignited by the United States in the region may strengthen the reactionary Islamic tendencies of the government.

The second challenge, thus, comes from Washington. Of late, Washington has been casually and dangerously throwing around the term *moderate Islam*[22] and using it to characterize pro-American governments throughout the region. During the first anniversary of the Iraq war, U.S. secretary of state Colin Powell said that Iraq would become an Islamic republic, just like Turkey and Pakistan. Further, Turkey has been lumped together, shockingly for many here, with pro-American Arab nations as an example of a "moderate Islamic" nation. In part, American government officials who use this term seem to believe that by demonstrating support for "moderate Islamic" nations they are proving that America is not opposed to Islam but only "radical" Islam or Islamic terrorism.

This terminology has dangerous connotations in Turkey. The Turkish Republic is not a country built on principles of "moderate Islam." The nation of Turkey has long chosen a secular identity. Characterizing Turkey as a "moderate Islamic" nation injures Turks' self-conception: the only democratic and secular majority-Muslim country in the region. Turkey, with all its shortcomings, has worked hard to embrace a secular, Western identity, and it does neither Ankara nor Washington any good to promote Turkey as a "moderate Islamic" nation. Such a characterization only gives support to those elements within Turkey who want to drive the nation away from its secular path and toward a fundamentally religious one. Murat Yetkin, in an editorial in the Turkish daily *Radikal*, stated, "Some ideologues, assessing that the Turkish example proves that democracy and free market economy can thrive in a Muslim society, try to elaborate the 'Turkish model' for Middle Eastern countries. . . . They seem to forget that the state of affairs has been possible only because Turkey chose the secular way."[23] The deputy chief of the Turkish General Staff, General İlker Başbuğ, registered the position of the Turkish Armed Forces in Washington by emphasizing that a "moderate Islamic state" is still only an Islamic state and is incompatible with democracy and secularism.[24] Americans who push for support of "moderate Islam" are playing with dynamite (one would think that Cold War support of Islamic extremists, including Al Qaeda and the Taliban, in Afghanistan would have taught American policymakers a lesson); they need to pay far greater attention to how such rhetoric—and related policies—plays in Turkey and other Islamic-majority nations that face complex internal political dynamics. The latest faux pas in cultural relations between America and Turkey was when the American Field Service exchange program administrators, in their infinite wisdom, began to place Turkish high school students with families of Muslim Malaysian or Indonesian origins in the United States. These families practiced Islamic rituals daily in their lives. They required the Turkish students to do the same, imposing strict dress codes on their female guests as well. Needless to say many Turkish students returned home in protest.

The third related challenge in Turkey is terrorism, both in its religious radical and PKK-separatist forms. While Ankara's and Washington's interests are confluent in the first case, it appears that they are not so in the second. Given that there are approximately five thousand PKK terrorists in northern Iraq living among the Iraqi Kurds, and that the latter is the only ethnic group that lends support to the American occupation of Iraq (as opposed to the Arabs), Washington and Ankara have a problem.

While American government officials are sensitive to Turkey's concerns about the PKK terrorists' presence in Iraq, this problem is not likely to fade away. It is and will remain a serious potential flashpoint in bilateral relations.

Last but not least among the challenges facing Turkey and the United States relates to Turkey's quest to become an EU member. In December 2004, the EU gave a date for accession negotiations to begin, and Ankara obtained the most desirable political balance in its Euro-Atlantic relations. The United States has been very supportive of a European Turkey all along, although the American pressure on the Europeans backfired on more than one occasion. However, while U.S.-Turkish relations vary, depending on conjuncture, EU membership is a civilizational issue of permanence. On the eve of the Iraq war in 2003, Ankara was at very critical crossroads, having to make a strategic choice between the U.S.-Israel camp and the EU. It chose the latter by instinct and precedent.

The Test of Will and Agency: The Iraq Crisis

Turkey's geography is aesthetically a blessing. It also makes Turkey integral to American's regional plans. Even before 9/11, American geopolitical strategists were overly enthusiastic about Turkey's utility in strengthening America power in the region. Ian O. Lesser, a policy analyst for the RAND Corporation, wrote:

> Beyond Turkey's potential to play a positive role in regions of importance to US strategy, the United States has an interest in Turkey as a direct contributor to US freedom of action—in essence, power projection—in adjacent regions. . . . The fact that the Özal government permitted the United States to use İncirlik base and other facilities for offensive air operations against Iraq during the Gulf War encouraged the belief that Ankara would welcome a more forward-leaning approach to access and overflight.[25]

Turkey's leaders and educated public were—and are—well aware that when the United States government looks at Turkey, it sees a forward base for its military adventures. Immediately prior to the Iraq war, debate in Turkey over its role in the forthcoming belligerency was heated and polarized. Some argued that Turkey had to be militarily involved in the Iraqi operation in order to have a say in its aftermath.[26] This position was particularly important for those who were eager to join the "coalition of the willing" in attempts to guarantee that an independent (Iraqi) Kurdistan would not emerge. Şaban Kardaş, a foreign policy analyst for the *Turkish Daily News,* presented another viewpoint:

> A choice is, therefore, being forced upon Turkey. Either it will try to become a so-called "stable" or regional power, in the service of some international interests, by maintaining and reproducing the current political culture, which is dominated by military and security considerations, or it will choose to become an ordinary, but democratic and self-sufficient state, in the service of its own citizens, by focusing on the necessary economic and political reforms and restructuring and transformation of its system.[27]

When the United States threatened to attack Iraq, even as rational debate continued, scenarios based on conspiracy theories became rampant in Turkey. A member of the Democratic Left Party (Demokratik Sol Parti, DSP) even argued in February 2003 that after the United States conquered Iraq for its oil, it would attack Turkey in order to seize our deposits of boracite as a future alternative fuel (Turkey holds 68 percent of the boracite reserves in the world).[28]

What caused a crisis between Washington and Ankara, however, was Prime Minister Erdoğan's encouragement of, and promises to, Washington, which *preceded* any parliamentary resolution that would allow U.S. basing in Turkey and open the northern front of attack to Iraq.[29] People in Turkey still wonder how and why Erdoğan had been invited to the White House in December 2002 when he did not even hold the portfolio of premiership and what he had been promised for helping the United States. When the resolution was rejected by two votes in the parliament on March 1, 2003, the American government, as well as much of the American mass media, blasted Turkey as some kind of ingrate or worse. William Safire of the *New York Times* wrote particularly vituperative articles.[30] In one, he stated, "The new, Islamic-influenced government of Recep Tayyip Erdoğan transformed that formerly staunch U.S. ally into Saddam's best friend."[31] In a broadcasted interview on CNN-Turk, U.S. deputy defense secretary Paul Wolfowitz blamed the Turkish military for not having taken a strong leadership role. He then asserted that Turkey would be badly hurt by its refusal to join the "coalition of the willing." His meaning was made clear when Washington cancelled its offer of a $6 billion grant, convertible to $24 billion in long-term, low-interest loans, which would have helped Turkey refinance its $145 billion state debt.[32] According to Wolfowitz, Turkey could only repair its relations with Washington if Ankara cooperated with the United States on resolving future disputes with Iran and Syria. Washington's idea of public diplomacy apparently did not rule out a public display of blackmail and threat.

The government prior to the AKP administration had hoped to finesse the crisis by convincing Saddam Hussein to comply with American demands. When that failed, Ankara asked Saddam to seek asylum abroad to save his people from war. It was to no avail. Afterwards, the AKP's strategic and foreign policy advisors, composed of cronies, had convinced the cabinet that the American armed forces could not attack Iraq without military basing in Turkey. Some in Turkey pointed out the economic costs of not complying with the United States and also suggested that having upwards of sixty thousand American troops in southeastern Turkey would be a financial boon for the ailing region. Still others feared that once the massive American troop deployment arrived, it might never leave. Overarching this debate was a general sense among many members of the parliament that the planned American attack on Iraq was not a just war. The Turkish president, Ahmet Necdet Sezer, publicly insisted on a UN Security Council resolution, because the Resolution 1483 did not authorize war.

Given the historical record and nationalist historiography of both sides, no affection is lost between the Arabs and Turks. But Turks do not find it easy to make war on Arabs. First of all, Turks have long understood Arabs to be the "chosen people" (*Kavm-i Necib*) because Islam was revealed to Prophet Mohammad. Second, to wage war on an Arab nation as an instrument of Western policy contradicts traditional tenets of Ottoman/Turkish foreign policy.[33] There is no compelling reason why that should change, even if the interlocutor of the nineteenth century, Britain, is reincarnated as the United States of America. None of the above, however, rules out war with an Arab country. But to make such a war, Turks must see how vital Turkish interests are at stake. No one could make that case. So, as a result, not without grave concern about confronting the massive power and leverage of the United States, Turkey—against the wishes of Prime Minister Erdoğan—turned down Washington's request for basing large numbers of American troops, though it did, as a gesture of goodwill, open its airspace for logistical support for the war.

In late summer 2003, after the American military mission was accomplished, Prime Minister Erdoğan volunteered troops for a peacekeeping mission, even as Iraqi resistance meant there was not yet a peace to keep. Erdoğan wanted both to restore U.S.-Turkish relations and to consolidate power over his party members in the parliament who had "failed" him dismally during the March 2003 voting. Using his political power, Erdoğan pushed a resolution through the parliament to send troops as a stabilization and peacekeeping force to Iraq despite overwhelming public opposition.

Of course, that deployment never happened. Turkey wanted to put its troops into the Dohuk, Kirkuk, and Tikrit area, to safeguard Kurdish issues,[34] whereas Washington insisted on the southern territory (Shiite territory). When the Kurds of northern Iraq and the Iraqi Ruling Council objected to any Turkish military presence, the Bush administration went along with their wishes, and the Turkish military did not enter Iraq.

As a result of this impasse, Washington has been, and is almost certain to continue, pressuring Turkey to allow the U.S. military to establish forward bases in Turkey for the Iraq conflict and whatever other regional use of force American planners foresee. According to news reports, plans were afoot to enlarge the İncirlik air base, deploy more weapons and military personnel, and build three naval bases on the Black Sea ports of Turkey.[35] The latter is not only in contravention of the 1936 Montreux Straits Convention, but in all probability would be deemed a hostile act by the Russian Federation. The saga is far from over. In 2006, the United States proposed to expand NATO's "Operation Active Endeavor" to the Black Sea. This operation had been activated in 2001, and the navies of Britain, Germany, Greece, Italy, the Netherlands, Spain, Turkey, and the United States have been monitoring commercial ships to deter potential terrorist activity in the Mediterranean. Russia and Turkey maintain that such a move would also compromise the Montreux Treaty of 1936. The multinational Black Sea Naval Force of the littoral states, which was established to do exactly what Operation Active Endeavor does, is already quite capable of carrying out such deterrence missions.[36] Such pressures contribute to anxieties in Turkey that the United States may yet cause other confrontations in Turkey's neighborhood.

Public Opinion in Turkey

The war in Iraq, America's continuing pressure on Turkey to cooperate in that war, and a general sense that the United States is not done asserting its will in the region has produced fear, anxiety, and anger in Turkey. As a partial result, a fierce nationalism is on the rise. It should be noted that these rising nationalist feelings, which range from genuine concern for the nation's safety and well-being to fascistic and xenophobic approaches are not just the result of American policies in the region. Different strata of the society are finding it very difficult to comply with everything that the European Union requires of Ankara, above and beyond the Copenhagen criteria for EU membership. Further, when major EU countries announced that even if and when Turkey fulfills all of this criteria, referenda will still have to be held in each EU country about Ankara's accession, many Turks were terribly disheartened. Moreover, Iran's nuclear challenge, which may attract American retribution, has also produced very strong public reactions.

The most obvious face of Turkey's heightened and often anti-American nationalism can be seen in its popular culture. Hypernationalist novels are all the rage, even among well-educated people. Thirty books, alone, on the Battle of Gallipoli during World War I—one of Ottoman Turkey's relatively recent battlefield victories—were published in the last two years. [37] Then came the infamous novella *Metal Storm* (*Metal Fırtına*), which has sold over half a million copies since its publication in 2004.[38] This trashy novel features a U.S. military attack on Istanbul and subsequent U.S. occupation of Turkey. Why? To take over the boracite mines, of course. Only by joining forces with Russia and the always helpful EU is Turkey able to liberate itself from the diabolical Americans. All kinds of conspiracy theories were hatched in Turkey over the publication of this book. Some argued that the "fiction" was part of U.S. psychological war on Turkey.[39] When rumor had it that *Metal Storm* had been approved for publication by the Turkish General Staff, the military felt obligated to issue a statement of denial.[40] The authors of the novella laughed all the way to the bank, and have produced other political thrillers such as *Lost Casket* (*Kayıp Naaş*), the story of Israeli agents who, during a fictional U.S. occupation of Ankara, steal Atatürk's casket and use his DNA to clone him. Thankfully this work and related fiction has not found an audience comparable to that of *Metal Storm*.

American officials did not react calmly to the popularity of *Metal Storm* and other anti-American screeds. On a visit to Turkey in February 2005, Undersecretary of Defense Douglas Feith asked that anti-American rhetoric cease. Nothing short of censorship, however, could have helped. Robert Pollock of the *Wall Street Journal* wrote an article condemning such attitudes in Turkey, entitled "The Sick Man of Europe . . . Again."[41] Yigal Schleifer of the *Christian Science Monitor* entitled his article, "Sure it's fiction. But many Turks see fact in anti-US novel."[42]

Despite such angry responses from the United States and the failure of more recent anti-American novels to find a mass audience, the public's affection for American villains has not come to an end. In 2006, a sensational movie, *The Valley of the Wolves—Iraq*, opened to widespread attention. The movie depicts American soldiers in Iraq as merciless killers who have a grisly side business as illegal traders of human organs extracted for transplant. The movie features a spicy revenge operation by Turkey's Special Forces against the American soldiers (this is a virtual retaliation against Americans who, in fact, arrested and hooded a group of Turkish Special Forces in Iraq in July 2004). In just a few months, four million people in Turkey paid to see this movie. Culture critic Vecdi Sayar, intriguingly, has argued that *The Valley of the Wolves* will not, as some have feared, fuel anti-Americanism in Turkey. He argues that, like the Hollywood films it imitates, it will just allow people in Turkey to let off some steam by harmlessly venting their frustrations over American actions in their region.[43] This may well be true, but the movie's success also reveals that a lot of people in Turkey are quite comfortable watching Americans portrayed as monsters—and this perspective is not something that would have been credible to people in Turkey even in the 1990s, let alone during the height of the Cold War.

By 2005, a BBC World News Service poll among twenty-one countries revealed that Turks ranked foremost (with 82 percent) among those who thought that Mr. Bush presented a threat to global security.[44] Nor did Americans fare well in the 2005 Pew Global Attitudes survey, where 53 percent of the Turks associated them with the word "rude," 70 percent with "violent," 68 percent with "greedy," and 57 percent with "immoral."[45] Since attitudes and opinion are amorphous and transient, one should be careful not to read too much into these surveys. Still, winning Turks' hearts and minds is made extremely difficult by the well-reported and devastating impact of American depleted uranium shells, cluster bombs, cruise missiles, bunker-buster bombs, and daisy-cutter bombs on the people of neighboring Iraq.

Conclusion

Turkey and the United States have been allies for more than half a century. And despite the powerful wave of anti-Americanism that has spread throughout Turkey, many in Turkey still hold a reservoir of good feeling toward American society and culture. Furthermore, despite the Iraq debacle, Turkey is not opposed to working with the United States to produce international peace and stability. In the post–Cold War period, Ankara participated in multilateral actions in the Balkans and Somalia. But for Turkey, operating in a dangerous region and working deliberately to foster proper relations with its neighbors, the EU, and the United States, legality, legitimacy, international law, and *pacta sund servanda* must be, as they have always been, the cornerstones of Turkish foreign policy. And at a time when questions about religion and politics affect so many nations around the world, Turkey must be vigilant in pursuing its traditional path of maintaining a secular state. Thus it is that both the government establishment and public opinion in Turkey grew so uneasy and so suspicious when the U.S. government, with the acquiescence of its citizens, used the excuse of the horrible September 11 terrorist attacks to carry out plans to transform the Middle East according to its own narrow and misguided self-interest. Now that the Iraq war has turned into a deadly quagmire that has increased security hazards in the region, people in Turkey are, generally, alienated by the United States.

For those in Turkey who believe that a good relationship with the United States is desirable and who, even more generally, want people in

Turkey to have reasons to respect the United States, it would be most desirable if the American government harnessed its ambitions of omnipotence and omnipresence for the sake of Turkish-American relations, and for the sake of the world.[46] But, for that to happen, Americans need to question the triumphalist attitude that since the Cold War seems to pervade not just the American government but American society, too. In his review of John L. Gaddis's book *The Cold War: A New History,* the British author Tony Judt stated, "It is one of the ironies of the cold war that America's victories in Europe were frequently offset by long-term damage to its reputation further afield, in Vietnam, for example, or the Middle East: the Soviet Union was not the only 'loser' in the cold war."[47] Lawrence Freedman turns this Cold War lesson to recent events in Iraq: "We have reached a turning-point in international politics as well as in Iraq. President George W. Bush is widely seen to have gambled on Iraq and lost. The impact of that loss goes well beyond Iraq. The United States has not been defeated in battle, and is unlikely to be. But it can no longer impose its will on Iraq because it lacks the moral authority to do so."[48] This loss of moral authority has been compounded by what the world has learned about American practices of rendering suspected terrorists to places where they may be secretly tortured, as well as the horrible treatment Iraqi prisoners have received directly at the hands of American soldiers. These incidents have captured worldwide attention, in part, because they appear to fit so perfectly with America's general defiance of international law[49] and pervasive attitude of arrogance and hubris. In sum, geopolitical or strategic thinking are not substitutes for moral authority, nor is the use of force without explicit authority. Maybe that is why no matter how attractive a democratic culture is, it does not automatically inspire political support. In the years ahead, Americans will have to find new ways to reach out to the people of Turkey to remind them of our two nations' linked past and the importance of our relationship for the future.

Notes

1. Niall Ferguson, *Colossus: The Rise and Fall of the American Empire* (London: Penguin Group, 2004).

2. "Istanbul," lyrics by Jimmy Kennedy, music by Nat Simon (of Tin Pan Alley), http://www.fastmail.fm.

3. İsmet Hulusi İmset, "Dünyayı dolaşan şarkı" (The song that travels the world), *Resimli 20. Asır,* June 11, 1953, http://www.medyakronik.com/arsiv/lightilave_220601.htm; "A sensual performer, Eartha Kitt," African American Registry, info@aaregistry.com; http://www.thelyricssite.com/song/Eartha+Kitt/Uskudara+Gider+Iken, accessed July 3, 2006.

4. Frances Stonor Saunders, *The Cultural Cold War: The CIA and the World of Arts and Letters* (New York: New Press, 1999); Penny M. Von Eschen, *Satchmo Blows Up the World* (Cambridge: Harvard University Press, 2004).

5. Mehmet Ö. Alkan, "Türkiye'de Amerikan İmajının Değişimi (1945–1980)" (The transformation of the American image in Turkey, 1945–1980), *Toplumsal Tarih* 118 (October 2003): 54–57.

6. Recorded interviews conducted by the senior class of 2004, Bilkent University, Department of International Relations as part of the Turkish Foreign Policy II course requirement.

7. The screenplay of *Khartoum* was written by Robert Ardrey, and the movie was a British-American coproduction in 1966. Heston played the role of General Charles Gordon, who in the end was executed by the "rebels" in 1885 (http://www.columbia.edu/~lnp3/mydocs/fascism_and_war/mahdism.htm, accessed July 3, 2006).

8. Rıfat N. Bali, "Azınlıkların Demokrat Parti Sevdası: Celal Bayar'ın Amerika Seyahati" (The love affair of the minorities with the Democratic Party: Celal Bayar's visit to the United States), *Toplumsal Tarih* 122 (February 2004): 14–21.

9. Bali, "Azınlıkların Demokrat Parti Sevdası," 54.

10. Discussion with Professor İlber Ortaylı, Bilkent University, May 2004.

11. For a concise history, see George S. Harris, *Troubled Alliance: Turkish-American Problems in Historical Perspective, 1945–1971* (Washington, D.C.: American Enterprise Institute for Public Policy Research, 1972); Nur Bilge Criss, "A Short History of Anti-Americanism and Terrorism: The Turkish Case," *Journal of American History* 89, no. 2 (2002): 472–84.

12. Nur Bilge Criss, "Sanction and Diplomacy," unpublished, 2006.

13. Nur Bilge Criss, "Mercenaries of Ideology: Turkey's Terrorism War," in Barry Rubin, ed., *Terrorism and Politics* (New York: St. Martin's, 1991), 123–50.

14. Alan Makovsky, "The New Activism in Turkish Foreign Policy," *SAIS Review,* Winter–Spring 1999, 92–113.

15. Recorded interview by Laden Fulya Özkan with Professor Duygu Sezer, Bilkent University, April 21, 2004.

16. Makovsky, "New Activism," 105.

17. Ali L. Karaosmanoğlu, "The transatlantic relations of the Afghanistan War and its consequences with regard to Turkey," *Turkish Daily News,* December 1, 2001.

18. Recorded interview by Daniel Blake with İsmail Topuzlu, April 29, 2004, Ankara.

19. Joshua Teitelbaum and Meir Litvak, "Students, Teachers and Edward Said; Taking Stock of Orientalism," trans. Keren Ribo, *Middle East Review of International Affairs* 10, no. 1 (2006): 23–43.

20. The ideology of political Islam, which has different manifestations, interpretations, and context, may be described as a desire to establish an Islamic state, which enforces traditional religious laws. In other words, it invokes an age-old controversy between secularism and the rule of religion, traditionalism versus modernity, and the struggle for power. Since the depiction has less to do with piety than with power in the name of religion, political Islam is not an absolute value system. Stripped of religious veneer, political Islam may even be interpreted as the struggle between the old elite and the younger aspirants to power.

21. A majority government tainted by political Islam in secular Turkey is an anachronism. However, the post-1980 election law curbs representation by a myriad of small political parties through a 10 percent national vote threshold. This precaution is meant to prevent small, extremist parties from becoming coalition partners by political bargaining; in the past they exerted more power, once in government, than the popular votes for them justified. Therefore, the AKP formed a majority government by 34 percent of the national vote, without recourse to run-off. The percentage also includes protest votes against mainstream parties that did little about corruption and unemployment.

22. The term *moderate Islam* was adopted by the Bush administration to mean the opposite of radical Islam, i.e., terrorism. See Yvonne Yazbeck Haddad, "The Quest for Moderate Islam," http://www.apomie.com/questforislam, accessed March 2, 2006.

23. Murat Yetkin, "Ilımlı İslam Modeli Tuzağı" (The trap of moderate Islam), *Radikal,* March 20, 2004.

24. "Ilımlı İslam Devleti?" (A moderate Islamic state?), editorial, *Cumhuriyet,* March 22, 2004; Mehmet Ali Kışlalı, "ABD İle İlişkiler," *Radikal,* March 23, 2004.

25. Ian O. Lesser, "Western Interests in a Changing Turkey," in Zalmay Khalilzad, Ian O. Lesser, and F. Stephen Larrabee, eds., *The Future of Turkish-Western Relations: Toward a Strategic Plan* (Santa Monica, Calif.: RAND, 2000), 71.

26. Sedat Sertoğlu, "Adam Geldi" (The Man has Arrived), *Sabah,* March 20, 2002.

27. Şaban Kardaş, "The Strategic Importance of Turkey after September 11," *Turkish Daily News,* May 25, 2002.

28. "ABD Türkiye'ye Savaş Açabilir" (The United States may declare war on Turkey), *Cumhuriyet,* February 9, 2003.

29. Fikret Bilâ, *Sivil Darbe Girişimi ve Ankara'da Irak Savaşları* (Attempts at a civilian coup and Iraq wars in Ankara) (Ankara: Ümit Yayıncılık, 2003); Sedat Ergin, "Bizden Saklananlar" (Information withheld from the public), *Hürriyet,* September 17–22, 2003; Murat Yetkin, *Tezkere: Irak Krizinin Gerçek Öyküsü* (Resolution: The true story of the Iraq crisis) (Istanbul: Remzi Kitabevi, 2004); Mustafa Balbay, *Irak Bataklığında Türk-Amerikan İlişkileri* (Turkish-American relations in the Iraqi quagmire) (Istanbul: Cumhuriyet Kitapları, 2004).

30. William Safire, "Advice to America from beyond the Grave," *New York Times,* March 4, 2003; "Turkey's Wrong Turn," *New York Times,* March 24, 2003; "Turkey's Wrong Turn Undermines a Genuine Friendship," *New York Times,* March 25, 2003; "New Take on Turkey," *New York Times,* May 29, 2003.

31. Safire, "Wrong Turn Undermines Friendship."

32. "Wolfowitz Hints at Support for Political Action by Turkish Military," http://www.@stratfor.com, accessed May 7, 2003.

33. Selim Deringil, "Aspects of Continuity in Turkish Foreign Policy: Abdülhamid II and İsmet İnönü," in *Turkish Foreign Policy during the Second World War: An "Active" Neutrality* (Cambridge: Cambridge University Press, 1989), 39–54. In 1881, when there was a nationalist uprising (the Urabi Pasha rebellion) against the khedive of Egypt (which was nominally still part of the Ottoman Empire) for squandering national wealth, the British asked Sultan Abdülhamid II to put down the insurrection. They were refused because the sultan had no interest in fighting fellow Muslims, nor did he wish to become a tool of Britain. In 1885, the British again asked the Ottomans to put down the Mahdi rebellion in the Sudan in return for territorial compensation from Somalia. Abdülhamid II also rejected this offer, stating that Somalia had never been part of the empire, and therefore the suggestion lacked legality and precedence.

34. Deringil, "Aspects of Continuity."

35. Mustafa Balbay, "ABD Yeni Üsler İstiyor" (The United States wants new bases), *Cumhuriyet,* May 17, 2004; Mehmet Ali Kışlalı, "Türkiye'den Beklentiler" (Expectations from Turkey), *Radikal,* May 21, 2004.

36. "Black Sea force divides Turkey, US," *Turkish Daily News,* March 1, 2006.

37. Ümit Bayazoğlu, review of *Children of the Dardanelles,* by Pierre Miquel, trans. Nuriye Yiğitler (Istanbul: Literatür Yayınevi, 2006) in *Radikal Kitap,* 4:261, March 17, 2006.

38. Orkun Uçar and Burak Turna, *Metal Fırtına* (Istanbul: Timaş Yayınları, 2004).

39. Behiç Gürcihan, "Metal Fırtına Hangi Senaryonun Alt Parçası?" (Which scenario does *Metal Storm* serve?), http://www.haberim.com, February 23, 2005, accessed March 6, 2006.

40. "Metal Fırtına ile İlişkimiz Yok" (We have nothing to do with *Metal Storm)*, sabah.com.tr/2005/02/18, accessed March 6, 2006.

41. Robert L. Pollock, "The Sick Man of Europe . . . Again," http://www .opinionjournal.com/editorial/feature, February 16, 2005, accessed March 6, 2006.

42. Yigal Schleifer, "Sure it's fiction. But many Turks see fact in anti-US novel," http://www.csmonitor.com, February 2005, accessed March 6, 2006.

43. Vecdi Sayar, "Kedi Gözü" (The eye of a cat), *Cumhuriyet*, February 10, 2006.

44. http://www.harrisinteractive.com/news/Wirthlin Report, March 2005, accessed March 2, 2006.

45. http://www.lonestartimes.com, February 7, 2006, accessed March 2, 2006.

46. Andrew J. Bacevich, "A Time for Reckoning, Ten Lessons to Take Away from Iraq," *American Conservative*, July 19, 2004, turkıstan-n@nıc.surfnet.nl, accessed July 14, 2004.

47. Tony Judt, "A Story Still to Be Told," review of John Lewis Gaddis's *The Cold War: A New History* (New York: Penguin, 2006), *New York Review of Books*, March 23, 2006, 11–15; Ellen Schrecker, ed., *Cold War Triumphalism: The Misuse of History After the Fall of Communism* (New York: New Press, 2004).

48. Lawrence Freedman, "America's battle to regain respect," ankam_turkfor pol@yahoo.com, accessed May 31, 2004.

49. Philippe Sands, *Lawless World: America and the Making and Breaking of Global Rules from FDR's Atlantic Charter to George W. Bush's Illegal War* (New York: Viking, 2005), 9.

BEAUTIFUL IMPERIALIST OR WARMONGERING HEGEMON?

□ □ □

CONTEMPORARY CHINESE VIEWS OF THE UNITED STATES

Yufan Hao and Lin Su

OVER the last few years, a new force has emerged within China: a semiautonomous, if still limited, public opinion. With the spread of the Internet, the rise of multiple media outlets in an emerging market economy, and the decreasing ability and, to a lesser extent, desire of the Chinese government to control people's political beliefs, an increasingly independent and forceful public is growing in China. Not surprisingly, this emergent public is primarily concerned with internal dynamics. But people in China, especially the urban, better-educated population, are also looking outward. In particular, they are fascinated by the United States and they have strong opinions about American foreign policy, America's complex role in the world, and the American way of life, insomuch as they understand it.[1]

Chinese interest in the United States is not new. But the role of Chinese public opinion is. And that increasingly assertive public is contributing to the formation of Chinese-American relations. Overall, those relations have dramatically improved over the last thirty or so years. Still, the relationship remains a fragile one. James Kelly, assistant secretary of state, could have been speaking for China, as well as the United States, when he aptly testified in the summer of 2003 before the Senate Foreign Relations Committee: "Neither we nor the Chinese leadership believe that there is anything inevitable about our relationship—either inevitably bad or inevitably good."

Since the September 11 attacks on the United States, the Chinese have, in general, looked more favorably toward the United States. In part, this more positive view has been fostered by a dramatic recasting of American government policy towards China. Soon after the attacks, the Bush administration, which had been responsible for a considerable worsening of relations between the two nations, turned to China for help against the terrorist threat. This gesture of goodwill and diplomatic outreach at a time of international difficulty was well received by China's leaders and its people.

Still, even as the threat of global terrorism has created solidarity between China and the United States, a majority of Chinese have expressed grave concerns about American unilateralism and warmongering. They fear that the United States may seek irresponsible and dangerous global domination in the name of its own national security. These international concerns are strongly influenced in China by specific actions the United States has taken toward China. Finally, Chinese perceptions of the United States are broadly affected by the American cultural presence in China and by the Chinese people's increasing ability to gain insights into the everyday life of the American people. At least among China's educated, emerging elite, views of America are no longer governed by simplistic images—either good or evil. Rather, an increasing number of Chinese see the United States as a powerful world leader whose culture contains useful elements, whose market savvy is worth emulating, and whose international relations demand careful, skeptical appraisal.

In developing this essay, as our introduction suggests, we will not base our claims on the usual kind of sources, which almost always run toward a gloss of political declarations by China's leaders. Instead, we bolster our account by offering a unique look into the opinions of a broad group of China's emerging foreign policy elite. We recently surveyed 261 randomly selected Chinese college students and midlevel bureaucrats enrolled in master of public administration (MPA) programs at Tsinghua University and Renmin University of China in Beijing and Inner Mongolian

University in Hohhot, the capital of the Inner Mongolian Autonomous Region.

We chose this group because, to a certain degree, they are emblematic of how the emerging governmental cohort in China views America. Right now, they are a kind of "sub-elite," concerned with what happens beyond China's borders but not yet in positions of authority.[2] Within a few years they will be.[3]

Chinese Perception of America: The Recent Historical Context

Like any people's perceptions of a foreign country, the Chinese see the United States through a time-specific cognitive conglomeration of understandings, values, and emotions. And, of course, a multitude of factors create differences in how individual Chinese feel about the United States. Still, at a general level, most Chinese, when they look at the United States, think about two broad concerns: how the United States affects China's modernization and how it challenges their nation's national security. As a result, Chinese tend to have a bifurcated image of the United States. They take America as the reference point for Chinese modernization since they believe that America is the world's most sophisticated, economically developed, full-fledged democracy. Then, too, they worry that America is a superpower that seeks world hegemony and, closer to home, might seek to undermine China's national security and social stability, possibly by interfering in China's policy toward Taiwan.

These concerns have historical resonances. So in order to better understand how America is perceived by China's emerging elite, we will take a brief detour and review the historic trajectory of Chinese perceptions of the United States.

A BRIEF HISTORY

Quickly characterizing historic Chinese perceptions of the United States is, as experts know too well, quite difficult, as it involves assessing multiple perspectives on a multitude of issues. In Jianwei Wang's thorough, historical study of China's perception of America, he argues that different groups of Chinese have held contradictory views of different aspects of America.[4] Still, we can make some generalizations.

Before 1949, numerous Chinese intellectuals viewed America as a model that China could emulate in its drive to modernize. However, these same intellectuals considered America to be an arrogant and selfish nation, no different than the other major Western powers. They noted: "the teacher always bullies the student."[5] These kinds of deep-rooted suspicions about the West's intention in China dominated intellectuals' views throughout most of the nineteenth century and during the first four decades of the twentieth century.

The Chinese masses, however, remained almost completely ignorant of and indifferent about America until the outbreak of the Pacific War. Suddenly, the United States was China's strong ally in its fight against the Japanese invaders. These friendly feelings only lasted until the Japanese were defeated. Gradually, they were replaced with bitter feelings, at least among those who supported the Communist struggle, after the Truman administration sided with Chiang Kai-shek during the Chinese Civil War. With the establishment of the People's Republic of China, America's wartime alliance against the Japanese was officially forgotten, and the United States became the number one state enemy.

The Korean War deepened this hostility, and the rift it created between the United States and China took more than two decades to heal. For most of the 1950s and 1960s, the bilateral relationship was characterized by bitter antagonism and military posturing. The Chinese government, not unrealistically, felt a keen sense of insecurity over Washington's policy of military encirclement and economic pressure. Yet the Chinese experience during the Korean War also made many Chinese believe that America was a "paper tiger," a phrase constantly used to mock the United States in Chinese government-controlled media.

President Richard Nixon's 1972 trip to Beijing had a massive impact on how the Chinese people viewed the United States. China's leaders embraced the Nixon olive branch and used their control of the mass media to soften their people's image of their longtime enemy in order to build domestic support for a dramatic policy change. Even today, Richard Nixon is remembered fondly, even by less well educated Chinese, and Henry Kissinger is still widely regarded in China as an "old friend."

In 1979, the government chose to speed up China's modernization by reforming its economic system and opening the country up to the rest of the world. This dramatic policy change, together with the normalization of U.S.-China diplomatic relations, opened a new era for U.S.-China relations. America was no longer viewed as an enemy or a de facto partner needed simply to balance the Soviet threat.[6] The United States was a trading partner, a source for capital, and an economic inspiration.

Many Chinese intellectuals, during this time, even looked with fascination at key aspects of American life, including the checks-and-balances political system, its developed market economy, its forms of advanced scientific and technological research, its highly sophisticated educational system, and its unique, globally attractive culture. All of these areas of American life became popular subjects in China. Chinese youth even began searching out Western media to learn more about the United States. In 1989 it was reported that more than 30 percent of Chinese university students listened to the Voice of America, and about 70 percent of those listening trusted VOA reporting, whereas 75 percent distrusted the official Chinese media.[7]

Throughout the 1980s, the United States enjoyed the best image a foreign country could have hoped for in China. A general consensus existed: China should have a good relationship with the United States and should learn from America in order to emulate its development model. America was viewed as not only welcoming the rise of China, but as a friend that was providing China with a helping hand.

This happy state of relations underwent a major change in 1989. In the wake of the June 4 Tiananmen Massacre, the American government began an unyielding campaign to pressure China to accept American notions of human rights. To put muscle into this campaign, the Americans began rigid economic, political, and technological sanctions against China, meant to stem the proliferation of weapons. These actions and accompanying harsh rhetoric suggested to most Chinese that Washington, yet again, had undergone a change of heart and, once again, wanted to hinder China's progress.

Chinese concerns that the United States had turned actively hostile were reinforced in the early 1990s by a series of unfortunate events. One of the most unpleasant occurred in the early fall of 1993 when the Chinese ship *Yin He,* which was carrying a load bound for Iran, was stopped in international waters by an American navy ship. American intelligence officers believed the vessel was carrying ingredients for chemical weapons. However, when the ship was inspected, no such cargo found. This incident was widely reported in the Chinese mass media, and the public was furious with the United States, especially after the American government refused to apologize for the mistake.

This event, together with U.S. efforts to block China's bid for the 2000 Olympic Games, annual scrutiny of China's most favored nation status, and Washington's constant objection throughout the 1990s to China's entry into World Trade Organization, were viewed by many Chinese as a continuation of nineteenth-century Western imperialism. Deep-rooted suspicions about American intentions toward China began, once again, to grow. The Beijing leadership perceived a new campaign to sabotage the Communist-controlled government. More generally, the public decided that the Americans, who had only a few years earlier offered a friendly hand, were now working against China's bid to become a modern, prosperous world power. In fact, many in China believe that since 1993 the United States has been deliberately casting China in the most negative light possible to create the impression that China is an adversary that needs to be checked and constrained at every turn.

THE SHIFTING VIEW OF YOUNG CHINESE

These increasingly hostile views of the United States were felt even more strongly by young Chinese. In May 1995, *China Youth Daily* conducted a survey entitled "The World in the Eyes of Chinese Youth." Some 120,000 young people participated in this survey, making it the largest poll of its kind in the history of the PRC. The survey produced a shocking portrait. While more than 74 percent of the respondents viewed America as having the most influence on China, 87.1 percent of them believed America to be the country least friendly to China. Fifty-seven percent of those surveyed considered America to be their least favorite country, 25.1 percent higher than runner-up Japan.[8] When asked about America's role in the 1991 Gulf War, an overwhelming majority (85.4 percent) believed that America fought the war for its own interests rather than for justice for Kuwait.[9] A similar survey conducted in December 1995 by the Research Center of Chinese Juveniles also found that

81.2 percent of the respondents believed that Washington "uses the promotion of democracy in the world only as an excuse, as its real goal is to establish its world domination."[10]

Anti-American sentiment culminated in 1996 when five young Chinese published a book entitled *China Can Say No,* which summarized the grievances that China had with other powerful nations, particularly the United States. The authors provided a long list of complaints, including the U.S. congressional annual scrutiny of China's most favored nation status, America's efforts to block China's bid to the 2000 Olympic Games, numerous occurrences of sexual harassment by foreign companies that had offices in China, and Taiwan leader Lee Tenghui's visit to America. The authors argued that the United States, as well as other foreign countries, had bullied China long enough; it was time for the Chinese to stand up and say no.[11]

The 1999 bombing of the Chinese embassy bombing in Yugoslavia by the United States greatly aggravated an already worsening bilateral relationship. Furious Chinese laid siege to the American embassy in Beijing for several days, and large-scale demonstrations took place all over China. McDonald's restaurants were attacked. The Western media portrayed these protests as government-manipulated events, aimed at diverting attention away from the tenth anniversary of the Tiananmen incidents. They were not.

The violent anti-American reaction was, in fact, a predictable result of the Chinese people's decade-long humiliation produced by the U.S. government's unrelenting criticism of Chinese trade practices and human rights policy.[12] The embassy bombing had a particularly strong impact on those young Chinese who had, until then, maintained a romantic view of the United States. As one Chinese scholar put it, "many of them [Chinese youth] may still love most things American; but that love is not blind anymore."[13]

Almost immediately after coming to power, President George W. Bush adopted a much tougher approach toward China. Well-educated Chinese believed he was responding to American public opinion, which had grown increasingly anxious about China's growing economic strength and industrial productivity. Bush rejected Bill Clinton's China policy, which aimed to mollify tense relations by elevating China to a status of "strategic partnership." Bush, instead, referred to China as a "strategic competitor" during his presidential campaign, and in his first year in office he administered a hard-line policy. Bush pushed for a National Missile Defense (NMD) system that Chinese perceived as aimed at them, increased criticisms of China's human rights abuses, and sped up advanced weapons sales to Taiwan.

On April 1, 2001, a U.S. EP-3 spy plane, while gathering intelligence off the Chinese mainland, collided with a Chinese jet fighter. The American plane landed on a Chinese island, where the crew was detained for eleven days. While the American public responded calmly to this incident, the Chinese public did not. Chinese were furious over the death of the Chinese pilot and the refusal of the American government to apologize for the situation. To make matters worse, even as this problem simmered, President Bush told a television interviewer that the United States would use whatever means necessary to defend Taiwan against a military attack by China. This statement was seen by many Chinese as a deliberate provocation.

THE IMPACT OF SEPTEMBER 11

Given this difficult relationship, it is striking how dramatically the September 11, 2001, terrorist attack affected U.S.-China relations. Suddenly, the Bush administration saw a vital interest in aligning itself with Beijing, which was perceived as a necessary ally in the fight against terrorism, particularly in Asia. Significant cooperation has since occurred on antiterrorism, Afghanistan, South Asia, and, most importantly, North Korea. It is quite understandable that many Chinese felt relieved that September 11 had suspended the debate in America, at least temporarily, on how to cope with China's increasing strength.

U.S.-China relations have been on a steady upward trend since September 11. Chinese were well aware when President Bush stopped calling China a "strategic competitor" and instead characterized China as a "constructive, cooperative and candid" nation. In a foreign policy speech delivered at George Washington University in September 2003, Secretary of State Colin Powell even characterized the bilateral relations as "the best they have been since President Nixon's first visit."[14]

Yet many problems remain, and disputes over a wide variety of issues continue. Many Americans, Chinese believe, continue to blame China for U.S. economic difficulties. Furthermore, America's pro-Taiwan policies are viewed in China as a potential threat to the region's stability and to China's security interests.[15] Indeed, media in both China and the United States have steadily developed stereotypes of each other for domestic reasons. China is portrayed in the America media as a "human rights abuser," "rogue state," "unlawful trade practitioner," "unfriendly competitor," and a "potential threat" to American global supremacy. In turn, China's media commonly shows the United States as an aggressive bully, eager to contain China, and prevent China's emergence as a great power. While American media have accused Chinese authorities of distorting the images of America to create an enemy for domestic political reasons, the Chinese media have accused the U.S. government and American media of "demonizing" China by turning a blind eye to China's progress and focusing solely on China's problems.[16]

This cross-cultural criticism extends deeply into policy experts dialogue, as well. American and other Western commentators assert that since the 1990s the Chinese people have become more nationalistic and increasingly anti-American. Western scholars seem only to differ on how they explain the sources of this anti-American nationalism.[17] Some view the rise as intrinsic to Chinese culture, which they perceive as irrationally xenophobic. Other scholars believe it is inherently reactive, as it is influenced by the current geopolitical climate and international events. Some scholars argue it was created by the authoritarian Chinese government to serve the survival goal of the CCP, while others argue that this anti-American nationalism is simply a disguised form of Chinese imperial ambition.[18]

Current Chinese Perception of America

Despite the grave concerns many Chinese have about American international policy, we do not think that Western scholars are right when they confidently charge that the Chinese people have become more anti-American. Based on our survey of China's emerging elite, we see a more complex set of attitudes emerging. We believe that China's better-educated younger generation is gaining a more objective, balanced, and reasonable understanding of the United States that will serve them well either in responding to their government's international policy or, in some cases, in directly contributing to the evolution of China's foreign policy.

At the most general level, the proto-elite groups we surveyed overwhelmingly had positive or mixed views of the United States, even after the United States invaded Iraq—a decision the Chinese overwhelmingly rejected. Some 47.5 percent of the MPA students we surveyed stated that they had an unalloyed favorable opinion of the United States, while 41 percent stated they had a mixed feeling of love and hate. Only 5.5 percent of those surveyed stated that they simply disliked America (with the remaining 6 percent offering no opinion). The college students were only somewhat more negative in their general views, with 26 percent having a totally favorable opinion, 50 percent holding mixed feelings, and 19 percent bluntly declaring a dislike of the United States (5 percent gave no opinion). Interestingly, while many of the people we interviewed readily admitted that their understandings of the United States were not comprehensive, almost everybody felt that their knowledge of the United States was far better than the understanding Americans had of China— an astounding 96 percent felt that way!

Regardless of how our respondents felt about the depth of their own knowledge of the United States, they were strikingly confident that they could distinguish between the attitudes of the American people toward China and the viewpoint of the American government. Overwhelmingly, for example, they stated that the American people have friendly feelings towards China (though the college students tended to be more suspicious of regular Americans' goodwill than were the slightly older MPA group).[19] They do not feel the same way about the American government (or at least the Bush administration circa 2003–4)—only about one in five believe the American government views China as a friend.[20]

Finally, to get a sense for where America fits in our Chinese respondents' global perspective we asked them to name the nation they most liked and the nation they most disliked. President Bush would be most disappointed by the result: France was easily the winner with one out of two people naming it as their favorite country. America did finish second with one out of five ranking it as their favorite. No other nation came close. Not surprisingly given the horrific events of World War II,

Japan still ranked as the least well liked nation in the world in the eyes of the Chinese—more than eight out of ten named it as their least favorite (among the college students, 6.8 percent ranked the United States as their least favorite country, while not a single one of the graduate students named the United States).

Based on our survey and interviews, we believe our respondents are right to believe that over the last few years they have gained a more thorough and less ideologically based understanding of the United States. In the 1970s and 1980s, Chinese still had a very limited knowledge of America, even as formal relations were improving. What knowledge existed came almost solely from a few translated American books and dubbed Hollywood movies and from official propaganda that few Chinese accepted as a trustworthy source of information. In China, through the 1980s, the United States remained largely a mythic place, which, despite often negative government propaganda, was widely seen as a land of wealth, freedom, and excitement. Not until a large number of Chinese students, businessmen, tourists, and officials went to America and brought back their personal experiences and understandings of the country did that happy myth begin to be tempered in the late 1980s and early 1990s by a more balanced view.

Today, Chinese have many ways to become familiar with America. Several million Chinese have visited the United States or have family members who have done so. Hollywood movies are now omnipresent in China; with DVD technology and the growing popularity of commercial piracy, nearly all popular American television shows and movies are almost immediately available in China. For example, *Friends, National Geographic,* and *Sex and the City* are massive hits throughout China.

Technological developments have also narrowed the distance between China and America. In 1997, there were only 620,000 Internet users in China, whereas, by the end of 2003, over 80 million people logged on regularly. Popular American books are easily purchased on numerous Chinese book websites, with some translated within weeks of their first release. Hip-hop music that comes out in New York today will be available to download with MP3 players tomorrow in Shanghai. Chinese youth are the most exuberant users of the new media, especially the Internet, and as a result are well versed in American culture and, to a lesser extent, the political and social realties of American life.[21]

We believe, too, that younger Chinese have a relatively benign, balanced, and calmly positive view of the United States because they are far less insecure about their own nation than were their elders. Even in the early 1990s, many Chinese believed that they could not stand up to the United States and that the future of their own nation might well be determined by external events. But from the mid-1990s onward, China began successfully to assert itself globally: in 1997 China regained control of Hong Kong; in 1999 Macao returned to China; and most recently China joined the WTO and was named host of the 2008 Olympics and the 2010 World Expo. The Chinese are well aware that the whole world is watching their flourishing economy and growing international power. The younger generation in China has come of age during this unsurpassed era of Chinese confidence, and they lack the defensiveness of prior generations.

Chinese confidence about their successful national path has resulted in a fair amount of pragmatism regarding China's external and internal government policy. Few Chinese see themselves, yet, as a global superpower (in our group only 9.2 percent), and few see the need to take on a global military role. Instead, by a huge margin, Chinese public opinion favors the continued effort to focus China's energy on increasing its economic power, and not its military strength (only 2 percent of our respondents believe that military buildup should be a national priority). Similarly, only 16.6 percent of the Chinese we interviewed believe that political reform should be a national priority. The Chinese people, rather remarkably, take a long view of China's rise to global power. Only 3.7 percent of the Chinese we surveyed believed that China would surpass the United States within twenty years, while roughly half calmly stated that China would need about a century to catch up and surpass the United States as a world power.[22] The Chinese proto-elite we surveyed seem remarkably composed and accepting of China's present economic and international path.

CONCERN ABOUT AMERICAN INTERNATIONAL BEHAVIOR

Thus, as the Chinese focus on their successful internal progress, their attitude towards the United States has become less oriented toward ideological positioning and political posturing. Instead, the United States is perceived as a complex reality that must be constantly gauged so as to ascertain its role in China's forward movement. Thus, our respondents, while generally positive in their view toward the United States, remain concerned about American foreign policy. Many are quite worried that America's recent projection of military power might lead to further destabilizing aggression that might have spillover effects on China. Specifically, when asked what major influence the United States has on current international affairs, 57 percent of those surveyed said the it practices "power politics that have made the world less stable," and only 9 percent believed that the United States contributed to "world stability." Moreover, 92 percent of the respondents believed that America practices an international double standard in which the American government constantly condemns other nations for repressive, violent actions even as the Americans practice such behavior. According to our survey, these concerns about American foreign policy are, increasingly, becoming the key factor in how the proto-elite in China perceive the United States, overall.

Our respondents view on the September 11 attack is in keeping with this perspective. A large percentage of those we surveyed viewed the event through the lens of what they saw as America's long-standing imperialist quest. Only 6 percent of the respondents said they fully sympathized with America for what happened, while 69 percent said that while they felt sympathetic and opposed terrorism, Americans needed to understand why the attack occurred.

We want to underline, however, that our respondents show far less concern about America's relations with peoples in the Middle East or Islamic nations than they do with American policy towards China. When asked which specific event had most affected their image of America, 33.3 percent mentioned the bombing of the Belgrade Chinese embassy, 24.2 percent said the double standard pursued by Washington, 15 percent mentioned the sanctions imposed by America against China since 1989, 6 percent said the U.S. refusal to sign the Kyoto Protocol, 6 percent said Taiwan's Lee Tunghui's visit to America, and 3 percent said the midair collision in 2001. Only 9 percent mentioned the U.S. war in Iraq.

To gain a more open-ended understanding of how our sample saw the U.S. role in the world, we provided them with a list of somewhat loaded terms by which they could identify America's global position. A very small number—around 2 percent—chose *impartial arbitrator,* and 11 percent picked *world leader.* Far more popular choices were *world hegemon* (53 percent) and *world police* (34 percent). We then provided our respondents with a wide range of words and asked them to describe with what image they would most associate America. The most frequent words chosen by the two groups were *hegemonic, powerful, open, democracy, freedom, beautiful imperialist, civilized, warmonger,* and *energetic.*

An important side note: while our respondents demonstrated in numerous ways a deep concern about America's approach to global relations, few felt any need to act on their concerns by boycotting American products; just the opposite. Hollywood movies remain extremely popular among young Chinese, and McDonald's fast food is still a popular treat. In fact, Hollywood movies seen in China counter the negative image that U.S. foreign policy produces in the Chinese public. We were intrigued to learn that a plurality of the people we surveyed believes American movies provide a positive image of the United States. The Chinese seem to love the Terminator as much as California voters.

Overall, although our respondents do not like American foreign policy, they remain confident about the state of Sino-American relations. Fifty-seven percent of those surveyed believe that Sino-American relations have somewhat improved over the last fourteen years, while 11 percent believe they have improved greatly. Only 12 percent view bilateral relations as having deteriorated, with another 12 percent say they have seen no change. Despite this generally positive appraisal, many Chinese state that they have only one major concern that could horribly damage U.S.-China relations: American policy towards Taiwan.

The Taiwan issue is not a new problem, but it remains a central one. Eighty percent of our survey respondents stated that they believe the United States supports the full and permanent separation of Taiwan from China. Exactly half believe that the United States will not publicly support Taiwan's fight for independence but will encourage Taiwan to take this path. Remarkably, not a single person we surveyed believed that the United States would support Taiwan's unification with China or stand by if such a policy were actively pursued by China. While Taiwan remains a hot-button issue for the Chinese we surveyed, it is critical to add that very few respondents believed that the Taiwan situation would result in a military confrontation between the United States and China.

Along those same lines, when asked if America policy, broadly under-stood, was any kind of "threat" to China's security and development, 38 percent said it was, while another 38 percent said it was not, with the re-maining 22 percent offering no opinion. When asked about their view of Sino-American relations over the next ten years, a majority of re-spondents agreed that they would stay about the same.

Overall, the students we interviewed, both those who are college age and those who are older, have a relatively calm and considered view of the state of U.S.-China relations. Taiwan is a problem in that relation-ship and our respondents demonstrated their concern, but they did not fall prey to hysteria or belligerent feelings over the issue; instead they look forward to a continued, nonviolent struggle to resolve the problem. And while the Chinese we interviewed do not share Americans' views on why the September 11 terrorist attacks occurred or on the war in Iraq, a large majority do not have an overall antagonistic view of the United States. Most want to see the United States and China continue to develop a good, mutually beneficial bilateral relationship. When asked bluntly if they would like to see China confront the United States over its inter-national policies, an overwhelming majority of the respondents rejected that option.

DECLINING ROLE OF GOVERNMENT

Western scholars have recently argued that the Chinese people are in-creasingly antagonistic towards the United States and other leading West-ern powers. While we see a reasonable concern in China over a variety of international issues, we do not find a turn towards xenophobia or ir-responsible anti-Americanism. Similarly, while many Western experts believe that government-controlled propaganda aims to produce xeno-phobia in general, and anti-Americanism in particular (to produce greater national solidarity and support for the Chinese Communist Party), we find that our respondents—who as future or present government bu-reaucrats should be particularly open to such propaganda—are not simply pawns of government information campaigns. In large part, such a campaign is not even possible anymore. While the Chinese govern-ment has historically played an overwhelmingly significant role in shap-ing public opinion about the United States through its control of the mass media and other forms of cultural production, that system is fast breaking down. Most of the party-controlled newspapers and publishing houses are now profit-making operations, and, thus, many have created lively mass-appeal papers and sensational tabloids and published a variety of books that have flourished on urban newsstands and in bookstores. Market competition among papers and magazines has become so intense that many headlines are now determined not by government decree but by what sells (though it is vital to state that China does not yet have Western-style freedom of the press; censorship and a licensing system are still firmly in place).[23]

As media content becomes freer, the Chinese people have come to take more stock in what is being printed, though they remain highly skeptical about the openness of newspapers, television reports, and other media that remain heavily influenced by the government.[24] Overall, we have found that the role of the government in shaping the image of America among the younger generation, although it remains strong, has become less of a determining factor than it was even a decade ago. People told us that they use the Internet, newspapers, books, movies, television shows, as well as government statements and school material to gain their own perspective on the United States.[25]

People's ability to gain a greater degree of independently produced perspective on the United States is, we believe, an increasingly important part of the government policy dynamic in China. In part because the current Chinese leaders lack the charismatic appeal that predecessors such as Mao Zedong and Deng Xiaoping enjoyed, they have been using claims of public support to legitimize their rule. Concrete evidence of this concern has come in the form of government-commissioned opinion polls that are explicitly aimed at learning what the public thinks on various issues so as to demonstrate the government's concerns about public preference. While in Western democracies such concern by the government about public opinion is a political given, in China it is news.

Second, factions within government policy elites have been increasingly using claims of public support to strengthen their own positions when the government is divided over the direction of policy. This has been particularly true regarding Sino-American relations, where, to put the matter schematically, some governing authorities believe the United States must be treated in a somewhat confrontational manner, while others believe that confrontation can be avoided by building mutual trust through cooperation and interaction. Chinese public opinion towards the United States could well be an important factor in determining the direction policy takes in this critic area, since the policy elite seems unable to gain a consensus. Overall, public opinion in China has become an interesting variable that has begun to affect policymaking by setting "boundaries of the permissible." This public opinion boundary-setting may well greatly influence the long-term direction of China's policy toward America.[26]

The location of that boundary as it relates to Sino-American relations is not fixed in place. Events have caused it to shift dramatically over the last sixty years. Right now, the majority of the Chinese emerging elite we studied have ambivalent feelings toward the United States.[27] Most see the United States as a two-faceted nation: Cultural America (America at home) and Superpower America (America in the world). The former image is mostly notably positive, while the latter is quite negative. Despite the deep disgust and anger over of the Iraq war and America's strident unilateralism, most Chinese are not turning directly against the United States. As our study shows, very few of our respondents are deeply antagonistic in their attitudes towards the United States, and almost none carry with them the almost ingrained dislike they feel towards Japan. The younger Chinese we interviewed mostly put the matter quite straightforwardly; they admire America's wealth, power, and vitality, but they dislike its hegemonic international behavior. On balance, most express warm feelings towards the United States, but their goodwill should not be taken for granted.

Conclusion

A few conclusions emerge from our study. First, the American war on terror, as it has been executed, is grossly unpopular in China. But our respondents, while worried about what that policy tells them about America's global ambitions, are far more concerned about the narrow set of policies the American government takes towards China. Many are deeply concerned that the United States will do more to constrain China's emergence as a prosperous country than it will do to help that emergence. In this regard America's symbol acts, such as the American position on China's right to host international events like the Olympics, or American responses to accidental events like the midair collision of planes, matter a great deal. More substantively, American policy on the Taiwan question is critically important in shaping public opinion. On the other hand, China's younger emerging elite has strong positive feelings towards American culture. To build on that goodwill, the American government should do what it can to increase its "soft power" by making its attractive culture more available to the Chinese people.

The Chinese people are extremely aware of how American decisions affect their nation. They are, to put the matter gently, wary of American unilateralism and bellicosity. While relations are generally good, both sides, with some reason, look at one another with suspicion and mistrust, which is made worse by misunderstandings. Although the Chinese emerging elite seems to be more confident and optimistic about the future of their country and about Sino-American relations than previous generations, their suspicions of America's global ambitions and fears that the United States will try to put roadblocks on China's path to prosperity could derail bilateral relations.

The American people need to realize the power they have in shaping Chinese images of the United States. They need to understand that China will become an ever greater force in the world and that working with China will produce far better results than working against China. With global challenges of all kinds ever present, America surely cannot go it alone, and in that regard it matters what the Chinese people think of the United States.

Notes

1. This chapter draws on the authors' essay "Contending Views," in Yufan Hao and Lin Su, eds., *Chinese Foreign Policy Making* (London: Ashgate, 2005). We are grateful to David Farber and Doug Macdonald for insightful comments and suggestions. This work was assisted by a grant from the Ford Foundation and a faculty research grant from Colgate University.

2. Defined by Joseph Fewsmith and Stanley Rosen as "public intellectuals, people who take part in public discourse and try to influence informed public

opinion and governmental policies on a range of issues." See "The Domestic Context of Chinese Foreign Policy: Does 'Public Opinion' Matter?" in David M. Lampton, ed., *The Making of Chinese Foreign and Security Policy in the Era of Reform, 1978–2000* (Stanford: Stanford University Press, 2001), 153.

3. To supplement our survey, we also sponsored another survey that consisted of simple questions asked among one hundred neighborhood committee cadres in Shanghai, the largest metropolitan area in China. Since this group of people is the linkage between the government and its citizens, our survey may reflect what both the Chinese people and Chinese officials at the grassroots level think of America.

4. Jianwei Wang, *Limited Adversaries: Post–Cold War Sino-American Mutual Images* (Oxford: Oxford University Press, 2000).

5. Niu Jun, "Suspicion: Assessing the Chinese View of America," *Zhongmei Changqi Duihua* (China–United States sustained dialogue, 1986–2001) (Beijing: Zhongguo Shehuikexue chubanshe, 2001), 81–88.

6. Yufan Hao and Huan Guocang, eds., *The Chinese View of the World* (New York: Pantheon, 1989).

7. J. H. Zhu, "Origins of the Chinese Student Unrest," *Indianapolis Star*, May 9, 1989, cited in Fewsmith and Rosen, "Domestic Context," 156.

8. *Chinese Youth Daily*, July 14, 1995.

9. Ren Yue, "China's Perceived Image of the United States: Its Sources and Impact," in Peter Koehn and Joseph Cheng, eds., *U.S.-China Relations Following the 1997–1998 Summits* (Hong Kong: Chinese University Press, 1999), 247–63.

10. Yue, "China's Perceived Image," 252.

11. Song Qiang et al., *Zhong Guo Ke Yi Shuo Bi* (China can say no) (Beijing: Zhonghua Gongshang Lianhe Chubanshe, 1996).

12. Charlotte Lloyd, "Pot of Resentment Has Overflowed," *Guardian Weekly*, May 16, 1999, 1.

13. Mobo C. F. Gao, "Sino-US Love and Hate Relations," *Journal of Contemporary Asia* 30, no. 4 (2000): 547–61.

14. Bonnie Glaser, "U.S.-China Relations: The Best since 1972 or the Best Ever?" *Comparative Connection*, Pacific Forum C515, October 2003, 1.

15. Arthur Waldron, "The Chinese Sickness," *Commentary*, July–August 2003, 36–42.

16. Liu Kang and Li Xiguang, *Yaomohua zhongguo de beihou* (Behind the demonization of China) (Hong Kong: Tai-Kung-Pao Publisher, 1997).

17. See Jonathan Unger, ed., *Chinese Nationalism* (Armonk, N.Y.: M. E. Sharpe, 1996); Allen Whiting, "Chinese Nationalism and Foreign Policy after Deng," *China Quarterly* 142 (June 1995): 295–316; Suisheng Zhao, "Chinese İntellectuals' Quest for National Greatness and Nationalistic Writings in the

1990s," *China Quarterly* 152 (December 1997): 725–45; Lowell Dittmer and Samuel Kim, eds., *China's Quest for National Identity* (Ithaca, N.Y.: Cornell University Press, 1993).

18. As Ross Terrill put it: "China now shouts its anti-hegemonism just as the China of Mao shouted its anti-imperialism; the tune is identical even if the lyric is adjusted. The song really means that a muscle-flexing China itself wants to be the hegemon." *The New Chinese Empire and What It Means for the United States* (New York: Basic Books, 2003), 267.

19. 52.5 percent of correspondents in both groups thought American people are friendly to China (50.2 percent thought them to be relatively friendly, and 2 percent thought them very friendly).

20. Sixty-nine percent believed Americans somewhat do not understand China, and 27 percent believed they do not understand China at all, with 4 percent having no opinion.

21. Zhaoxi, "Jin shinianlai zhongmei guanxi diaochazhong de minjian renzhi" (Societal consensus from the survey on Sino-American relations in the last ten years), *New Weekly Magazine*, May 22, 2003, http://www.sina.com.cn.

22. The survey among the one hundred neighborhood committee members agrees with this perspective. Twenty-seven percent selected forty to fifty years, 53 percent selected fifty to sixty years, 8 percent selected twenty to thirty years, and 4 percent selected ten to twenty years.

23. According to the editor of *Global Times*, a mass-appeal paper created by the *People's Daily*, their editors give a few tentative headlines from which the street vendors choose those they like most, as some eye-catching headlines prompt street vendors to double the number of retail copies purchased.

24. See J. M. Chan, "Commercialization without Independence," in J. Y. Cheng and M. Brosseau, eds., *China Review, 1993* (Hong Kong: Chinese University Press, 1993), 25.1–25.21; Xu Yu, "Professionalization without Guarantees: Changes of the Chinese Press in Post-1989 Years," *Gazette* 53, nos. 1–2 (1994): 23–41; Chen Huailin, "Bird-Caged Press Freedom in China," in J. Cheng, ed., *China in the Post-Deng Era* (Hong Kong: Chinese University Press, 1998), 645–68; Yuezhi Zhao, "From Commercialization to Conglomeration: The Transformation of the Chinese Press within the Orbit of the Party State," *Journal of Communication* 50, no. 2 (2000): 3–26.

25. This seems to be in line with the poll taken by Global Scan in December 2003 concerning public attitudes toward media and press in China: a plurality of 42.6 percent of the Chinese public does not trust press and media (21 percent have no trust, 18.42 percent not much trust, 2.66 percent no trust at all ["no trust" and "no trust at all" appear to be the same category), while 31.5 percent trust Chinese press and media, and 23 percent have some trust.

26. Fewsmith and Rosen, "Domestic Context," 174–75. Perhaps the most obvious example of the impact public opinion has had on Chinese policy towards the United States occurred during 1999 crisis in Sino-American relations. Negotiations between Washington and Beijing over China's bid to join the WTO had been deadlocked for years. China wanted to enter the WTO as a developing country, while the United States insisted that China should join as a developed country with a shorter period of adjustment before Beijing opened its lucrative market to American products. On the eve of Premier Zhu's visit to America, Beijing suddenly demonstrated its readiness to strike a deal for its WTO membership. However, President Clinton did not grasp the chance. Zhu left Washington empty-handed after he made significant concessions to U.S. demands. To make the situation worse, the United States Trade Representative posted an outline of the trade commitments China had made on the Web, and the Chinese government lost control over the flow of information. Almost immediately the Internet was filled with denunciations of Zhu, accusing him of "selling the country down the river." When Chinese public opinion was inflamed, the internal strife within the Chinese government became apparent as the minister of information industries tendered his resignation. It was at this moment that the American bomber attacked the Chinese embassy in Belgrade. Public outrage was so extreme that the Chinese leadership had no choice but to yield to it, having to refuse America's apology and explanation for the embassy bombing.

27. Harold R. Isaacs, *Scratches on Our Minds* (New York: John Day, 1958).

FROM THE

COLD WAR TO

A LUKEWARM

PEACE

❏ ❏ ❏

RUSSIAN VIEWS OF SEPTEMBER 11 AND BEYOND

Eric Shiraev and Olga Makhovskaya

I N Russia, few world events in the past decade generated such a robust public reaction as the terrorist acts of September 11, 2001, and the America-led war on terrorism that followed. At the beginning of this millennium, nearly free of political censorship, Russian society was still very young as a democracy but already mature enough to embrace a wide range of diverse opinions expressed unreservedly. Scores of Russians, from powerful politicians who made serious official statements, to pundits expressing themselves in flamboyant newspaper editorials, to passersby making remarks in live television interviews—all responded passionately to the unfolding events and their ramifications for Russia, U.S.-Russian relations, international terrorism, and the future of the world. Some of these responses echoed the fears of the confrontational and ideology-driven "old school" of thinking formed during the Cold War. Others were obviously sympathetic towards America and Americans. Yet other reactions reflected a dynamic, contradictory, and at times confused mixture of love-hate beliefs founded on rational assessments, passing emotions, political alliances, or other personal commitments. Despite such a perceived diversity and eclecticism of opinions,

Russia's reactions to what happened on September 11 in America, and then later on in Afghanistan, in Iraq, and in the world, were rooted in a solid, relatively coherent ideological and cultural foundation. This nearly consensual climate of opinion had been forming for several decades and was firmly shaped during the post–Cold War period after 1991. To put it bluntly, decades of Russian frustration over the economic gap between Western nations and Russia and a widely held fear of American power and suspicion of American arrogance, combined with Russians' long-standing belief in their nation's own exceptionality, desire for cultural autonomy, and international leadership, created a widespread feeling within Russia that America, while deserving of sympathy following September 11, was not to be fully trusted with an international war on terrorism.

A View from the Past: The Cold War

All modern Russian leaders try to walk a fault line that runs between two tectonic plates: on the one side is a great majority of Russians' comfort with a predominantly traditionalist and backward provincial way of life, isolated from the outside world, and on the other is Russians' long-standing admiration for Western capitalist dynamism and world-dominant culture. For generations, Russian leaders and scores of domestic thinkers have attempted to find a strategy that would allow Russia to overcome its economic inferiority without losing its cultural heritage. This predicament created chronically ambivalent attitudes toward Western countries. In particular, for decades, many Russians have perceived the United States as more advanced and "civilized" than Russia, even in the thick of the Cold War. Such ambivalent attitudes were glaringly obvious among the Russian elite throughout many years of pre-Soviet, Soviet, and recent Russian history. Today, suspiciousness and resistance to everything Western is miraculously combined with an attraction to and acceptance of its customs, beliefs, symbols, and most elements of the Western way of life.[1]

Discussing their lifestyle, culture, technology, and hopes for the future, Russians seldom compare themselves with their eastern or southern neighbors, such as Turkey, China, Iran, or India. Russia, as a nation, has always been keen to measure itself against the West. Despite its ambiguous geographic location, people of this country persistently, and especially in recent history, considered nations located westward as closer to them culturally than all of the territories, kingdoms, caliphates, emirates, and empires to the east and south. Part of this mind-set is also the symbolic tradition of singling out one Western country at a time in history to be a paragon for acceptance and imitation. Never has this role been handed over to China, Afghanistan, or Korea. These functions were historically assigned to countries such as the Netherlands, France, Prussia, or England. In the second half of the twentieth century it was the United States' turn to serve in this symbolic role.

Since the 1940s, during the Communist years, Russian attitudes about the United States were based on the fortified pillars of a totalitarian and anti-Western ideology. The attitudes were reinforced by the generally limited access of the Soviet people, because of censorship, to any truthful information about the West. In public schools and through the government-controlled media, the Soviet people were given some facts about technological and economic achievements of Western democracies. Yet the main message conveyed to the Soviet people that the West was chronically ill and all its material success was temporary and superficial. The free-market economic system and liberal democracy, according to the official Soviet ideology, had no future.[2] The notorious remark, "We will bury you," made by the Soviet premier Nikita Khrushchev in 1956, was not necessarily a reflection of the belligerent intentions of the Soviet regime but rather a deep-seated belief in the inevitable implosion of capitalism. The Soviet ideologists also vigorously promoted the view that Western capitalism wouldn't die without a fight and that the United States and its allies would do anything to prolong their agony by trying to dominate the world. Soviet leaders were genuinely afraid about the spread of a Western-style democracy and commonly labeled U.S. foreign policies as "imperialist," "colonialist," "militarist," and "aggressive." In the press, the distinction was often made, however, between "good" ordinary Americans, especially the working class, and the "evil" elite, including the military-industrial complex, big property owners, decadent intellectuals, and government officials.[3]

Despite the systematic institutional effort to develop strong anti-Western and, subsequently, anti-American attitudes in the Soviet people and especially in the younger generations, the outcome of such ideological brainwashing was not what officials had expected. Although the majority of the Soviet people by the end of the 1970s and the beginning of the 1980s maintained negative or nonsupportive attitudes about U.S. foreign policies, most people saw clearly the advantages of the American and West European political and social system.[4] No reliable poll results exist to support this observation because surveys were heavily censored in those days, but based on retrospective work by an array of Russian social scientists, we can generalize using the rule of the thirds: about one-third of the Soviet people generally accepted the anti-American attitudes prescribed by the government; about one-third rejected most of the critical information conveyed via the media about the United States; and the remaining third either did not care at all or had a mixed set of opinions.[5]

The coming of Mikhail Gorbachev to power in 1985 signaled a major shift in Soviet domestic and foreign policies. Gorbachev's perestroika meant a serious shift, as well, in the official ideological perception of the West. Gorbachev pushed a more positive Soviet view of the United States, in particular, to provide a reformist framework for restructuring of socialism at home. However, the initial plan of gradual improvement of the socialist economy set forth by Gorbachev failed. The government-controlled economic system and social institutions rapidly collapsed. The reforms in foreign policy led to the end of the Warsaw Pact, which was the political and military alliance of the socialist countries, the withdrawal of the Soviet troops from Eastern Europe, and the normalization of the relationship between Moscow and Washington. These changes in the late 1980s affected the Soviet people's attitudes toward the West in three ways.

First, most people who carried deeply seated suspicions about the United States became even more distrustful. They blamed the pro-Western policies of Gorbachev for the failure of Communism and the collapse of the Soviet Union as a superpower. On the other hand, those people who already had developed pro-Western views saw the ongoing social changes as a true blessing and the long-awaited confirmation of their reformist views.[6] Second, a significant number of people who maintained mixed or indifferent views about the West, witnessing an inevitable collapse of an inefficient regime, sided with the "pro-Western" viewpoint; they believed it was the only alternative to the ideology-driven, pro-Communist, and anti-Western doctrines of the past. Third, most pro-Western attitudes, the expression of which had been virtually prohibited before 1985, were easily conveyed during the period of Gorbachev's reforms via a growing number of independent media outlets. Anti-American views in the late 1980s and early 1990s were virtually shut down by the government, and the distribution of such views was limited to a few significantly weakened media sources supported mainly by disjointed prosocialist and nationalist groups.

In Russia's new atmosphere of ideological pluralism and diversity, the United States became an important cultural symbol. For many Russians, having either a negative or a positive attitude about America was an essential part of their ideological orientation and cultural identity. Especially for most representatives of Russia's new educated middle class in the late 1980s, America by default had become the natural antipode of the past: the inefficient, bureaucratic, and backward Soviet Union.[7]

Getting Closer: Post-Soviet Developments

Since December 25, 1991, the date when the official "death certificate" of the Soviet Union was issued, the administration of Boris Yeltsin, the new Russian president, began to act openly and exuberantly on pro-American attitudes. When Yeltsin spoke before the U.S. Congress in June 1992, he effusively praised the United States for helping Russia slay the dragon of Communism. Yeltsin was not speaking just from the heart. He hoped that his post–Cold War pro-Americanism would, literally, pay off for the Russian people. Many Russians expected the United States to provide them with a massive program of economic assistance, similar to the Marshall Plan of the 1940s in Europe.[8] These expectations turned out to be wishful thinking. Russians' excited hopes for a massive influx of American and Western assistance to help their society rebuild after the defeat of Communism has never materialized.

Russia's encounter with severe economic difficulties in the early 1990s chastened Russian optimists (never a large number) who had held out the Western free-market model as the panacea for Soviet economic failures. Social disenchantment with American-style market reforms grew after 1992 due to social and personal insecurity, shortages of money, rampant inflation, skyrocketing prices, and epidemic corruption.[9] The United States provided the Russia people with no massive economic help, and both elites and common folk bitterly realized that their country would face its overwhelming problems using its own, limited resources. To make things worse, the Russian economy after a period of recovery in the mid-1990s took a deep and painful dive again in 1998, thus further damaging Russians' faith in the power of a self-regulating free market to create prosperity for more than a few oligarchs. One of the psychological consequences of this period of economic difficulties was a sustained growth of an anti-Western mood, deliberately "beefed up" by antimarket political opposition, mostly Communists, populists, and nationalists. By the late 1990s, anti-Western attitudes had gained considerable strength in Russia. America's apparent indifference to Russia's troubles and well-reported decisions not to provide assistance angered the average person. America's prosperity, strength, and selfishness were seen as a sign of arrogance. Many Russians believed that their nation's loss of superpower status was good for America but bad for Russia.

To millions of Russians, the fall of the Soviet Union created an immeasurable psychological gap between past and present. Once they were citizens of a gigantic multinational superpower, both respected and feared around the world. Then, by the early 1990s, Russia had become a shrunken, second-rate nation unable to compete on the international stage. History gives only too many examples of how apparent national humiliation coupled with devastating economic collapse sparks explosions of xenophobia. The rise of Russian-grown chauvinism and nationalism coincided with the collapse of the Soviet Union. The main target for Russian chauvinism was, not surprisingly, the West and its most powerful country. A new form of xenophobic Russian isolationism emerged. The ugly chimera of Cold War ideology was resurrected by the supporters of Russia-grown national socialism, a popular version of "Stalinism without Stalin."[10] Others followed the example of Alexander Solzhenitsyn, the famed writer. Although he passionately advocated anti-Communism, he also maintained anti-Western and nationalistic views based on historical, philosophical, religious, and moral grounds.[11] Another nationalistic school of thought embraced a popular idea of Russia's historic Eurasian mission as a pathbreaker and beacon of humanity designated by a special historic calling.[12]

Attitudes about the West and the United States began to play a role in domestic political battles. A pro-Western foreign policy course chosen in the early 1990s evoked persistent disdain from the domestic political opposition to the Kremlin policies. Anti-Americanism and anti-Western attitudes were used as a political card to achieve specific goals at home. To be accused of being unpatriotic became dangerous for any politician running for reelection in the 1990s and after. On many occasions, Russian policy toward the West fell hostage to domestic political considerations. Nationalists and Communists, despite ideological differences between these movements, were among the main carriers of anti-Western and anti-American attitudes. According to many surveys, about a third of Russians shared these hostile views.[13]

Several international developments further contributed to anti-American sentiment in Russia. First, many Russians believed NATO's westward expansion in the mid-1990s to be an anti-Russian demonstration of disrespect for their country's security concerns. The Russian mass media portrayed the United States as a major coordinator of NATO expansion and accused the United States of deliberately attempting to undermine the post–Cold War strategic balance in Europe. Next, a majority of people, including Russian top officials, perceived Western military intervention in Bosnia as an attempt by Americans and their European "puppets" to punish small and "innocent" Serbia and establish American control over the Balkans.[14] The negative image of the United States was further darkened during the U.S.-led NATO military campaign against Serbia in 1999. Russians were especially irritated by what they called arrogant and irresponsible actions of the Western powers against a sovereign country in the heart of Europe. The mainstream Russian media repeatedly called NATO an aggressor and a threat to Russia. This powerful anti-Western mood crossed party lines. Even cautious moderate politicians began to issue statements against the perceived dangers of American and NATO policies.

In the wake of the war in Serbia, by the end of the 1990s, opinion polls yielded a steady 60 percent national average of anti-Western attitudes (which doubled the ten-year average for anti-Western sentiment). Even small bilateral or international issues suddenly began to matter to an increasingly large proportion of people. The United States was frequently accused in the mass media of selling poor-quality products. Russian consumers began to be bombarded by newspaper stories about U.S. corporations ripping them off. One of the most remarkable cases was a media campaign that supported the boycott of American frozen chicken legs (called in Russia "Bush's Legs," a reference to President George H.

Bush, who was president when the frozen food product was first imported into Russia).[15] Despite this increasing hostility towards the United States, as soon as the situation in Kosovo calmed down, negative attitudes towards America declined steadily to an average 30 percent national average. More importantly, the sudden rise to power in 1999 of a former security officer from St. Petersburg, the relatively young and pragmatic Vladimir Putin, was viewed by most Russians as a sign that Russian foreign policy would be based on common sense, rational calculations, and reliable and mutually beneficial relations with the United States.

September 11 and After: The Media and Elites' Reactions

The Russian government responded almost instantly to the September 11 attacks on the United States. President Putin condemned the attacks in a special appearance on all Russian television networks. He called the terrorist acts "barbaric," emphasized that they were directed against innocent people, and referred to the feelings of "indignation and revolt" directed against the perpetrators of the strike. Putin sent a telegram to George W. Bush that not only expressed sympathy to the American people but also stated that be believed that the attacks must not go unpunished.[16] The Kremlin issued a decree to lower Russian flags to half-mast and observe a moment of silence throughout Russia at noon Moscow time on September 13. On that day, Putin again held a telephone conversation with Bush and discussed joint actions. Russia and NATO issued an extraordinary statement expressing anger at the devastating attacks on the United States and calling for international efforts to combat global terrorism.

Top public officials from the Defense and Foreign Affairs ministries also issued statements and made public remarks that echoed Putin's comments of September 11. Sergei Lebedev, head of the Foreign Intelligence Service, the general who usually keeps a very low profile, stated publicly that his agency was working closely with national security offices of other countries to prevent new attacks. He also called for renewed attempts to fight international terrorism.[17] Boris Nemtsov, the leader of the Union of Right Forces, known for his conciliatory approach to conflict, was reported to have said on September 13 that Russia should come down hard on terrorism to prevent future attacks against the Kremlin. Grigory Yavlinsky, the leader of the Yabloko party recognized for his long-term support of the principles of liberal democracy, said on September 15 that the terrorist attacks in Washington and New York were the beginning of a new era in which close cooperation between the largest countries, such as the United States and Russia, in the sphere of combating international terrorism, was inevitable.

Other politicians, however, had different ideas. Alexander Shokhin, head of the Duma's finance and crediting committee, was quoted in *Kommersant* on September 12 predicting, with regrets, that the United States would not listen to reason and would choose to punish their enemies unilaterally. Another deputy speaker of the Duma, Vladimir Zhirinovsky,[18] known for his flamboyant behavior, said with apparent joy that the terrorist attacks signaled the end of U.S. dominance. The leader of the Russian Communist Party, Gennady Zyuganov,[19] voiced concern about the Islamic world, Arab countries, and Russia's neighbors in Central Asia. Some politicians' worries over a possible international conflict led to the Duma's resolution of September 19, which stated that any use of force, presumably by the United States, must be rigorously monitored and should not provoke any destabilization in the region.

Russian newspaper headlines on the morning of September 12 were more than dramatic. "Armageddon Now," read the *Kommersant,* a respectable daily newspaper. The paper then warned about the ongoing market collapse and a chaotic situation in currency exchange operations. The word *Armageddon* was used by other printed sources, including the popular newspaper *Izvestia,* which also proclaimed the beginning of the war of civilizations. Similar apocalyptic doom-and-gloom metaphors were featured on the front pages of most newspapers. *Vremya MN* issued a headline that read, "The Apocalypse Happened Yesterday." *Komsomolskaya Pravda* referred to a third world war started by terrorists. The vast majority of articles contained negative, condemning, and disapproving comments referring to cruelty, murder, extremism, insanity, and evil of those who perpetrated the attacks. As an example, *Izvestia* put together the following sequence: "Armageddon. Big country. Big sorrow. Big suffering." Only a very few papers, such as the ultranationalist *Zavtra,* published articles justifying the murderous actions taken against the United States.

Instant Opinions

Most Russians could watch the unfolding events of September 11 on CNN (Fox News and MSNBC were not available to them, yet). Ten years earlier, in 1991, Americans were anxiously sitting in front of television screens following the live CNN coverage of the dramatic events of the August putsch in Moscow. Americans were concerned, puzzled, and hopeful that the fragile Russian democracy would survive and people would not die. Now, in 2001, it was Russians' turn to watch the live coverage. Numerous conversations and interviews with Russians of all walks of life revealed that the most common emotional reaction was shock and fear coupled with deep concerns for the Americans. The American embassy in Moscow and the U.S. consulate general in St. Petersburg drew huge crowds of people bringing flowers, leaving compassionate notes, or simply standing there in silence. People lamented and prayed during spontaneously organized candlelight vigils and regular church services all over the country.

Results of opinion polls were published as early as on September 13. A majority of the Russian people sympathized with the Americans. In a national poll taken September 15–16 by the Public Opinion Foundation, 77 percent of respondents said that they experienced strong emotions when they first heard about the attacks. Only 8 percent of the respondents said they did not care about the events in America. At the same time, about 15 percent reported their satisfaction. Predictably, more than one-third of the respondents satisfied about the attacks identified with the Communist Party.[20] A large number of Russians believed that the attacks against America were somewhat warranted. According to a survey conducted on September 11 and 12 by the Moscow Academy for Humanitarian and Social Issues (MGSA), 21 percent of the respondents agreed that the attacks were a justified punishment for the Americans. A similar question asked by the All-Russia Public Opinion Study Center (VTsIOM) showed that 35 percent of Muscovites polled two days after the events spoke of the terrorist act as a punishment of Americans, which they deserved for the bombings of Hiroshima and Nagasaki, Iraq, and Yugoslavia. However, in both surveys, more people disagreed (37 percent and 61 percent respectively) with the idea that the attacks were justified punishment. Opinion polls also showed a wide range of opinions about what the United States should do in terms of its military and nonmilitary responses.[21] Russians didn't have a predominant opinion about whom to blame for the devastating terrorist attacks.

Whom to Blame and What to Do?

More than a half of Russian newspaper publications in September and October 2001 immediately pointed at Islamic militants or fundamentalists including bin Laden and Al Qaeda, and another 10 percent mentioned Arab terrorists in general.[22] In the search for instant evidence, reporters quoted mostly foreign information services. Most paper reports underlined the international nature of the sophisticated plot.[23] Approximately one-third of published references included a variety of guesses, including America's own government or "homegrown" American terrorist groups.[24] To illustrate, Vladimir Zhirinovsky, leader of the Liberal Democratic Party of Russia, drew parallels between the September 11 attacks and the burning of the Reichstag, the House of Parliament, in Berlin in 1933, after which Hitler assumed dictatorship in Germany. Zhirinovsky predicted during a television interview on October 18 that, in a fashion similar to what Hitler had done, the United States would identify an innocent scapegoat and would attack it. General Boris Agapov, a distinguished specialist on Afghanistan, also expressed reservations about Afghan groups as perpetrators of terrorist acts. He said that it was impossible to imagine how "primitive" organizations such as the Taliban or bin Laden followers could have executed such a complicated and large-scale act of terrorism as flying airplanes into buildings.[25] Other commentators raised doubts about the evidence that pinpointed Arab terrorists, as did Leonid Shebarshin,[26] the former chief of the Soviet Foreign Intelligence. But these skeptical reactions were largely published by pro-Communist newspapers such as *Sovetskaya Rossiya* and *Zavtra.* In other papers, including the mainstream *Moskovsky Komsomolets, Komsomolskaya Pravda,* and *Trud,* more than 70 percent of references described the perpetrators as Islamic or Arab militants.

The tragic events overseas also sparked immediate concerns about similar attacks against Russia. For instance, on September 13 an influential Moscow newspaper discussed whether a kamikaze pilot could hit the Kremlin or any other strategic target in Moscow and whether such a criminal action was preventable (*Komsomolskaya Pravda,* on September 13). Some articles urged Russia to accelerate its military buildup to reduce the probability of such suicidal actions.[27] Dmitry Rogozin, chairman of the State Duma International Affairs Committee, said it was the time for the United States to agree with Russian requests and reconsider its nuclear defense programs in face of unconventional threats from terrorist groups.[28]

America Is Hit, but What about Us?

Gradually, comments shifted to one of Russia's most serious domestic problems: the breakaway republic of Chechnya. In the past, Moscow had repeatedly accused bin Laden and the Taliban of helping the Chechen guerrillas. Hours after the attacks in the United States, Russian politicians were already drawing comparisons between the U.S. tragedy and the troubling situation in this southern region of Russia. On September 11, Rogozin said that that the events in the United States could and should change Western attitudes toward Russia's policy in Chechnya: America would finally see the rebels as terrorists, not freedom fighters.[29] Sergei Yastrzhembsky, the presidential spokesman on Chechnya, Nikolai Kovalev, deputy chairman of the Committee of the State Duma for Security, and Nikolay Patrushev, director of the Russian Federal Security Service, made similar comments.[30] Russian politicians, including those who had earlier urged conciliatory policies in Chechnya, had become distinctly hawkish since the attacks against the United States. Boris Nemtsov, one of a few active supporters of a political settlement in Chechnya, had changed his position.[31] In an interview with the Moscow newspaper *Moskovsky Komsomolets* on September 13, Nemtsov sounded very skeptical about negotiations and insisted on the toughest measures against terrorist of all kinds. Scores of columnists and television commentators began to make harsh remarks about Chechnya, insisting on tough measures against the terrorists. The reports also reminded readers that Russia had repeatedly claimed in the past that there was a connection between international terrorist groups, on the one hand, and Chechen terrorists, on the other.

Several themes appeared in the interviews given by politicians and in articles written by commentators. Russia was commonly perceived as an equal partner of the United States in the war against terrorism. In September 2001, Putin stated that Russia was ready to cooperate with the United States during the antiterrorist campaign.[32] More importantly, Russia perceived itself as an increasingly essential partner in any international coalition. As early as October 2001, the Russian media started to discuss direct and indirect benefits that the country could and should receive for its support of the United States and the war on terror.[33] Russian defense minister Sergei Ivanov emphasized the importance of profitable arms deals with the anti-Taliban Northern Alliance in Afghanistan;[34] publications started to appear in which the West was criticized for the lack of benefits given to Russia for its cooperative role.[35] A new course of events was believed to have affected specific problems related to the NATO expansion eastward, American plans to develop the strategic defense system, and Russia's tough approach to the Chechen problem. Repeatedly, these issues were mentioned as now being resolved favorably for Russia, given the new changed world.[36]

Some, including Deputy Foreign Minister Georgy Mamedov,[37] suggested hopefully that the tragic events in the United States could stimulate the development of a new world order, with Russia actively participating in a stronger UN, a nonideological NATO, the World Trade Organization, and an efficient G-8.[38] Some also recommended the creation of a new antiterrorist coalition, modeled after the anti-Hitler coalition of the 1940s and on the basis of NATO. In that coalition, Russia was anticipated to take a leading position alongside the United States and draw closer to the West.[39] Some argued that if Russia did not approach the West, it would face huge debts, hostilities to its southern borders, and fierce competition from China.[40]

The Campaign in Afghanistan: "Yes, But . . . "

While the Bush administration's plans for the war on terror were not clear in the fall of 2001, the Russian media almost immediately after September 11 began to publish commentaries about a definite military action against Afghanistan.[41] Although President Vladimir Putin and

Foreign Minister Igor Ivanov made statements about the importance of balanced and intelligent decisions, they did not rule out the possibility that the United States would use force in the fight against terrorism.[42] Politicians began to discuss the "price" the Kremlin had to demand for its involvement in the forthcoming war, as was done in a radio interview by the head of the Foreign and Defense Policy Council, Sergei Karaganov.[43]

Meanwhile, cautions and antiwar voices were also becoming stronger. Military experts expressed an overall positive opinion about a forthcoming retaliation from the United States. However, they warned about many difficulties that awaited any military force in Afghanistan. Moscow Region governor Boris Gromov, who had served as a top commander in Afghanistan during the Soviet occupation in the 1980s, ruled out any movement of infantry. Even the U.S. Special Forces, he believed, would suffer heavy casualties.[44] Similarly, most politicians and commentators supported, in general, the position of Washington, but expressed serious reservations about potential loss of life among peaceful populations.[45] All these ambivalent opinions about a military action against Afghanistan launched by the United States generally reflected the views of the public. In October, different sources published similar reports about how divided public opinion was about potential air strikes against Afghanistan.[46]

After the Kremlin had promised to support the military campaign in Afghanistan and possibly elsewhere,[47] officials began to spell out possible limitations to what Russia and other countries could do. Early in the fall, several Russian officials had ruled out the use of Russia's ground forces. Defense Minister Sergei Ivanov told *Russia TV* that Russia was not planning to participate in attacks against terrorist bases in Afghanistan.[48] This official Russian opposition stood in stark contrast to the decisions of the governments of several former Soviet countries that chose to participate in American-led actions against international terrorism. Anatoly Kvashnin, head of the General Staff of the armed forces, said it was highly unlikely that Russian troops would take part in an antiterrorist operation, and Ivanov insisted that there was not even any hypothetical ground for a possible NATO deployment in central Asian states.[49] Dmitry Rogozin suggested that the result of any military action initiated by the United States would be innocent victims and further terrorist retaliatory acts.[50]

During the late fall of 2001, then, the moderate majority of Russian political elites was split between supporters of the course chosen by President Putin and those who were already wary about it for various reasons. Of course, some individuals vehemently supported the new foreign policy of Russia. They voiced their opinion mostly through a few consistently proliberal, pro-Western media, such as TV channel 6, the newspaper *Kommersant,* and the weekly *Itogi.* Top military officials and intelligence bureaucrats, however, were unhappy about the possibility of a war and the deployment of NATO troops in central Asia. The "open letter" of a group of Russian generals and admirals published on November 10, 2001, criticized Putin's policies and his alleged pro-Western course. Left-wing political parties expressed a similar disdain. They all stood firmly against any form of Russian military participation in the evolving antiterrorist coalition.[51] Most politicians saw in Putin's support of America a threat to their dream to rebuild Russian independence, keep its distance from the West, and strengthen its military power.[52] Some lobbyists predicted a potential loss of business with partners in the Middle East or central Asia.[53] Duma speaker Gennady Seleznev earnestly expressed a common objection in a television interview; he declared on September 18 that Russia should distinguish between governments and simple people and not deliver blows against entire nations.[54] Some extremist and nationalist politicians did not hide their direct hostility against the West. For instance, Zhirinovsky in his usual flamboyant fashion said that the only way for Russia to become a great power again was not to support the United States but to side with the Taliban and create an alliance with the Arab world.[55]

What was the general reaction of the press? Overall, as the analysis of the publications in major daily newspapers shows, unilateral military actions of the United States were supported in fewer than 15 percent of publications. It was common for the media to doubt the effectiveness of military actions and to suggest that Russia to stay away from the conflict.[56] *Komsomolskaya Pravda* was among the most pacifist-oriented newspapers, with basically all publications related to the events appealing to sobriety of judgment, self-restraint, and nonviolent solutions. Pro-Communist *Sovetskaya Rossiya,* while leaning toward the noninterventionist approach (18 percent of articles) and suggestions about how the

United States should change its foreign policy (30 percent), displayed a greater variety of opinions. The vast majority of newspaper publications conveyed a negative opinion about a possible war in Afghanistan. Possible outcomes of the war, such as the liquidation of the terrorist camps, replacement of the oppressive political regime of Taliban, and the creation of a democratic government in Afghanistan, were practically ignored by the Russian media.

The majority of Russians were skeptical about the military actions in Afghanistan. Most people did not have access to diverse information and were fed from sources that conveyed a one-sided opinion about the war on terror. Not surprisingly, many individuals perceived the Afghan war as an aspect of America's imperialistic ambition and its desire to dominate the world. To these people, the events of September 11 were a convenient justification for the future war. Others, although they understood the defensive nature of the military actions, insisted that the war was launched on behalf of American interests. President Bush's claim that the war was being waged to bring ideals of democracy to Afghanistan was too distant and unacceptable to many Russians, who were struggling from payday to payday as they reeled from the economic insecurity caused by free-market uncertainties. Yet other groups understood the necessity of the war but did not see any reason for Russian forces to join in: people remembered the Soviet military's gruesome experiences in Afghanistan in the 1980s. Numerous articles in Russian newspapers and magazines contained personal accounts from Russian officers who fought in Afghanistan and who predicted a tough time for the American troops in that country. Plenty of warnings came from former military veterans who referred to the U.S. inability to learn from other countries' mistakes, like ones that the Soviet Union committed in Afghanistan in the 1980s, where the Soviet military suffered at least fifteen thousand deaths.[57]

U.S. Foreign Policy Assailed

By late September 2001, after the shock and uncertainty caused by the terrorist acts had faded, media reports began to focus on the United States' foreign policy. Comments about perceived U.S. arrogance and overconfidence were common on newspaper front pages and in editorial columns. America was frequently ridiculed for overestimating terrorist threats and of ignoring international law. Yuri Baluyevsky, first deputy chief of the General Staff, said that the ability of rogue states, including Afghanistan, to deploy weapons of mass destruction was grossly exaggerated and, therefore, that military strikes against such countries were unjustified.[58] Russian political scientist Gleb Pavlovsky, head of the Fund for Effective Policies, referred to the "traditional" U.S. policy of demonstrative retribution, which the Americans resorted to time and again to show the world how tough they were.[59] Some publications suggested that the war on terror was a general excuse to fight an aggressive war against any state that dared to express anti-American attitudes.[60] America was commonly accused of bullying the rest of the world into submission.[61] Other reports questioned the ability of American people to persevere in the face of adversity. For example, Yulia Latynina, a journalist with *ORT,* called Americans intellectually lazy and incapable of fighting to the bitter end. She also said that the U.S. government always removes its soldiers from the places that were too frightening for them.[62]

The most negative opinions came from nationalist and Communist sources, which blatantly accused the United States of barbaric actions, hegemonic policies, and disrespect for international law.[63] But even in more liberal publications a distinct anti-American sentiment surfaced. In the wake of September 11, at least three of these liberal newspapers, *Izvestia, Obshchaia Gazeta,* and *Novaia Gazeta,* published several poorly substantiated, openly prejudicial articles filled with racist remarks that suggested that their authors were taking pleasure in the American tragedy.[64]

Policy after 2002: Prospects in Cooperation

Russian foreign policy-making, formalized in the 1993 constitution, is dominated by the president. President Putin, since taking power, had maintained a pragmatic foreign policy aimed at an effective, although somewhat limited, partnership with the United States. Putin's willingness to fight terrorism together with the United States, especially after the tragic events in 2004 in Beslan took the lives of more than three

hundred hostages, his interests in regional stability, support of nonprolif-
eration policies, and the pursuit of a greater economic stability for Russia motivated most of Russia's governmental relations with the United
States. Since 2001, the Kremlin and the White House had shared similar
attitudes on at least five common foreign-policy-related issues.[65]

The first issue that brought the United States and Russia closer together was the possibility of joint actions aimed at forming an antiterrorist coalition. This coalition, Putin believed, could create a convenient
basis for the broader U.S.-Russian relationship. An umbrella of "collective action" would allow Moscow and Washington to pursue independently their national objectives, namely, fighting terrorism.

Second, both countries shared a common concern over proliferation
of weapons of mass destruction. The Russian government was and is
genuinely alarmed by the nuclear weapons programs of North Korea and,
especially, Iran. After September 11, both nations felt even more vulnerable to horrific attacks, and both governments began to work on programs to secure nuclear, chemical, and biological materials in their own
countries, as well as all over the world.

Third, both nations had major concerns about regional security and,
in particular, the situation in Afghanistan after 2002, in Iraq after 2003,
around Iran after 2005, and in the Middle East. On Iraq, Putin stated on
several occasions that Russia had no interest in a U.S. policy failure. Although Russia, as a member of the Security Council, did not support the
war in Iraq, officials believed in 2004 and after that a forced withdrawal
of U.S. troops from Iraq would create a highly dangerous situation, too
close to Russia.

The fourth shared issue was oil-related. Because Russia has large oil
reserves and because of its renewed hopes for efficient economic relations with the West, Russia has become one of the most reliable suppli-
ers of oil for the West. OPEC, with all its diverse interests and past use of
oil as a political weapon, is, arguably, a less reliable supplier. The "oil card"
has increasingly played a serious role in Russian foreign policy, which is
likely to tie together Russian and Western interests.

And, finally, the fifth and most controversial concern affecting Russian and American interests was the question of international cooperation. After losing its superpower status, Russia became more dependent
on arenas of joint cooperation. In particular, the Russian government

looked to the United Nations as a means of magnifying its own international influence. Thus, Putin pursued measures to create a stronger and more effective United Nations and to take advantage of Russia's seat on the Security Council. Here, Russia and the United States, in practice, were often moving in different directions.

The Obstacles

Even as Putin worked to emphasize common American-Russian interests and to de-emphasize areas of difference, a series of events, unrelated to the war on terrorism, worked to divide the two nations. A few critically important examples are worth mentioning. The Bush administration's decision to walk away from the Anti-Ballistic Missile Treaty was wildly unpopular in Russia. Overwhelmingly, Russians considered Bush's move to be unwise and dangerous; it evoked old Cold War concerns about the United States seeking unilateral advantages at the expense of Russia. Second, during the campaign in Afghanistan and then as a result of the larger war on terrorism, significant numbers of American troops were deployed near the Russian border in Georgia and central Asia. This forward troop deployment is widely perceived by Russians as a dangerous development that threatens Russian national security. Even apparently insignificant American developments have produced quite unexpected reactions in Russia. For most Americans, the 2002 Olympic Games in Salt Lake City and the 2004 Games in Greece were quickly forgotten. A majority of Russians, however, were very upset over several Olympic incidents, especially the treatment of Russian figure skaters and gymnasts (considered "mistreatments" in Russia), and these incidents have remained sore spots in Russian attitudes about the West and the United States. Seventy percent of Russians, right after the winter 2002 Olympics, told pollsters that they considered the United States an unfriendly country. While this anger faded with time, it reappeared again when the United States prepared to invade Iraq in 2003.

Thus, Russian perceptions of the United States had gotten significantly worse at the end of 2002 while the debate over the looming war in Iraq intensified. Criticism of the U.S. actions reached an apogee in the media, which even some Russian commentators called "hysteria." By late

2003, after the invasion, only 4 percent of Russians said that they sided with the American decision to go to war, while 48 percent said they sympathized with the Iraqi people.[66] This public opinion was not unexpected. When Saddam Hussein was in power, many Russian politicians and officials from the Russian Orthodox Church had visited Iraq, citing their desire to help Iraq to cope with UN sanctions. These visits were widely discussed in the Russian media, and it was reported that certain Russian companies were allegedly given the right to purchase Iraqi oil in exchange for political support in Moscow. As a result of these Russian-Iraqi connections, which included economic interests and humanitarian concerns, a number of influential voices that ranged from Communists to nationalists to key Kremlin officials opposed the U.S. invasion. Zhirinovsky was among the most vehement opponents of the war in Iraq. He not only claimed a friendship with Saddam Hussein, he also had strong business contacts with the Iraqi government and the ruling party. Not surprisingly, Zhirinovsky considered the war to be an exercise in raw American power. He publicly praised the strength of the Iraqi army and determination of the Iraqi people; he predicted various doomsday scenarios for Americans. When the war was almost inevitable, he switched tactics and began to criticize his own government for inaction, insisting that Russia should deploy its troops in Iraq and split the country into several zones of occupation. He argued that if Russia did nothing, America would establish control over Iraqi oil and deny Russia access to Iraqi resources.[67]

When the U.S.-led coalition forces invaded Iraq in 2003, Russian-American relations reached their lowest post–Cold War point. President Putin publicly disagreed with President Bush on the war, its causes and possible consequences. Many Russians argued that the war proved traditional arguments about American expansionism, imperialism, and desire for the world domination. In addition, Russians argued that the war revealed a new American "clash of civilizations" doctrine. The events in Iraq were seen by some as evidence of a new crusade by the West against Muslims all over the world, including in Russia. Konstanin Zatulin, director of an influential Moscow think tank and host of a popular television show, *Materik,* said that a new holy war had been declared by the West against the East and that the task of all Orthodox Christians was to resist the aggression of Catholicism and Protestantism.[68]

Zatulin based his view on a theory. However, a strong pro-Islamic lobby has also emerged in Russia in the early twenty-first century. This movement represents a range of interests and is gradually gaining strength. No powerful organization spearheads this movement. Nevertheless, a common set of principles unifies this diverse crowd of pro-Islamic officials, journalists, and influential nongovernmental organizations. All support Muslim emigration into Russia from states such as Azerbaijan, Uzbekistan, Kazakhstan, Tajikistan, and even Afghanistan. Many of these pro-Islam advocates in Russia are supported by business groups associated with oil and other lucrative businesses in the Caucasus region of Russia, as well as in Azerbaijan and other central Asian countries. They not only sponsor immigration to Russia but also build Islamic schools and mosques.[69] An avalanche of classic anti-American rhetoric is found in the essays of one of the most popular representatives of this movement, Geidar Jamal. Commenting on international events, he typically fires a barrage of sarcastic shots at the United States' geopolitical ambitions, Russian undemocratic elections, the chaos in the Middle East, Russia's weakness in the international arena, and Putin's inability to maintain a firm foreign policy. Jamal also tries to persuade his readers that the United States has become a totalitarian country after September 11 and that its citizens no longer have political freedom. There are few original thoughts in his claims. Like other radical critics, he argues that the Bush administration started the war in Iraq to enhance its own reelection chances and because of the Pentagon's desire for world domination.[70]

Since 2003, there has been no shortage of opinions expressed by leading Russian foreign-policy experts regarding the future of U.S.-Russia relations. Alexei Bogaturov, director of the influential Institute of the USA and Canada and a firm believer in geoeconomics, has argued that America is dangerous not because of its global political ambitions but rather because of America's ability to "steal" economic partners from its competitors. Gleb Pavlovsky, who established his high reputation under Boris Yeltsin, was more optimistic and believed in Soviet-American cooperation. On the other hand, one of his opponents in media discussions, Stanislav Belkovsly, president of the Institute of National Strategy, has expressed grave concern about America's growing influence in the former Soviet Asian republics. Viacheslav Nikonov, president of the influential think tank Politika and former member of the Duma, has been more pragmatic in his attitudes and has suggested that Russia should get closer to the United States and Great Britain to gain access to Iraqi oil.

The Russian people have demonstrated some interest in these debates. Unfortunately, emotional assessments usually overshadow any attempts at rational criticism. A trendy book series, sold in street booths under an unambiguous title, "Great Confrontation: America against Russia," has become a bestseller. Its authors, Krupnov and Kalashnikov,[71] have created a five-hundred-page mixture of paranoid beliefs, panicky conclusions, and blatant misinterpretation of pseudo-facts to convey their main idea that Russia has already lost four world wars (World War I, World War II, the Cold War, and the war for economic superiority). The fifth war, they argue, will be the most decisive of all. This war has already begun: its first blows are the expansion of NATO and the antiterrorist campaign of the United States. The authors conclude that Russia has been knocked out of its eastern markets and suffocated by a variety of subtle but powerful economic sanctions administered by the West.

Public Opinion: Ambivalence, Bitterness, and Hope

While the pundits and reporters were busy writing their columns critical of U.S. foreign policy, most Russians paid little attention. There is nothing uniquely Russian in this position. As in many other countries, Russians cared less about America than about their own economic aspirations. They watched reruns of *Sex and the City* on Russian television, checked their TV guides for the next NHL or NBA game, and downloaded (often illegally) the music files of the latest American hip-hop or rock sensations. Jack Daniels was served in Moscow bars, and Jeep Cherokees and Lincolns moved down narrow Russian highways. Russians rented American movies on DVD and did not boycott American cigarettes because of the war in Iraq. Neither did they pour Pepsi in the Volga River in protest over American expansionism.

Surveys taken by the Public Opinion Foundation between 2001 and 2006 showed that Russians' attitudes about America are significantly influenced by immediate events and their coverage in the media. The more negative the coverage of the U.S. involvement in an international issue, the worse are their attitudes. From the beginning of 2001 through 2002, on average, according to the same polling company, more then one-third of respondents considered the United States a friendly country.[72] In March 2003, however, when the war in Iraq begun, surveys showed that only about 17 percent of Russians believed that America was a friendly state. However, soon thereafter the numbers returned to average levels. Only 16 percent of people consider Russian and the United States equal partners. Twice as many view these two countries as partners out of necessity. About 40 percent of Russians said they would like to visit America. Among young people, the percentage of those who want to visit the United States is close to 55 percent.[73] However, overwhelmingly Russians in 2004 (74 percent) stated that their nation should not participate in a UN multinational peacekeeping force, if the decision was made to send such a contingent to Iraq.[74] Throughout the first years of the twenty-first century, approximately two-thirds of the polled Russians say they liked Americans as people. Yet approximately 70 percent of Russians said they did not like the actions of the U.S. government.

As in the late 1980s, a substantial proportion of people today associates America, more than any other place, with wealth, prosperity, and advanced technologies. In surveys, people typically refer to America as the country where "the law works," and as a "free, civilized, democratic country." Most negative evaluations of the United States (27 percent) point to U.S. foreign policy; America is compared to "a boa constrictor who ate a half of the world" or is called the "world's executioner." Some Russians are quite emotional in discussing the United States: "I wish this country was covered with water"; "I wish I had a hand grenade to throw on them." Overall, Russians respect American economic success and are impressed by its democratic form of government. But they are fearful of its international ambitions. The Iraq attack only hardened those core beliefs.[75]

Most Russians remain proud about the country's victory in World War II in 1945. Russians know that America has never fought a war against a foreign power on its own territory, at least a major war compared to those Russia has encountered during its long history: the Mongol rule, the Polish invasion, the war against Napoleon, millions dead during World War I, and many more killed during World War II. These reflections on their history give many Russians a sense of moral superiority over Americans, who have not really, as the Russian old saying goes, "sniffed the gunpowder" on the battlefield. But more and more, in Russia, nostalgic feelings of superiority and security have been replaced by a sense of both personal and national insecurity. Many ordinary Russians maintain the view that the United States represents a general threat to Russia's national security (significantly diminished since the end of the Cold War (but still a threat. Surveys conducted by leading polling organizations show that many Russian, up to 50 percent, believe that since America was so quick to bomb Afghanistan and Iraq, there is a strong likelihood that given a small pretext, F-16s and B-2s might drop bombs on Russian military bases and that armored Humvees could well roar on the streets of the republics of the former Soviet Union. This fear is exacerbated by the expanding NATO presence in eastern Europe. Although 32 percent of Russians did not believe that the new expanded NATO was a threat to the country, about 60 percent of Russians believed in April 2004 that the inclusion of new NATO members was a "definite" or "somewhat" certain threat for Russia.[76]

As these and other surveys demonstrate, when most Russians look at the United States, they distinguish two basic features. The first one is that the United States is the world economic leader and a country in which most people are prosperous. But in addition, they see a nation driven by an aggressive foreign policy. Most Russians still believe that a main objective of the United States government is to create a weak and obedient Russia. As a result, Russians have ambivalent feelings about the United States. Thus, specific events, such as the wars in Bosnia and Kosovo in the 1990s, or the Iraq war, or the United States' tough position related to Iran's nuclear ambitions, drive Russian public opinion back and forth from pro- to anti-American sentiments.

Conclusion: What's Next?

Although President Putin confirmed his country's strong support of the United States on September 11, 2001, top officials in the Kremlin quickly articulated the conditions under which Russia would participate in the war on terror. They clearly signaled that Russia was not giving America a carte blanche and that Moscow would support Washington, but not on all occasions. In Washington, such ambivalence was accepted. The Bush White House understood that Putin, to protect his political base, needed to appear presidential and independent. Key elements of the Russian mass media echoed the Kremlin's measured support of America's foreign policy in 2001 and after.

However, many opinion leaders of the conservative wing in Russia did not care about which direction the political wind was blowing from the Kremlin. They remain committed to the anti-Western attitudes of the Soviet era. The United States, as the most powerful representative of the Western world, is the most obvious and convenient target of their extreme dislike of capitalism and everything that is associated with it. Nowadays, instead of the old, one-dimensional Soviet-era Communist ideological platform, contemporary anti-American views of this crowd are based on a wide variety of beliefs including nationalist, fascist, racist, and chauvinist attitudes. The only solid psychological foundation remaining from the past was the all-encompassing, visceral, and broiling dislike of capitalism, the United States, and most things American. These leaders support internationalism and multilateralism largely because such approaches are the only way for Russia to have a meaningful foreign policy role in the world.

Another type of Russian anti-Americanism comes from a different ideological and political crowd. These are members of the Russian opinion elite, largely former or current officials, renowned pundits, and respected journalists, many of whom during Gorbachev's perestroika held pro-Western, liberal attitudes, but who were galvanized by the developments in the early and middle 1990s that left the United States the world's only superpower and Russia a subordinated player on the world stage. They still believe in Russia's great potential to play a leading, if not unilateral, role in the world.

Despite the obvious political and ideological charge of the elites, most ordinary people in Russia in the early twenty-first century remained politically indifferent. "Serenity, peace, and order" was the key slogan used by the pro-Putin United Russia Party during the parliamentary election year of 2003. About 46 percent of those Russians who voted for the first time in the parliamentary elections of that year cast their votes for Putin and his ruling party. There is nothing unusual in voting for a party of status quo. This new young generation of Russians, however, has embraced social conformity and political indifference as the answer to their aspi-rations. Surveys show that they prefer to occupy a middle ground and not to engage in anything that could radically transform their lives.[77]

Things changed in Russia after September 2004. In the wake of the worst terrorist attacks on the Russian soil, including suicide bombings in Moscow, airplane crushes, and the killing of hundreds of children and adults in Beslan, most Russians supported central authorities' pledge to take worldwide unilateral actions against terrorism. A majority of Russians also supported the subsequent antidemocratic reforms that strengthened the Kremlin's power to fight both terrorism and other forces of disorder. Many of these proauthoritarian Russians feel that their country, unlike the United States, is handcuffed by international criticism and barriers, especially those raised by the United States, in their fight against terrorism. This proves to many that the United States applies one set of rules to its own policies and another set of rules to other countries' struggles to create domestic security.[78]

For most Russians, the United States still stands as a kind of cultural symbol of individualism and self-responsibility: in America, Russians widely believe, people are successfully taught to be self-reliant. The lib-eral reforms that began in Russia in the mid-1980s attempted to incul-cate a similar ideal. But after two decades of struggle, insecurity, and un-certainty, an increasing number of Russians have come to doubt that American principles of free-market capitalism and individualistic civil liberties can take root in the Russian soil. People are tired of being poor and helpless. They are frustrated by Russia's omnipotent bureaucracy, corruption, crime, and constant, failed social experimentation. As a re-sult, America, once an inspiring model for many, has become a power-ful irritant, a constant reminder of how far their nation has fallen and of how poorly suited the American model seems to be for their society. Similarly, they watch in anger but also in resignation as America uses its military might to force its will on the rest of the world, refusing to be judged or to concede its errors. Russia, they know, for many reasons can-not act similarly to protect itself or to assert its will internationally. That knowledge hurts.

Russian journalists now routinely depict the United States as an arro-gant and greedy monster. The images are not much different from those Soviet citizens saw regularly at the height of the Cold War. Apparently, some cultural images do not easily change. In the 1970s, the official line was that the Soviet people did not hate Americans; they only disliked America's social system, its government, and its policies. Likewise, in the first years of the twenty-first century, as Russians bury their own victims of terrorism, most Russians say they empathize with the American people's fear of terrorism. But few Russian have any sympathy for the American government, and they categorically reject American international unilateralism. History, at least in Russia, it seems, can repeat itself.

Notes

1. Vladimir Shlapentokh, "The Changeable Soviet Image of America," in Thomas Perry Thornton, ed., *Anti-Americanism: Origins and Context* (Newbury Park, Calif.: Sage, 1988); Eric Shiraev and Vlad Zubok, *Anti-Americanism in Russia: From Stalin to Putin* (New York: St. Martin's/Palgrave, 2000).

2. Evgeny Vasiliev, "Moment of Truth: The Kremlin Had Better Revise Its Foreign Policy and Defense Doctrines," *Vremya MN*, September 14, 2001.

3. Alexander Kukharkin, *Po tu storony rassveta* (On the other side of sunset) (Moscow: Politicheskaya Literatura, 1974).

4. Vladimir Shlapentokh, *Soviet Public Opinion and Ideology: Mythology and Pragmatism in Interaction* (New York: Praeger, 1986).

5. Shlapentokh, "Changeable Soviet Image"; Erik Shiraev and A. I. Bastrykin, *Trends, Idols, and Self* (Leningrad: Lenizdat, 1988).

6. Shiraev and Zubok, *Anti-Americanism in Russia*.

7. Betty Glad and Eric Shiraev, eds., *The Russian Transformation* (New York: St. Martin's, 1999).

8. Georgy Arbatov, "Rescue Russia or Else!" *Newsday*, October 25, 1992, 1–2.

9. Janine Wedel, "Harvard's Role in US Aid to Russia," *Boston Globe*, March 25, 2006; Boris Grushin, "Is Peace at All Possible in Today's Russia?" *Mir Mnenii i Mnenia o Mire*, December 1994, 8–12.

10. Shlapentokh, "Changeable Soviet Image," 162.

11. Alexander Solzhenitsyn, "Ugodilo Zernishko promezh dvukh zhernovov," *Novy Mir* 9 (1998): 47–125.

12. Alexandr Dugin, *Osnovi Geopolitiki* (Fundamentals of geopolitics) (Moscow: Arktogea, 1998).

13. Eric Shiraev and Deone Terrio, "Russian Decision-Making Regarding Bosnia: Indifferent Public and Feuding Elites," in Eric Shiraev and Richard Sobel,

eds., *International Public Opinion and the Bosnia Crisis* (Lanham, Md.: Lexington Books, 2003).

14. Shiraev and Terrio, "Russian Decision-Making."

15. Shiraev and Zubok, *Anti-Americanism in Russia.*

16. Interfax, September 11, 2001.

17. Ana Uzelac, "Terror May Be Tie That Binds," *Moscow Times,* September 13, 2001.

18. Vladimir Zhirinovsky, "An Interview," September 14, 2001, www.strana.ru.

19. Gennady Zyuganov, "An Interview," *Nezavisimaya Gazeta,* September 13, 2001.

20. www.fom.ru, September 20, 2001.

21. Andrei Stepanov, "Russian Public Opinions in New Political Realities," *Vremya MN,* November 14, 2001.

22. Eric Shiraev, "Sorry, but Not Sorry," in Vladimir Shlapentokh, Joshua Woods, and Eric Shiraev, eds., *America: Sovereign Defender or Cowboy Nation?* (London: Ashgate, 2005).

23. Elena Ovcharenko and Yevgenii Umerenkov, "Those Who Bombed Moscow Have Reached the United States: In a New Era, the World Realizes That Terrorism Is No Joke," *Komsomolskaya Pravda,* September 12, 2001.

24. Boris Kagarlitsky, "Bin Laden? Better Be Sure," *Moscow Times,* September 18, 2001.

25. Boris Kagarlitsky, "A Need for Honest Answers," *Moscow Times,* October 30, 2001.

26. Leonid Shebarshin, "A War for an Audience," *Vremya MN,* October 17, 2001.

27. Sergei Ptichkin, "Is the Kremlin Protected Against Air Attack?" *Rossiyskaya Gazeta,* September 14, 2001; Gleb Pavlovsky, "Are We Prepared to Wait until the Enemy Hits Us as It Hit America?" www.strana.ru, October 24, 2001.

28. Dmitry Gornostaev, "Will Bush See That His Myths Are Dispelled?" posted on www.strana.ru, September 13, 2001.

29. Dmitry Rogozin, interview, *Russia TV,* September 11, 2001.

30. ORT: Public Russian Television, September 15, 2001; Nikolai Kovalev, "The U.S. Would Thus Repeat the Bitter Experience," www.strana.ru, September 14, 2001.

31. Boris Nemtsov, "An Interview," *Moskovsky Komsomolets,* September 13, 2001.

32. *RIA Novosti,* September 24, 2001; *Komsomolskaya Pravda,* September 24, 2001.

33. Georgy Osipov and Kirill Palshin, "Russia Invited to Participate in the New Split of the World, but Will It Get Anything Out of It?" *Izvestia,* October 2,

2001; Sergei Markov, "A War Has Been Declared! Who Is the Enemy?" September 22, 2001, www.strana.ru.

34. gazeta.ru, October 29, 2001.

35. Vyachceslav Nikonov, "Partnership or Renunciation? Russia Risks Assuming the Whole Burden of the Operation in Afghanistan," *Trud*, October 27, 2001.

36. Pavlovsky, "Are We Prepared?"

37. ITAR-Tass, September 17, 2001.

38. Alexei Bogaturov, "Love's Comeback: Russia's Second Attempt at Partnership with the West," *Vek*, September 28, 2001.

39. Markov, "War Has Been Declared!"

40. Vasiliev, "Moment of Truth"; Victor Khamrayev, "The Duma against Carpet Bombing," *Vremya Novostei*, http://www.vremya.ru/2001/172/, September 20, 2001; Yury Alexeyev, "Russia's Participation in Anti-terrorist Operation in Afghanistan May Be Substantial; Non-military Russian Experts Believe That Active Participation of Russian Secret Services in Operation May Ensure Its Success," www.strana.ru, September 18, 2001.

41. Gleb Pavlovsky, "Terrorists' Aim Is World War," www.strana.ru, September 12, 2001.

42. Interfax, September 15, 2001.

43. Ekho Moskvy, September 17, 2001.

44. Russian Information Agency, September 18, 2001.

45. Alexei Arbatov, "Press Conference with Vice Chairman of State Duma Committee for Defense," Federal News Service, September 18, 2001, www.fednews.ru.

46. Dmitry Shusharin, "The President's Loneliness: President Putin Has the Courage to Make Unpopular Decisions," *Vremya MN*, October 26, 2001.

47. *Russia TV,* September 15, 2001.

48. ORT, September 13, 2001.

49. Nikolai Ulyanov, "Russia Will Not Actively Participate in New Afghan War," www.strana.ru, September 19, 2001.

50. Rogozin, "An Interview."

51. Ulyanov, "Russia Will Not Participate."

52. Vladimir Shlapentokh, "Is Putin a Pro Western Lone Ranger?" *Johnson's Russia List,* No. 5609, December 20, 2001.

53. *Komsomolskaya Pravda,* September 25, 2001.

54. www.ortv.ru, September 18, 2001.

55. Khamrayev, "Duma against Carpet Bombing"; *NTV International,* October 2, 2001.

56. Vahtang Shelia, "The Wrong War," *Novaya Gazeta,* October 11, 2001.

57. Ruslan Aushev, Interfax, September 17, 2001.

58. Yuri Baluyevsky, "An Interview: Equal Russia-U.S. Partnership a Necessity of Gobal Stability," *Krasnaya Zvezda,* December 9, 2001.

59. Pavlovsky, "Terrorists' Aim."

60. Alexander Dugin, "An Interview," *Nezvisimaya Gazea,* September 13, 2001.

61. Yuri Pankov, "The United States Is Not Ready to Fight International Terrorism," *Krasnaya Zvezda,* September 18, 2001.

62. Yulia Latynina, "Plato on Fate of Modern Civilization," *Moscow Times,* September 19, 2001.

63. Zyuganov, "An Interview."

64. Shlapentokh, "Putin a Lone Ranger?"

65. Dmitri Trenin, "Russian-American Relations: Two Years After 9/11," Carnegie Moscow Center Briefing Paper, vol. 5, no. 8, August 2003, www.carnegie.ru/en/staff/56232.htm.

66. Public Opinion Foundation, national poll taken May 21, 2004, www.fom.ru/topics/426.html.

67. E. Trofimova, "Zhirinovsky: Russia Should Occupy Iraq," Ytro.ru, March 11, 2003.

68. K. Zatulin, "An Interview," http://www.emeeting.ru/, March 25, 2003.

69. Andrei Krotkov, "Mosques from Tver to Moscow," *Ogonek,* June 22, 2003, 48–51.

70. G. Jamal, "Elections in Russia and the Arrest of Saddam," http://www.kontrudar.ru/article_43.html.

71. Y. Krupnov and M. Kalashnikov, *The Ork's Rage* (Moscow: Astrel, 2003).

72. P. Bavin, "Russians about America and Americans about Russia: A comparative analysis of survey results," www.fom.ru/topics/141.html.

73. Public Opinion Foundation, national poll taken on September 11, 2003, www.fom.ru/topics/119.html.

74. *ROMIR Monitoring,* All-Russian survey, May 2004.

75. FOP, March 22, 2003.

76. *ROMIR Monitoring,* All-Russian survey, April 15–20, 2004.

77. Olga Makhovskaya, "It Is Boring to Live in Russia," *Ogonek,* June 22, 2003, 17–18.

78. N. Rudensky, "Comments on G. Bush's Remarks," *Grani,* October 16, 2004, www.grani.ru.

NUESTRO ONCE DE SEPTIEMBRE

❑ ❑ ❑

THE KINGDOM OF THE COMMA

Fernando Escalante-Gonzalbo and Mauricio Tenorio-Trillo

ON THE MORNING of September 11, 2001, Mexican poet and historian of science Carlos López Beltrán woke up in Manhattan, not far from the Twin Towers. "Each one of those beings," he recollected, "who opted out, accelerating death by throwing themselves into the air . . . could have been us." Indeed, the victims "were us, alas with a tiny variation in the bifurcations of the past." López Beltrán, like so many, felt the powerful pull of empathy for those who were lost. He felt, too, the odd coupling of solitude and solidarity that so many experienced in New York as they poured into the streets, trying to make sense of what was happening: "To be together, to have and to be company became the edge, the basis, the harbor, and the only firm ground." López Beltrán also watched as Americans, in visceral display, hung their national flag, red white and blue, in storefronts, in apartment windows, and on street corners. Even as he understood the need, as a historian and an intellectual he worried that "underneath that patriotism [was] the menacing tooth of future massacres." While his heart went out to his American neighbors, he feared what their need for vengeance and security might bring.[1]

All over the world people responded to the September 11 terrorist attacks in sundry combinations of empathy, rational caution in the midst of fear, and the poetic impulse that floats up even in the cruelest of "Waste Lands." In Mexico, even in the immediate aftermath of the attacks, many people revealed only their disdain for an America they reviled. A few well-known opinion makers clamored to announce that those who died somehow deserved to be killed. Others, as in many parts of the Spanish-speaking world, panicked by the slaughter, echoed the "war of civilizations" proclamations of political theorist Samuel Huntington. Some voices in Mexico, Spain, and Argentina, relatively few, called for less passion and more reason as they struggled to offer plans for a new internationalism. And in the immediate aftermath of the attack, television broadcasters repeatedly showed images of emotional American preachers heatedly calling on God, while more weighty media sources turned to international intellectuals such as Jean Baudrillard, whose pseudo-poetic declarations about the United States were translated into Spanish—he declared that September 11 was a collective "counterphobic delirium to exorcize evil, which indeed is there, everywhere, as an obscure object of desire."[2]

As the horrors of September 11 became encapsulated within the Bush administration's evermore expansive and unilateralist war on terror, almost everywhere around the world simple anti-Americanism replaced people's complex responses to the original attacks. In 2002, as the Bush administration prepared Americans for the invasion of Iraq, people throughout the Spanish-speaking world rejected Americans' bellicosity.[3] Only the conservative government of José María Aznar in Spain, against all odds, took a strong pro-Bush position, and this was done in the face of massive domestic opposition. By 2004 those visceral anti-Americanists who had even in the immediate aftermath of September 11 blamed the United States, appeared to many in the Spanish-speaking world to have been right all along. In view of U.S. policies in Iraq and elsewhere in the world, Mexican and Spanish anti-Americanists could smugly state, "We told you so," and those relative few who had spoken out cautioning about the problems of terrorism and in sympathy to American people, or who had even supported the American government's first responses to the terrorist attacks, were roundly dismissed, especially in Mexico, as at best naive or at worst reactionary sellouts to the American Empire.

In this essay we want to focus not on Mexican and the larger Spanish-speaking world's responses to the Iraq invasion but on the more immediate post–September 11 situation. In the first months after September

11 the deep divide between the United States and the Spanish-speaking world was, once again, revealed. But we believe that during this brief period an opportunity also existed for Mexicans, in particular, to forge a new relationship with the United States and to overcome some of the dangerous and mythical civilizational barriers that divide the Americas. The days after September 11, at least in Mexico, challenged the nature of Mexico-U.S. relationships and forced Mexican opinion makers to face their own contradictory views of the meaning of Mexico as non-*gringo*.

The overall immediate reaction to September 11 in Mexico, as in Argentina and Spain (which we will examine to contextualize a close analysis of Mexican reaction), was that of the "Kingdom of the Comma"— very rarely did a writer or speaker of any kind simply come out and condemn the terrorists who attacked the United States. Instead of disapproving of the terrorists and then coming to a simple and eloquent full stop, they would condemn terrorism, then add a comma and one or more of three possible arguments that people must understand: (*a*) *El que a hierro mata a hierro muere,*[4] that is, the United States deserved the attacks; (*b*) "it is wrong to put things into good versus evil, reality is too complex, but undoubtedly the United States has produced lots of evil in the world; thus the terrorists are not totally to be blamed but instead we should condemn —— (choose one or all: capitalism, neoliberalism, Wall Street, poverty, globalization, military industrial complex, Israel)"; or (*c*) "violence has a logic," thus the search of causes and logics as a way to answer, "What is next?"[5] This final argument was particularly potent and blended with sharp positions on whether to follow President Bush's messianic reaction to September 11. But in fact, the idea that "violence has a logic" ought to have been considered carefully, especially by Mexican opinion makers in view both of the irrational nature of terrorism and of the complex and integrated relationship that exists between Mexico and the United States.

Al otro día . . .

In the Spanish-speaking world, the mass media provided blanket coverage of the September 11 terrorist attacks in the United States. During those first hours of coverage and in the initial newspaper reports almost no one anywhere welcomed what had happened. The media paid particular attention to the multinational nature of the casualties. Reports zeroed in on the dead from the Spanish-speaking world, a number that would reach 120—as if passports made a difference in death. From the beginning, however, commentators discussed the attacks on the World Trade Center and the Pentagon as symbolic attacks on American military and economic power. And frequent comments, which carried elements of schadenfreude, were made about the surprising vulnerability of the United States, the world's superpower. In Mexico, most opinion makers bluntly explained the attacks as a response to American imperialism. This callous assertion did produce a reaction among a few analysts and intellectuals who were astounded by such a blatant and unthinking anti-Americanism. In Argentina and Spain, too, commentators also routinely explained the attacks as a consequence of U.S. "historical" guilt, though media in those countries, in the immediate aftermath of September 11, were not as quick as those in Mexico to dismiss the terrorists attacks as an unfortunate but not unreasonable response to American imperialism. In Argentina, most opinion makers, sensitive to their country's own experience with terrorism in the 1990s, were much more sympathetic to the American victims and not so quick to follow every condolence with an explanation that blamed them for their own deaths. Similarly, Spaniards' experience with the terrorist Basque organization ETA tempered Spanish response, though a deep-rooted anti-Americanism prevailed in the long run.

While the Mexican media reacted ambivalently to the terrorist attacks, several important Mexican intellectuals who happened to be in New York at the time of the attacks, López Beltrán, Enrique Krauze, and Jesús Silva Herzog Márquez, called for a radical and unequivocal condemnation of the attacks and for Mexican symbolic and political support of the United States. Mexican minister of foreign affairs Jorge Castañeda, too, spoke out immediately after the attacks, offering full and untempered condolences to the American people and angry condemnation of the terrorists. Similarly, Guadalupe Loaeza, a respected columnist for the influential newspaper *Reforma*, asked for the end of intellectuals' ambivalence and insisted that Mexican president Vicente Fox speak out strongly against the attacks. In her column, she called for a candlelight vigil at the U.S. embassy in Mexico City. However, only five people showed up that evening at the embassy.

On the other hand, that same day, a consortium of civic groups and student organizations called for a different rally, one with the motto "We are all Arabs." At least two hundred people attended that gathering, during which the respected leftist leader Rosario Ibarra demanded that Mexicans boycott McDonald's and AT&T, even as corpses were being recovered from the ruins of the World Trade Center. Carlos Fuentes, Mexico's international luminary, offered a related perspective two weeks after the attack when he rather oddly noted that Mexico was indeed a partner of the United States, but "we are not the United States' *achichincles* [servants]," as if Mexico in the immediate aftermath was being asked for troops or money and not for simple but important symbolic and political support.[6] In sum, while a few Mexican opinion makers offered symbolic support to the United States, for most the context was more important than the events, and the context was endemic and constant U.S. aggressions, a list that included without nuance or distinction the War of 1848, Hiroshima, Cuba, Nicaragua, Chile, and Kosovo. Indeed, U.S. aggressions for annalists constituted a twofold cause: it was a motif and a logic, a material precedent. Violence and terrorism were granted rational and—somehow—historical justification.

Those Mexicans who used incidents of past American aggressions to contextualize or even justify the terrorist attacks turned out to be, relatively speaking, the moderates in the anti-Americanist camp. Others dug even deeper into the mire of anti-Americanism for explanations. The attack was terrible, wrote Guillermo Almeyra in *La Jornada* on September 12, 2001, but (comma) "doubt is legitimate." The Nazis, the author explained, burned the Reichstag and then blamed the Communists in order to justify repressing their enemies. Americans, perhaps, had done much the same. Who, after all, but the United States, could have masterminded such a cleverly diabolical plot? The same day, *La Jornada*'s editorial page was adamant: "It is too soon and would be wrong to point out who is to be blamed, but the cultural profile (*matiz*) of yesterday's horror in the neighbor country seems to be neither Arab, nor Islamic, nor Asian, but, perhaps, profoundly American." *La Jornada* played this card for weeks, only incrementally accepting evidence of Al Qaeda involvement. Of course, the pages of *La Jornada* represent an extremist position in Mexican public life. But even in centrist newspapers, such as *El Universal*, some commentators in the first week after September 11 maintained similar hypotheses about American government involvement in the attacks.[7]

Proponents of another school of thought in those immediate post–September 11 days argued that Mexico simply needed to stay aloof from the whole mess since, in essence, America's problems were its own and had nothing to do with Mexico. Gustavo Esteva in *Reforma* opined that the September 11 terrorists and the vengeful Americans who claimed to be antiterrorists offered a "perfect symmetry." Thus, Mexico could not side with either one. Sergio Aguayo in *Reforma*, September 14, 2001, used a similar logic to criticize President Fox after he seemed to offer the Americans some timid sympathy (he had canceled some of the September 15 and 16 independence days' celebrations) and Minister of Foreign Affairs Jorge Castañeda for supporting the United States. Aguayo sonorously observed that despite the gravity of the situation "we ought to remember the existing distance between the [Mexican] government and what [the Mexican] society thinks—[Mexican society] finds no place for the United States in its project of nationhood." Despite millions of Mexicans in the United States, despite billions of dollars sent to Mexico by Mexicans working in the United States, despite Mexico and the United States sharing a complex common history, Aguayo believed Mexican society had no reason to reach out to the United States during its dark hours, that such sympathy would somehow impinge on Mexican ontology. Luis Javier Garrido wrote to the same tune in *La Jornada* on September 14, observing that "Black Tuesday was black also for the new Mexican government, for if Bush Jr. showed no great stature as president, Fox once again missed the opportunity to remain silent. His unconsciousness betrayed him once again—he canceled the Independence Day celebration, as if the insults [the terrorist attacks] had been directed to him." According to this logic, the terrorist attack was not a tragedy against humanity but simply payback against the United States, and whether the United States or the terrorists were most culpable for what had happened, well, that was not for Mexico to decide.

Overwhelmingly the anti-American consensus that dominated the Mexican mass media asserted that while the dead were to be mourned, the United States had brought the terrorist attack upon itself. No one, the Mexican public was warned, should look at these tragedies through the fundamentalist religious eyes of Donald Rumsfeld, Dick Cheney, or

President Bush, for in the final analysis the tragedy had been caused by the profound inequality that characterized the world, and that inequality rested at the doorstep of the United States, which was also responsible for terrible acts of destructions in Japan, Korea, Vietnam, Guatemala, Chile, Nicaragua, Mexico, Kosovo, Palestine . . . History, *magistra vitae,* had come back to haunt the United States. Even the bishop of Chiapas, Felipe Arizmendi, jumped on the bandwagon: "Now they [Americans] harvest what they have sowed." A drum beat of opinion pieces pounded home this logic, so much so that by the time the United States invaded Afghanistan and was preparing public opinion for the Iraq war, this claim had become a morally certifiable piece of conventional wisdom in Mexico. Very few voices made any attempt to recognize the difference between, say, the vital political role played by the United States in Kosovo—in the midst of European irresponsible inaction—and the U.S.-supported military coup d'état in September 11, 1973, in Chile. All American acts of foreign intervention were disdainfully treated as imperialist acts of aggression that paved the way for the terrorist attacks of September 11. In Mexico, few recalled the great solidarity showed by the U.S. government and civil organizations during Mexico City's massive earthquake in September 19, 1985, when the Mexican government seemed unable to handle the situation. When some analysts did point out President Clinton's support of Mexico during the 1994 financial crisis, others dismissed the aid as nothing more than venal American self-interest.

Such cynical, historically confused, and morally suspect anti-Americanism did not go entirely unanswered. Roger Bartra, a prominent scholar, lambasted his fellow Mexican intellectuals for using September 11 to recycle dangerous "patriotic and nationalistic myths."[8] It was a disgrace, he argued, that in Mexico so many were willing to dismiss the horror of September 11 by asserting "that bin Laden's terrorism is provoked by Washington state terrorism." For Bartra, reactions to September 11 underlined the crisis of the Left in Mexico; unable to create a democratic agenda, the Left took refuge in demagogic anti-Americanism and in nationalism. Historian Enrique Krauze agreed: "Past [U.S.] historical abuses do not justify our lack of moral solidarity." "Therefore," he continued, "and in view of the nature of our bilateral agenda, I believe that President Fox ought to show a clear sign of sympathy toward the American people."[9] Foreign Affairs Minister Jorge Castañeda, as already noted, had responded rapidly to the attack, asking his fellow citizens to show their solidarity with the United States, but as a result two major parties, the center-left PRI (Institutional Revolutionary Party) and the leftist PRD (Democratic Revolution Party), asked for his resignation. President Fox did not follow the lead of his foreign affairs minister, even on the night of September 15, when the Zocalo, Mexico City's main plaza, was full of people and he could have expressed at least a note of sympathy for the U.S. dead. But he gave no minute of silence, no official condolence. Fox probably said nothing at the advice of his political team, who watch public opinion polls like hawks. To sympathize with the United States, even in those immediate post–September 11 days, those advisors undoubtedly feared, was to challenge the nation's reflexive anti-Americanism and risk political backlash.

By late September, a very few Mexican opinion makers began to do a sort of double take and to articulate a kind of anti-anti-Americanism as they pondered the underlying anti-Americanism disseminated by the great majority of Mexico's media. Rafael Ruiz Harrell in *Reforma* called for the end of "commas" and ambivalence and for strong gestures of solidarity.[10] Enrique Krauze provided a lesson in logic: "U.S. historical abuses are one thing and the irresponsible blending (which is being done) of those abuses with the causes of Islamic terrorism is another thing, as if bin Laden or the Taliban (who could care less for the social and economic well-being of people, beginning with their own people) were the champions of anti-Imperialism. Blinded by ideological hate, some Latin American intellectuals (particularly Mexicans) once made the inexcusable mistake of supporting Hitler and Stalin just because they were enemies of the Yankees."[11] Krauze called for a new kind of Mexican Americanism that recognized historic problems and contemporary predicaments but did not blindly lash out at the United States in order to side with murderous terrorists. So did at least a few other important intellectuals and journalists, including Ariel Dorfman, Andrés Oppenheimer, and Mario Vargas Llosa; their essays were published in Mexico, Spain, Argentina, and elsewhere. Even Mexico's most prominent leftist intellectual, Carlos Monsiváis, broke with the anti-American consensus, warning about the global danger of terrorism and calling for Mexicans to support the American people.[12]

The entire Spanish-speaking world did not respond to September 11 as did Mexico. Argentina followed a different path. The government of President Fernando de la Rua responded promptly to the attack with gestures of solidarity, and several key opinion makers followed suit. "The future is very dark," argued Carlos Escudé in *Página 12* (Buenos Aires) on September 12, "and Argentina is a part of it; it already was a victim of huge terrorist attacks in the 1990s; that is, no one is safe in today's world. It is in our own interest to be strong allies of those who have more means than us to defend the free world." Though this kind of reaction was too pro-American for some Argentines, it was not an uncommon reaction in the first weeks after September 11. In an "Open love Letter to the American People"—a title never seen in Mexico—an essay by Mempo Giardeninelli, published in *Página 12,* on September 14, the terrorists were strongly condemned and readers were asked to show their solidarity with the American people, even as the author criticized the U.S. government's foreign policy. The leftist writer Atilio Borón concurred, arguing in *Página 12* on the sixteenth that the terrorist attacks were "absolutely unjustified," especially, he claimed, from a socialist point of view. Undoubtedly, the recent history of state terrorism in Argentina and recent fundamentalist terrorist attacks in Buenos Aires affected Argentinean reaction across much of the political spectrum.

There were, of course, extreme reactions in very radical Argentinean circles.[13] When the Organization of American States under the auspices of Brazilian president Fernando Henrique Cardoso came out in strong support of the United States in its fight against terrorism, Hebe Bonafini, a well-known leader of the Madres de la Plaza de Mayo movement in Argentina, together with other intellectuals, claimed to be very happy about the attacks in New York and Washington. According to Bonafini, the bombers had helped to balance the scales of justice against the murderous Americans. The terrorists, she said, were "courageous men and women" who "gave their lives for us."[14] Mainstream media, however, kept a much more moderate position, and the Argentinean government, together with that of Brazil, led continental support of the U.S. government in the days following September 11.

In Spain, experience with ETA terror moderated but did not negate a strong Spanish tradition of anti-Americanism—a sort of Spanish imperial nostalgia. The day after the attacks, in Spain's major newspaper, *El*

País, Enrique Gil Calvo gave full-throated voice to the anti-American side: "In sum, in the final analysis the cause of everything that has just happened is American arrogant power, which, with excessive faith in its military hegemony and its scientific supremacy, is believed to be independent from the rest of the world. . . . Thus, now the rest of the world's peoples also undertake their own unilateral policies, not necessarily military, economic, or scientific, but often religious, cultural, or ideological, and of course always depredatory, aggressive, and revenge taking." But, unlike Mexico's major left newspapers, the editorial page of *El País* condemned, without the "comma," the September 11 terrorists: attacks "of hyperterrorism have reached us all. Yesterday's smoke, in which Manhattan was submerged, brings tears in all *biennacidos* [well-bred, those of goodwill] world's citizens." One of Spain's most distinguished social scientists, Manuel Castells, unhesitatingly added his voice to the call for a reasoned response to the attacks, insisting that people distinguish between the evil of terrorist attacks and the necessary antiglobalization and anti-neoliberal struggles (*El País,* September 16, 2001). Various Spanish analysts used the phrase "Now we are all New Yorkers," without trying to find, as Miguel Angel Aguilar put it, "the remotest sign of justification" (*El País,* September 18, 2001).

In Spain, this show of solidarity did not, however, last long. In response to Bush administration unilateralism and Prime Minister Aznar's arrogant rejection of Spanish public opinion, much of the Spanish intelligentsia reverted back to a characteristic anti-Americanism. Rossana Rossanda provided a typical response in her "Notes by an anti-American" (*El País,* September 28, 2001): "Bush es un loco," and though she claimed to feel the pain of mourning American citizens, she acidly concluded, "I don't like that they believed themselves to be beyond the consequences of what their country does in the world." Ergo they deserved it?

More radical publications, such as *Viejo Topo,* piled on, asking, "Who is the enemy?" The answer was predictable: "It is important to be aware that without justice, peace is weak and fragile, and that the policies with which the globalizing Western world has ruled the globalized world are a source of infamy, injustice, and death." It is necessary, therefore, to address the hurts done to the "desperados" before "their desperation forces them to savagism; to attend their reasons, to ease their suffering, to eliminate the outrageous injustices which have subdued them."[15] The September 11 attacks were explained as a logical outcome of U.S. government imperial policies, and the American people were charged, too, as guilty for not stopping their government's brutal international policies: "The ignorance of a large part of U.S. society is childish. . . . The United States is responsible for a system that produces misery in two-thirds of humankind."[16] Santiago López Petit's aphorisms characterized the response of part of the Spanish Left: "The events of September 11 have been the most nihilist gesture in history. As the most nihilist gesture in history it has demonstrated the greatest truth about power: that power is a lie. . . . The events of September 11 not only show the truth about power. They also show the truth about resistance. This nihilist gesture is not mine. But what option is there?"[17]

In the weeks and months after September 11, some prestigious Spanish publications resisted the turn to a simplistic anti-Americanism and, instead, dedicated whole issues to nuanced views on the meaning of the terrorist attacks. They offered multiple perspectives and included the views of American, as well as other European, writers, including Michael Ignatieff, Michael Walzer, Norman Birnbaum, Giovanni Sartori, and Ryszard Kapuscinski.[18] Analyses of U.S. vulnerability, the role of NATO, and various views on the Islamic world were provided. In such mainstream publications as *Revista de Occidente* and *Claves de razón práctica* balanced opinions prevailed. In the former, Fernando Reineras forecasted the emergence of megaterrorism that would threaten Western democracies. (Of course, he was right; three years later, on March 11, 2004, Madrid was the target.)[19] Fernando Vallespín and Rafael del Águila, in *Claves*, wrote two of the best analyses in Spanish about the consequences of September 11. Vallespín hoped that the tragic September 11 attacks would provide an opportunity to "design more active and better articulated mechanisms both of international cooperation and of global governance . . . [to do so] it was necessary that the United States . . . leave behind its quasi-isolationist absorption in being the only superpower."[20] For Vallespín, a new Hobbesian pact was necessary after September 11 in order to create forms of identity and citizenship beyond "civilizations" and nations. Del Águila called for a pragmatic notion of justice in order to opt for a safer and yet minimally just world. But by the end of 2003, all these ruminations seemed like old stories in the face of Aznar's involvement in the Bush coalition and the strong Spanish anti-war position that fueled a rough anti-Americanism.[21]

Explaining the Reactions: The Paradoxes of Anti-Americanismo

Outside of the United States, anti-Americanism has been a conspicuous and long-standing characteristic of the intellectual and the scholar, often a key part of his or her social role. Anti-Americanism is also—but in complex, varied, and difficult-to-capture ways—a popular feeling, especially in Mexico, where all classes and sectors of the society have for more than a century and a half been affected by the "U.S. question." September 11 and its aftermath made visible a characteristic of anti-Americanism in Mexico: the smug generalities of anti-Americanism showed how much we lack a strong, indispensable, well-articulated, and intelligent criticism of the United States. Rather than provide a reasoned critique of America's role in the world that could differentiate between specific policies and their specific consequences, too many anti-Americanist opinion makers in Mexico offered only a shotgun analysis that blasted everything the United States has done in the world. Bin Laden and his minions are, in this analysis, no different from peaceful protesters against American neoliberal policy in Bolivia; all are right to be angry with the United States and have the right to fight back. How much more useful would be a pragmatic and knowledgeable criticism of the United States. Instead we are treated to an often nonsensical, nationalistic, vituperative anti-Americanism that provides little more than a puffed-up kind of finger-pointing that always castigates the United States and always cheers those who attack it. The nature or character of evil is made nonsensical by Mexican intellectual-like anti-Americanism just as it is made ridiculous by Bush-like pseudoreligious unilateralism.[22]

A second characteristic of anti-Americanism in Mexico, as revealed by the post–September 11 commentary, is its insensitivity to location and timing. We readily agree that a strong dose of critical analysis is something Americans need to hear far more often. While residing in the United States we ourselves have been frequently dismayed by the jingoistic quality of news coverage, and we were particularly troubled by the lack of critical public inquiry during the Bush administration's preparations for a war on Iraq. Even when we read U.S. academic studies, with their careful, even baroque analyses of issues of race, class, and gender and their constant nods to jargon, we are struck by their profoundly parochial, often nationalistic attitudes and their assumption that American domestic hysterias are universal phenomena. So we readily understand why intellectuals outside of the United States feel the powerful need to offer a corrective to Americans' own self-image and the power those widely disseminated self-images have in the world. Still, there is a time and a place for such criticisms. Why did Mexican intellectuals believe that the immediate aftermath of September 11, when thousands of people in New York and Washington had been brutally killed by a terrorist religious organization financed by fanatic millionaires, was an appropriate time for callous anti-Americanism? Why did so many opinion makers in Mexico—and so many other places—think that their first duty was to find a rational justification for such irrational violence? It was not the moment, not the place.

We believe that widespread ignorance of the United States in Mexico, despite its proximity, explains, in part, why so many found it easy to excuse and even justify the terrorist attacks. In Mexico, as well as in Spain, almost no one studies the United States. In Mexico, no undergraduate or graduate programs or research centers exist for the rigorous study of the "monster." We wonder if it would be possible to be so conventionally anti-Americanist in Mexico or Spain if more people had a more profound historical understanding of the United States (and it would surely be useful if far more people in Mexico understood something about the very real dangers of terrorism). We trust it is possible and necessary to reinvent a comprehensive critique of the United States without falling into the simplistic, one-dimensional, and one-sided conventions of Mexican or French or Spanish anti-Americanisms. Scholars in Mexico—and elsewhere—need to produce a critique of the United States, just as they need to have sophisticated analyses of their own nations. In fact, given the contemporary power and reach of the United States, no internal, national evaluation is really complete without an understanding of the development and roles of the United States, which serves, for better and for worse, as a kind of international cross-reference.

Another characteristic of the flamboyant anti-Americanism of the post–September 11 days was its conflating or equating of the United States with destructive Americanization and, thus, the September 11 attacks as a blow against aggressive global Americanization. In Mexico, as in Spain or France, many intellectuals argue that "Americanization" (a.k.a., globalization) is the antipode of far more authentic and salutatory forms of "good" collective identity or forms of integration such as "Europe" or "Latin" America or "local communities." The United States is treated as a malignant carrier of excessive modernity that destroys healthy societies and rich cultures around the world. In this narrative the United States becomes the embodiment of vulgarity, anti-intellectualism, consumerism, rudeness, fatness, and simple-mindedness. This kind of argument has been promulgated for decades in books read widely in intellectual circles throughout Europe and Latin America; for example, Leo L. Mathias's *i.e. Entdeckung Amerikas anno 1953 oder das geordnete Chaos* (1954) or Jean Baudrillard's *L'Amérique* (last edition 2000), or the prizewinning book by Spanish intellectual Vicente Verdú, *El planeta Americano* (1997).

Similar anti-American images have been offered by Mexican writers for more than a century. Manuel Gutiérrez Najera had already decided by the early twentieth century that Mexico had become Americanized, by which he meant it had become corrupt, materialistic, and utilitarian; it had lost its great spiritual superiority. Octavio Paz, in the 1960s, complained that unlike Mexico, which in its very cuisine (mole was his example), demonstrated a rich amalgamation of wonderful flavors, the United States offered people the pragmatic cultural equivalent of a hunk of unseasoned beef and tasteless iceberg lettuce.[23] The logic of conventional intellectual anti-Americanism in Spain or Mexico is unambiguous. U.S. people are provincial, imperialistic, racist, ethnocentric, without history, religious fundamentalists, inane salesmen, lovers of money, obscene, ignorant, childish, drug addicts, gluttonous eaters, and fat. Europeans and Mexicans, of course, are exemplary citizens, urbane inhabitants of civilized cities, sane proponents of a life harmoniously balanced between work and play, profound communitarians, secular, not racist, champions of historically rooted and sophisticated culture, gourmets, and, surely, slim and beautiful. We construct our Europe or our Latinness, protected by these beliefs doggedly articulated.[24]

When September 11 came, Mexicans took easy refuge in our picture of how different we were from the people of the United States, whose ugly culture had undoubtedly contributed to the attacks. Anti-Americanism understood as anti-Americanization is for many intellectuals a short-hand truism that needs no detailed explanation, even as its proponents have no real knowledge of the United States. In Mexico, in particular, this formulaic scorn for American culture made the peculiar Al Qaeda dynamic at work during the September 11 terror attacks impossible to understand and easy to ignore. Mexican opinion makers' conventional ugly anti-American picture was, alas, given immediate shape and texture by the crude rhetoric of the Bush administration, which fit perfectly with the anti-Americanist mind-set.[25]

Explaining the Reaction: Mexico's Political Culture

The fierce anti-Americanism so many intellectuals and opinion makers promulgated in the immediate aftermath of September 11, as we have already demonstrated, was a historically conditioned response. Cold War animosities in which Americans demonized the Mexican Left played a vital role in that conditioning. And the Mexican Left's particular decades-long encounter with CIA actions fueled some of the more spec-tacular accusations made in the Mexican media, such as the claim that the American government was actually responsible for the September 11 attacks. These extreme reactions, along with the general tone of feverish anti-Americanism in the post–September 11 days and weeks, while in-fluential in intellectual and political circles, were not, by any means, fully accepted or shared in by the general population of Mexico.

The United States has been and will continue to be imbued in the lives of millions of Mexican in a way that intellectuals' anti-Americanism barely touches. Popular anti-Americanism, the kind shared by large sec-tors of the Mexican population, is neither so Machiavellian nor so fiercely negative. Common "Mexicans," said Enrique Krauze, comment-ing on Mexican intellectuals' anti-Americanism, "take from U.S. culture whatever is convenient for them and discount the rest. Despite all clichés, Mexicans' attitude toward the U.S. is reasonably healthy."[26] Healthy, however, does not mean necessarily friendly or inviting. But it is not as ideological as the anti-Americanism of many Mexican intellectuals. Indeed, popular Mexican anti-Americanism tends to be more like the kind of hostility or simple rivalry that exists between any neighboring countries—as, for instance, the cultural antagonism between the French and Spaniards—though in the case of Mexico there is the added difficulty of profound economic inequality, a condition that ironically produces both attraction and repulsion. Mexican popular anti-Americanism, thus, combines elements of hate and even love for the United States; it is the common, primary-school-like, definition of Mexicanness as not-*gringo;* it includes the hopeful possibilities of the North; it is the benign anti-Americanism that is heard in the roar of rival *futbol* fans in soccer matches in which the Mexican national team plays in Chicago or Los Angeles; and it is the complex feelings produced by the billions of dollars sent every year by Mexicans in the United States to their families back home.[27] According to a sample of more than six hundred people interviewed in Mexico a week after September 11, 78 percent claimed to feel solidarity with the United States as a result of the terrorist attacks, and 79 percent agreed that the attacks not only touched the United States but affected world freedom and democracy. At the same time, a great majority (89 percent) opposed Mexico's military involvement in any retaliation, though 73 percent agreed that Mexico should share intelligence and cooperate with the U.S in fighting terrorists. There was nothing extraordinarily pro- or anti-American about these feelings. Historian Alan Knight's insightful comment about Mexico in the 1930s—"Recalcitrant people, revolutionary government"[28]—could be used today, with only slight modification, in commenting about the Mexican people and Mexico's intellectuals' respective feelings about the United States.[29]

Anti-Americanism is one of the oldest habits in Mexico's nationalist ideology (paralleled, it need be said, throughout the nineteenth and twentieth centuries by anti-Spaniard and anti-Chinese sentiments). It is a trend nurtured loosely by the history children learn in public schools, and reinforced by people's daily experience of U.S. power and influence in their way of life—even as the United States is also admired, incorporated, and celebrated. To be sure, Mexican popular anti-Americanism is based on stereotypes that are the result of ignorance about the United States, or information about the United States received through biased nationalistic education, as well as the intermediacy of millions of migrants who periodically come back and tell stories of life in the United States that produce envy, admiration, and bitterness. Truth be told, Mexican prejudices about the United States are very similar—and a reaction and a stimulus to—U.S. prejudices about Mexicans. In the twentieth century, on both sides of the border, we tried to ignore each other, pretending that the neighbor did not exist or was not important, or was farther away—culturally and politically—than was actually the case.[30] Almost two centuries of mutual stereotyping, racialization, and the raising of civilizational barriers have resulted in all sort of fantasies and prejudices. These feelings have been only strengthened by academic and popular works in the United States that have condemned Mexicans either as racially or culturally inferior to Americans (early twentieth century) or a "Hispanic challenge" to the "American creed" (early twenty-first century); views that make of Mexico either the paradise of indigenous, non-Western, non-American, small communities or the site of genetic corruption. The anti-American excesses of the Mexican reactions to September 11 was, in part, an echo of those long-standing noises of prejudices and false senses of distance between the two nations.[31]

Mexican anti-Americanism, as exhibited in the post–September 11 days, is not just a reactive process or an outward response to the policies—real or imagined—of the Colossus of the North. Mexican anti-Americanism emerges from Mexico's internal political and institutional dynamics and its carefully nurtured revolutionary traditions and claims. First, to understand why the Mexican media so tightly embraced anti-Americanism right after September 11, why it jumped so far ahead of Mexican public opinion in expressing anti-Americanism, we need to consider the problematic nature of Mexican journalism and the twisted structure of Mexican public space.

For almost the entire twentieth century, Mexico did not have a truly free press. Newspapers, radio, and television stations existed under the shadow of state sponsorship and censorship. Only in the last two decades has Mexico achieved a fully free media, and yet, even now the media lacks a high level of independent professionalism, and it is not held publicly accountable for its performance. Mexican newspapers and electronic media offer almost no space for knowledge-based expertise. Nor has the Mexican mass media developed a capacity for, or interest in, investigative journalism. Few articles demonstrate a professional level of research and fact-checking. Analytic pieces are highly ideological, full of sound bites and conventionalities that offer little or no expert knowledge that could contribute to an informed public opinion. These failures are particularly serious in coverage of international issues. Typically the same people who write or broadcast about the most recent political scandal of Mexico's president's wife also report on international events. Our opinion makers have limited knowledge, but they do have an opinion about everything. Therefore, clichés and stereotypes abound, and superficiality reigns.

While an occasional expert in international affairs does appear in the mass media, analyses of international events are overwhelmingly provided by politicians, writers, journalists, or anchorpeople. They necessarily depend on long-held prejudices and ready-made explanations for any situation. In the case of the September 11 terrorist attacks, rather than delve into the motives of the specific perpetrators, the Mexican media analysts zeroed in on the "true cause" of the attacks. Thus, rather than learn about Al Qaeda and how and why it chose to fly airplanes into buildings and kill thousands of innocent people, the Mexican people were told, in simplistic terms, about the events of 1848, Vietnam, Kosovo, and Chile. So much interest in "context" and true causes led to ridiculously few assessments of the nature, structure, and history of Islamism and its strategies. Mexican analysts had virtually nothing to say about the convoluted politics of the Middle East and the trajectory of fundamentalist Islamism.

State control and censorship of media has diminished in Mexico in the last decade but over that same period a highly concentrated media industry has emerged, and that new media industry has embraced a star system of opinion makers who provide a narrow, largely uniformed, and highly conventionalized perspective on both domestic and international events.[32] The rise of freedom of the press in Mexico has resulted in a blizzard of political opinion shows broadcast on television but, ironically, on those shows no more than fifteen opinion makers are used to convey "informed" views of the issues of the day.[33] As a consequence, a narrow range of voices represent "the voice of the civil society" and structure Mexico's public space. Not surprisingly, this tight circle of opinion makers rarely understands a given topic in depth; instead they tend to explain not the mysterious new subject but rather do their best to articulate what Mexican founding father José María Morelos called "the nation's feelings." Once the star system opines, the rest of the nation's opinion makers, at the regional and local level, tend to follow (perhaps, this system was not so different from that of the United States in the months previous to the invasion of Iraq?).[34] Hence, the immediate reaction to September 11 in the mass media, at least, was improvised, stereotypically anti-American, mechanical, and superficial not only because of the nature and magnitude of the events, but because of the characteristics of Mexico's public space.

This formulaic and abstract response, we should add, was intensified by Mexicans' relative lack of familiarity with international or even domestic terrorism. Except for a brief and limited episode in the 1970s, Mexico, unlike Argentina and Spain, has not experienced terrorism firsthand. Instead, Mexicans, or at least Mexican opinion makers, related the September 11 attacks to those kinds of revolutionary acts of violence that are held in high esteem in their nation's historical memory and ideological construct.

Mexican opinion makers, and much of the public, almost reflexively express a favorable view of guerrilla groups, insurrectionism, and protests, even including terrorist acts, in any part of the world, against any state authority. Examples abound: the Mexican intelligentsia celebrated the FMLN in El Salvador, the FSLN in Nicaragua, the URNG in Guatemala, all Palestinian organizations, and even ETA in Spain. In the Mexican political imagination, or at least in the imaginations of most of its intellectuals, state institutions (if not Mexican state institutions) are highly suspect, and violent responses to the state are to be respected. Throughout the twentieth century, the postrevolutionary Mexican state proudly embraced this stance, so long as it did not mean internal rebellion.[35] The most visible exception to this trend is rather illuminating: the until very recently consensual support of the Cuban state, because supporting it was, and is, supporting the Revolution, and it was, and is, opposing the United States—a perfect combination in Mexico's twentieth-century political culture.

In public elementary education, nationalist historiography, and the everyday rituals and rhetoric of Mexico's political culture, the nation's revolutionary tradition is insistently and repeatedly championed. Modern Mexico is hailed as the product of revolutions: the revolution against the Spanish empire (1810), the revolution against the power of the church and military leaders (1857), and the famous Mexican Revolution against the three-decade-long dictatorship of Porfirio Díaz (1910). Other nations, including France and the United States, similarly call on their revolutionary heritage to explain their nationhood, but for almost the last century in Mexico a revolutionary heritage has not merely been a part of nationalist identity but integral to the very legitimacy of the PRI, the nation's official party (called, by the way, the party of the "institutionalized revolution"). This revolutionary identity is so strong that it became critical to the claims of the opposition, as well, which has always tried to gain political traction by insisting that the PRI has betrayed the revolution. Political struggle in Mexico is almost always fought within a simple dualism: the people versus the state. Mexico does not have a revolutionary Jacobin discourse—not a centralizing, authoritarian, institutional ideology—but a populist discourse with anarchist features and Maratist characteristics.[36] In Mexico, all parties claim to support a revolutionary tradition that stands against all forms of controlled institutional hierarchy and authority and for the claims of the always virtuous People. In the Mexican political formula, the People are always in need of help and protection but the state is always an oppressor. Because of these political conventions, Mexican opinion makers are quite comfortable defending the People, social justice, and even the nation, but they have no available ready-made discourse that defends the state.

Thus Mexican opinion makers essentially turned the September 11 terrorists into freedom fighters. They did not seem to care that the authors of September 11 were not poor peasants or victims of the IMF but were, instead well-trained South Arabians supported by a fanatic religious millionaire with no social agenda at all. In Mexico, in the aftermath of September 11, the facts mattered little. Instead, opinion makers reverted to what they knew and offered a symbolic field where the terrorists could be made righteous brothers with every other revolutionary guerrilla, anti-imperialist, and "popular" freedom fighter. Not only did this kind of reasoning explain very little to the Mexican public, it actually accepted the system of representation advanced by the terrorists as an explanation of their deeds.[37]

This same logic has been used before and after in Mexico; it is not just a form of anti-Americanism. Very few Mexican opinion makers in the last three decades articulated a clear-cut defense of the Spanish state against ETA. Ditto for the Columbian state's struggle with terrorists. And next to no one has offered support to Israel in its struggles to stop terrorists from blowing up men, women, and children on buses and in restaurants. Not even the Peruvian government was offered support in its fight against the Shining Path, even though that particular group had few fans in Mexico.[38]

Small wonder, thus, that the Mexican reaction to the terrorist attacks in Madrid, in March 11, 2004, was not very different from that to the attacks in 2001. In the week following the Madrid attacks, nearly one hundred pieces were published by opinion makers in Mexico. Except for a very few, all opinion pieces followed a similar scheme: they condemned terrorism but, once again, "comma" and then "context." And the context for almost all of the opinion makers was Iraq. All talked about President Bush as someone to be blamed and about the evil of U.S. aggressions, about the people killed by allied forces in Baghdad, and almost all ended considering the attacks a consequence of the policies taken by Spain's chief of government, José María Aznar. That is, somehow, the terrorist attacks had a legitimate logic. Thus, even without anti-Americanism as a context, Mexican opinion makers responded to March 11 in Madrid similarly to how they had responded to September 11.

Not surprisingly, influential Mexicans responded similarly to the London terrorist attacks in July 2005. Both President Vicente Fox and the leader of the opposition, Andrés Manuel López Obrador, told their fellow Mexicans that they need not fear similar attacks because Mexico respects intentional law, does not intervene in armed conflicts, and maintains friendly relationships with all countries. Both politicians implied that badly behaved countries bring terrorist attacks upon themselves. Here, too, for Mexicans anti-Americanism was secondary to their deep-rooted understanding that violent attacks by relatively weak nonstate actors should be understood as legitimate insurrections against oppressive regimes.

In fact, just as the deployment of troops overseas immediately creates an automatic rally-around-the-flag effect in the United States (at least for a while), Mexico's opinion makers almost automatically rally around just about anybody whom they perceive as rebelling against an established state. At the same time, Mexican opinion makers—and even more so, the Mexican public at large—are not crude, knee-jerk advocates of violence, even against the state. Mexico's own experiences with criminality and lawlessness work against a cheerful acceptance of violence. Thus, very few commentators openly support political violence, though the 1994 Chiapas rebellion and the September 11 attacks brought some commentators close to such support, as they argued in both cases (wildly different, as they were) that legitimate revolutionary violence might be the only tool available to fight such powerful forces as, respectively, Mexico's corrupt PRI state and U.S. imperialism.

More commonly, whether it is the Chiapas rebellion or the September 11 attacks or the March 11 bombs in Madrid, opinion makers offer a kind of apology for the rebel force's violence and then insist that state authorities recognize their culpability for the violent outburst (i.e., the true cause of the rebellion), and then show their good faith by negotiating a settlement with the perpetrators of the violent acts.[39] Mexican opinion makers practice an "accusatory pacifism" in which they wash their hands of violence but just as quickly insist that rebel violence can only have been caused by the state's failure to act justly with the aggrieved parties who are assumed to be stand-ins for the People themselves. Sometimes, of course, this perspective is quite reasonable. But it is not always correct. This logic played out perfectly in the immediate aftermath of the September 11 attacks. Commentator after commentator insisted that the U.S. government should not respond to the attacks militarily—or even through the simple enforcement of the law—but should instead admit its responsibility for the attacks and negotiate with the terrorists in order to resolve the political problems that precipitated the slaughter.

Mexico's revolutionary tradition has placed the government and opinion makers in an odd situation. On the one hand, Mexico has for many years maintained a good, stable relationship with the United States that has historically included the sharing of intelligence information and security concerns. On the other hand, during the Cold War and after, Mexico has yearned to demonstrate its independence from the United States and its allegiance to revolutionary struggles throughout the world. Thus, Mexico has pointedly kept a strong friendship with Fidel Castro's Cuba and has offered political exile to all sorts of revolutionary groups, including ETA terrorists and Central American guerrillas. When, after September 11, Foreign Affairs Minister Castañeda rejected that balancing act by unequivocally condemning the September 11 terrorists and forthrightly standing with the American people, he was attacked from all sides—and received no support from the rest of the government—for failing to maintain Mexico's fabled independent path and revolutionary tradition—which had been neither very transcendental nor really neutral vis-à-vis either revolutionary movements or U.S. military and intelligence goals.

Conclusion: The Dangers of Ninguneo

Americans have adopted many words from Spanish: fiesta, siesta, guerrilla, cacique, caudillo, sombrero, and "No Way Jose." It is too bad they have not also adopted the word *ningunear* (or its noun form *ninguneo*). *Ningunear* has several connotations: to humiliate, to make less, to misplace, to discriminate, to ignore, to put down, and to patronize. It is a very useful term for understanding Mexican-American relations.

Ningunear is what the Bush administration and the U.S. media, too, have done to Mexico and the rest of the continent after September 11. Not that Mexico or the rest of the continent had been a vital priority in the United States before September 11, but after the democratic turn in Mexico—with the election of the first non-PRI president—and the election of the supposedly pro-Mexico George W. Bush, a window of opportunity seemed to be wide open. Certainly in Mexico, people expected great things. President Fox appointed as minister of foreign affairs Jorge Castañeda, a man with excellent leftist credentials who wanted to strengthen relations with the United States and who brought with him a team of experts who, for the very first time in Mexican history, knew the United States and were willing to overcome both traditional Mexican anti-Americanism and the cozy and corrupt polygamous marriage of mutual convenience that had long existed between U.S. intelligence agencies and trade officials, private interests, and the Mexican government. President Bush, too, seemed powerfully motivated to make useful changes. During the 2000 campaign he had insisted that he was uniquely prepared as the former governor of Texas and as a friend of

President Fox to improve relations with Mexico. Once elected, Bush proved to be as good as his word: President Fox was the first foreign leader received by President Bush, and the Mexican people watched appreciatively as the red carpet was rolled out and Bush did his best to speak words of greeting and respect in Spanish (and while it was not good Spanish, Bush was the first U.S. president to give it his best shot on international television). Fox and Bush made plans for immigration agreements, for new agendas, and for a new treatment of Mexico by the United States.

By September 12, 2001, this very short-lived era of good feelings was over. Mexico had become, once again, a *ninguneo*. General Bush had a battle to fight, and Mexico saw no role for itself in this bully war.

September 11 could have been an opportunity for Mexico and the United States to ponder how intertwined the two nations have long been. So much talking of global wars and clashes of civilizations should have been a good opportunity for people to realize that, as compared to what was happening elsewhere in the world, between Mexico and the United States there is already—nothing to do about it—only one shared past, one shared present, and one shared future based increasingly on intertwined cultures, economies, and people. But in the hypernationalistic and self-absorbed ethos of post–September 11 America, the Bush administration forgot about Mexico, and Mexico reverted with a vengeance back to the anti-Americanism that is so much a part of its modern nationalistic identity. Now, as the two nations, once again, fight openly about old problems, especially the meaning of the border for Mexican workers, some Americans, well represented in a powerful faction of the Republican Party, are fighting furiously to shorten the conceptual distance between a Mexican and a terrorist. Americans, in their tragedy, did what seems to come so easily to the powerful: to see others not as real people caught in their own webs of history, culture, and interests but only as subordinates who will stand "with them or against them." And, just as importantly, during that time of the blood-dimmed tide, few Mexicans were able to make the empathic leap and understand as Carlos López Beltrán did, that, as for those who died in the Twin Towers, "Each one of those beings . . . could have been us . . . were us, alas, with a tiny variation in the bifurcations of the past."

Notes

1. Carlos López Beltrán, "Pies en polvorosa," *Fractal* 21 (April–June 2001): 95–104.

2. Jean Baudrillard, *L' esprit du terrorisme* (Paris: Éditions Galilée, 2002).

3. The authors acknowledge Miquel Valls's help in collecting data for this essay.

4. Popular Mexican saying—those who kill with the sword (knife) will be killed with the sword (or knife)—used several times by various journalists and intellectuals; see for instance, Luis González Souza in *La Jornada,* September 15, 2001.

5. Sergio Aguayo, "El ataque a EU: Las viñas de la ira," *Reforma,* September 12, 2001. An emblematic expression of the kingdom of the "comma": "I do not hesitate in condemning the attacks perpetrated against the U.S. population. It is equally important to isolate some of the chords of the symphony of irrationality. Violence has a logic, and to understand it is indispensable in order to control it."

6. *La Jornada,* September 26, 2001.

7. See Ricardo Alemán, "Itinerario Político. Quién fue y por qué. ¿El enemigo en casa?" *El Universal,* September 13, 2001. The author claimed that only radical or interest groups within the United States could have done it, as they had killed John F. Kennedy.

8. Roger Bartra, "Las redes imaginarias del terrorismo politico," *Letras Libres,* May 2003, 98–103.

9. Enrique Krauze, "Ataque a Estados Unidos: Odios teológicos," *La insignia,* September 25, 2001, www.lainsignia.org/2001/septiembre/int_125.htm.

10. Rafael Ruiz Harrel, "La mezquindad quiere pretextos," *Reforma,* September 29, 2001.

11. Krauze, "Ataque a Estados Unidos."

12. Carlos Monsivias, "México desde el 11 de septiembre," *Fractal* 22 (July–September 2001): 11–35.

13. About this see Carlos Malamud, "América Latina después del 11 de septiembre," *Revista de Occidente,* special issue, November 2001.

14. All data quoted and analyzed in Malamud, "América Latina después del 11 de septiembre."

15. Miguerl Riera, "¿Quién es el enemigo," *Viejo Topo,* October 2001.

16. Juan Carlos Monedero, "Las plegarias oídas de Bin Laden," *Viejo Topo,* November 2001.

17. Santiago López Petit, "El acontecimiento 11 de septiembre. Polifemo busca a su enemigo," *Viejo Topo,* November 2001.

18. See, for intance, *Revista de Occidente,* special issue, November 2001; *Revista Temas,* October 2001 (dedicated to global terror); *Claves de razón práctica,* November 2001 and December 2001.

19. Fernando Reinares, "¿A qué obedece el megaterrorismo?" *Revista de Occidente,* special issue, November 2001.

20. Fernando Vallespín, "Las torres de Babel. Reflexiones en torno al 'choque de culturas'"; and Rafael del Águila, "Tras el 11 de septiembre. Dilemas y paradojas de la globalización," both in *Claves de la razón práctica,* December 2001.

21. The Catalan media followed their own form of anti-Americanism, also stimulated by the U.S. policies in the months and years following September 11. In 2005 Catalan writer and television commentator Vicenç Villatoro published, in Catalan, a novel (*La dona a la finestra. El Born, 10 de setembre de 1714)* that somehow equated New York's September 11 with Barcelona's September 11 –the date in 1714 in which the Bourbons defeated the Catalan resistance, and thus today's official national day of Catalonia. In the novel, a U.S. Jewish black film director tries to re-create the life of a Catalan woman in Barcelona during the day before the final defeat in 1714—constantly echoing the director's memory of the 2001 terrorist attacks with the Bourbon attacks, though the 2001 terrorist attacks were very different in nature than the Spanish War of Succession, which lasted nine years, ending with the defeat of the Catalan nobility, which had signed a treaty with England and Genoa against the Bourbon Spanish king Phillip V. This is the legacy of September 11 at the service of Catalan nationalism. As in many other parts of the world, in Catalan, September 11 was digested locally.

22. See Fernando Escalante Gonzalbo, *In the Eyes of God: A Study on the Culture of Suffering,* trans. Jessica C. Locke (Austin: University of Texas Press, 2006); Richard J. Bernstein, *The Abuse of Evil: The Corruption of Politics and Religion since 9/11* (Malden, Mass.: Polity Press, 2005).

23. On Paz, see essays in Octavio Paz, *El ogro filantrópico: Historia y politica, 1971–1978,* 2nd ed. (Mexico City: J. Mortiz, 1979).

24. See Federico Romero, "The Twilight of American Cultural Hegemony: A Historical Perspective on Western Europe's Distancing from America," in this volume; Alan McPherson, ed., *Yankee no! Anti-Americanism in U.S.-Latin American Relations* (Cambridge: Harvard University Press, 2003); Jean François Revel, *L'obsession anti-américaine: Son fonctionnement, ses causes, ses inconsequences* (Paris: Plon, 2002); Philippe Roger, *L'ennemi américain: Genealogie de l'antiamericanisme français* (Paris: Seuil, 2002). For an emblematic U.S. nationalist view of anti-Americanism, see Paul Hollander, *Anti-Americanism: Critiques at Home and Abroad, 1965–1990* (New York: Oxford University Press, 1992); and the analysis of the emergence of U.S. nationalism as a "good" nationalism

vis-à-vis other, "bad" nationalisms, in Liah Greenfeld, *Nationalism: Five Roads to Modernity* (Cambridge: Harvard University Press, 1992).

25. We should note that, just as Mexicans have created their version of the United States, so have U.S. scholars, writers, activists, and journalists been inventing and reinventing their own private Mexico that they use to critique both modernist and postmodernist trends. Mexico is for some "The Hispanic Challenge." For others, Mexico is a land of pureness and authenticity where everyone can find their own Frida Kahlo or Tepoztlán or Chiapas. European scholars and writers have done the same, also consuming a "genuine" Mexico that stands in direct contrast to the giant to the North. The Europeans never seem to see that they are consuming an already Americanized product, from the arts and crafts they buy to their fascination with indigenous peoples. It is like buying an authentic pre-Hispanic piece, so as not to be Americanized, Westernized, only to find at the back of the piece, and in small font, the logo "Made in Mex-America." At the same time, let us be clear, Mexican arts and crafts, Mexican muralism, or Mexican indigenism were and are not less Mexican because they exist as complex cultural interactions in which the U.S. factor was essential.

26. Various authors, "La Roma Americana: Filias y fobias," *Letras Libres*, October 2001.

27. On the different historical presentation of Mexican anti-Americanism, see Alan Knight, *U.S.-Mexican Relations, 1910–1940: An Interpretation* (La Jolla, Calif.: Center for U.S.-Mexican Studies, University of California, 1987); Miguel Basañez, *Human Values and Beliefs: A Cross-Cultural Sourcebook* (Ann Arbor: University of Michigan Press, 1998); Ronald Inglehart, Neil Nevitte, and Miguel Bazañez, *The North American Trajectory: Cultural, Economic, and Political Ties among the United States, Canada, and Mexico* (New York: Aldine de Gruyter, 1996); Robert Earle and John Wirth, eds., *Identities in North America: The Search for Community* (Stanford: Stanford University Press, 1995); Douglas Lawrence Taylor, *El nuevo norteamericano: Integración continental, cultura e identidad nacional* (Mexico City: Tijuana, 2001); Mauricio Tenorio-Trillo, "Historia . . . ," in *De cómo ignorar* (Mexico City: FCE, 2000).

28. Alan Knight, "Revolutionary Project, Recalcitrant People: Mexico, 1910–1940," in Jaime Rodríguez, ed., *The Revolutionary Process in Mexico: Essays on Political and Social Change, 1880–1940* (Los Angeles: UCLA Latin American Center, 1990).

29. *Reforma*, September 24, 2001.

30. See Tenorio-Trillo, *De cómo ignorar*.

31. Samuel P. Huntington, *Who Are We: The Challenges to America's National Identity* (New York: Simon and Shuster, 2004); and our reactions in Fernando

Escalante-Gonzalbo, ed., *Otro sueño americano. En torno a ¿Quiénes somos? de Samuel P. Huntington* (Mexico City: Paidós, 2004).

32. See Jordi Nadal y Francisco García, *Libros o velocidad. Reflexiones sobre el oficio editorial* (Mexico City: FCE, 2005); André Schiffrin, *The Business of Books* (New York: Verso, 2000); Gabriel Zaíd, *Crítica del mundo cultural* (Mexico City: El Colegio Nacional, 1999). During that same period, journalism programs and the social sciences in Mexican institutions of higher learning have been re-organized into a market-oriented style of education. This change, too, has diminished the critical capacity of Mexican civil society.

33. See Claudio Lomnitz, "An Intellectual's Stock in the Factory of Mexico's Ruins," in *Deep Mexico, Silent Mexico* (Minneapolis: University of Minnesota Press, 2001).

34. See Mark Danner, *The Secret Way to War* (New York: New York Review of Books, 2006).

35. Though, in this case, too, there were those who suggested that the attacks were planned by the Spanish intelligence agencies because "for state terrorism the crime in Madrid is rational and functional, as it benefits Bush and Aznar." Guillermo Almeyra, *La Jornada,* March 14, 2004.

36. Among the features of Marat's language that have echoes in the conventional political discourse in Mexico are the idea that popular sovereignty manifests itself in riots, the idea that needs are the source of rights. See, for instance, Olivier Coquard, *Marat* (Paris: Fayard, 1989).

37. A counterexample is illuminating: the Mexican media does not know how to explain Iraqi sectarian attacks that are clearly not against the United States but against Iraqi civilians. The People vs. the State formula does not work. So the mass media laments the violence, but here there is no "comma"; no one seems comfortable or, perhaps capable, of explaining the context for this kind of violence. So instead there is mainly silence.

38. The internal struggle in Chiapas is a much more complicated story, but it, too, was eventually treated as a righteous indigenous movement against illegitimate state authorities. See, for instance, Pedro Pitarch, "Los zapatistas y el arte de la ventriloquía," *Istor* (Summer 2003), 95–132.

39. See, for instance, Pitarch, "Los zapatistas."

THE TWILIGHT

OF AMERICAN

CULTURAL

HEGEMONY

A Historical Perspective on Western Europe's

Distancing from America

❑ ❑ ❑

Federico Romero

FIRST, a flashback. In April 1999, the NATO alliance, keystone of Euro-American cooperation, celebrated its fiftieth anniversary with the most momentous changes in its long history. It peacefully expanded eastward, into what had long been "enemy territory," and it waged its first actual war, against Serbia's Milošević regime. Poland, Hungary, and the Czech Republic (not to mention the many others that would come later) were then joining West Europeans in entrusting their security to a collective pact based upon a substantial delegation of power, responsibility, and leadership to a distant, strategically superior ally. Meanwhile, the alliance itself was fighting over Kosovo a war pivoted on a doctrine never before expounded in such explicit and proud terms, a doctrine claiming that the boundaries of national sovereignty were not always sacrosanct, and should take second place to the primacy of universal human rights and democracy. In other words, it was a Wilsonian war if ever there was one. An outright crusade for universal rights, it pitted that arch-Wilsonian agent, "a community of power" grounded in democratic ideology, against a brutal but admittedly sovereign regime.[1]

Whatever one thought of the wisdom of either of those initiatives, one thing seemed starkly clear to the historical-minded observer. Europe, or most of it anyway, had come a long, long way from the nation-based view of international order that had shaped its history throughout the entire modern era. It not only rejected that view (by and large this had already happened in the years after World War II) but now embraced the alternative American view, lock, stock, and barrel.

In many ways, the 1999 crisis over Kosovo seemed to illustrate and epitomize the depth of Europe's internalization of the American world-view—especially if one looked at the peculiar coalition of statesmen (and spin doctors) who articulated NATO's message. The alignment of Britain's New Labour with America's democratic universalism might not have been terribly surprising. But the advocacy of a Wilsonian war for democracy and human rights by French Gaullists and Socialists, as well as politicians who had come of age protesting against the American war in Vietnam, like ex-Communist Italian prime minister Massimo D'Alema and ex-radical German foreign minister Joschka Fischer, was quite unprecedented. And the outlook was not dramatically different in the media and public opinion at large. Opinion polls registered large majorities in favor of such a war's rationale in every country but Italy (where opinions were split fifty-fifty), and the Czech Republic and Greece (where opposition to the war prevailed).[2]

In the photo-opportunity pictures at the April 1999 Washington summit—national flags hanging in the background—NATO leaders were beaming their optimistic belief in the universal rights upheld by NATO weaponry (and hiding their anxiety for a conflict whose victorious ending was not yet in sight at that point). Was it really surprising that those smiling representatives of a "baby-boom" generation that had finally found its way into the halls of government—the Clintons and Blairs, the Schroeders, Fischers, and D'Alemas—would see eye to eye and speak the same conceptual language? Was the eruption of a common mind-set—articulated in the classical language of American liberal internationalism—such an unpredictable event?

The Wilsonian code had been gradually internalized over a long period in different but connected struggles for a more inclusive view of democracy, equal opportunities, multiculturalism, and global human rights, but now—resurrected in the 1990s by the Clinton administration—it had come to saturate the moderate-to-leftist spectrum of European politics. Whether or not one ranks Antonio Gramsci as the theorist of choice, this was cultural hegemony made as apparent as it can get. The American reading of international rules and values had triumphed by metamorphosing into a shared transatlantic culture with no apparent internal barriers and boundaries. It looked as though Woodrow Wilson had won even Georges Clemenceau, eighty years after their Versailles discussions, over to his side. The half-century of American leadership in Western Europe—and now a larger Europe—had reached an unprecedented peak.

An optical illusion? Fast-forward to the spring of 2003, and that peak actually looks like an apogee, soon followed by a precipitous descent. What had changed so drastically in just four years?

Just Old, Stale Anti-Americanism?

When trying to account for the deep, massive, passionate clash between Europe and America in the winter and spring 2003—or, to be precise, between the vast majority of Europeans and the U.S.-led initiative to invade Iraq—scholars and pundits have come up with a variety of explanations, not always incompatible.

International relations experts stressed the long-term change wrought by the end of the Cold War. America's security policies are no longer focused on Europe, which is therefore less relevant and central. At the same time, Europe[3] feels less dependent upon America and less closely bound to its leadership. Whether the stress is on the historical and systemic change associated with the end of bipolarism, on the contingent and abrupt change brought by the Bush administration's security strategy, or on the long-term evolution of an unprecedented European philosophy of institutionalized peace,[4] these arguments stress the role of mutual perceptions and, even more cogently, of self-perceptions. Interests might be less similar than they used to be; nonetheless they still remain largely communal and shared. Europe and the United States certainly do not threaten each other's vital interests.

What has truly changed is the international role each polity attributes to itself and its society. A new transatlantic bargain might, and yet might not, be struck in the near future on the basis of overriding common interests and goals, but the protagonists on both sides of the Atlantic no longer share the common mind-set that had kept them together for fifty years.[5]

In a different strain of scholarship, historians and cultural analysts of European anti-Americanism[6] have traditionally grappled, without conclusive answers, with the complex relationship between culture and power that is at the foundation of the phenomenon itself.[7] That the power imbalance was a key factor became clear quite soon after September 11. Even when solidarity with America was most widespread and warmly expressed, even when large portions of European public opinion were still supporting the notion of the "war on terror" (and were perhaps perplexed by, but not opposed to, the campaign in Afghanistan), opinion polls were revealing a contrary undercurrent. Sixty-six percent of West Europeans and seventy percent of East Europeans—roughly in sync with opinions expressed in the Middle East or in Latin America—apparently believed that it was a "good thing" that the United States now felt vulnerable. In other words, they sympathized with terror-struck America, they supported its response, but they also joined many other parts of the world in appreciating—or should we say relishing?—America's new sense of vulnerability.

Since the countries we are considering are among the richest in the world, their attitude cannot be simplistically explained away as the bitterness felt by the powerless towards the powerful. It was rather the result of more complex intra-Western jostling about the distribution of such power. Rather revealingly, in the same poll West Europeans stood out as the most convinced critics of American multinational corporations. In Asia, Latin America, or the Middle East criticism of the United States was not so clearly focused on the nefarious activities of Nike, McDonald's or Microsoft, but West Europeans believed this to be a major reason to dislike the United States. A bit odd—to say the least—since European multinationals are the major counterpart, worldwide, of the American ones; and European societies are not the most but the least vulnerable to the disruptions that multinationals can bring upon a community. It can be inferred that Europeans did not so much criticize American multinationals as such, but rather the fact that they are more globally mighty and emblematic than the European ones.

If the analogy holds, West Europeans by and large did not dispute the strategic or moral implications of the "war on terror"—at least before Iraq became its main focus—but its unilateral management, the lack of consultation with European governments, the fact that Washington did not conceive of cooperation as a two-way street. In short, what Europeans were criticizing in the early post–September 11 stage was the inbuilt, glaring inequality of the transatlantic partnership, made ever more visible (and distressing) by the abrasive unilateralism displayed by the Bush administration. Indeed, when asked to list the factors that contributed to public dislike of the United States, West Europeans topped the world league in pointing to "resentment of U.S. power" as the primary, crucial element.[8]

That such resentment (and the alleged "ingratitude" that goes with it) was at the center of European anti-American opinions throughout the twentieth century has always been a staple of the critics of such anti-Americanism.[9] It is certainly easy today—far too easy and tempting—to read the recent transatlantic crisis in the light of the catalogue of anti-American tropes and stereotypes that anti-Americanism has built up over more than a century.[10] But confounding different phenomena in a soup conveniently labeled as anti-Americanism is not a particularly useful tool for analysis. The anti-Americanism that is nowadays decried in many headlines is a complex but also limited phenomenon that requires closer scrutiny.

A poll of French citizens taken at the end of 2001, for instance, tells us that "structured anti-Americanism" embraced only about 10 percent of the population, primarily intellectual and professional white collars, mostly on the left politically, with strong concerns for threats to cultural identity. At the opposite end, a quarter of the population was defined as very sympathetic to the United States and quite confident that Europe could sustain a friendly competition with it. In between, the vast majority of those polled proclaimed various degrees of mild interest or indifference, but no hostility.[11] Surveys of Italy revealed a similar picture once you take into account the more polarized politics of that country: here the anti-American group was a bit larger and included also a sizable chunk of blue-collar workers, while the explicitly pro-American wing of the population was more robustly stable at around 40 percent.[12]

It is true that images and languages can recur, and most public criticism of the war in Iraq reverberated with the well-established slogans and metaphors of traditional anti-Americanism. It would have been truly surprising if, in the midst of the deepest Euro-American crisis since World War II, that language had simply vanished without a trace. But it is just as clear that something new is also afoot. Traditional anti-Americanism articulated by conservative intellectual elites in the interwar period, and then reelaborated by leftist intellectuals in the early Cold War era, was premised on the pessimistic sense that Europe was being overrun by a modern juggernaut, that its society (or "civilization") was to be swallowed up and changed beyond recognition by American capitalist modernity. This was the frightened anti-Americanism that posited a Europe without future, and saw its decline as historical catastrophe. Such doom-and-gloom anti-Americanism, however, no longer appears central or even important. As Mary Nolan recently argued:

> What is new about anti-Americanism and anti-Europeanism is less the substantive issues in dispute, which have been rather consistent over the past two decades, than the context in which they are being articulated. . . . Capitalist modernity in Europe and America has diverged and many parts of Europe embrace a different conception of social justice and not just a different conception of international law and cooperation and of post-national development. America has not been marginalized by any means—how could a country with so much military and economic power be ignored—but it has been decentered as an economic model, a cultural mecca and a political beacon. The new anti-Americanism both reflects and is intensified by Europe's tendency to look to the real and imagined Europe, rather than to America, when debating its modern future.[13]

Many indicators suggest that America is still (and perhaps even more) resented for its awesome and multidimensional power: strategic but also economic, technological, and cultural. However, such public feelings are no longer coupled with the impotent fear of Europe's decline, and the ensuing bitter conviction that the United States embodies Europe's inevitable future.

At the opposite end, what used to be the discourse of Americanism in Europe has changed as well. Historians have reached some kind of consensus on the features, actors, and dynamics of Americanization in postwar Europe, and it goes roughly like this. Postwar generations of young, urban West Europeans adopted parts of American mass culture, molded it into a specific language of their own, and adapted it to their own goals and purposes. They appropriated and used American culture in order to wage their conflicts for freedom from traditional authorities: church, family, school, state. They deployed it for their own collective and individual assertion within the contexts of national cultures still shell-shocked by the self-inflicted disaster of World War II. They turned it into a vehicle for modernizing many features of their own societies—not only production, commerce, and technology, but communication, education, art, lifestyle, politics.[14]

Nowadays the highly educated, more cosmopolitan European youth of the new century are experiencing a rather different process of cultural and political identification. They need not borrow from America their most innovative cultural icons in order to mobilize them against a local context of conservative traditionalism. Those icons—however American their historical origins might be—are largely perceived as denationalized components of a fully global culture that we all partake of—willingly for most, unwillingly for many. Nor are European social structures and cultural patterns usually interpreted as suffocating legacies of a past to be overcome, or suffered as a cage that needs to be pried open in order to be—as the 1960s had it—"liberated" and "authentic."

A New Self-Perception

The main public opinion indicators suggest quite the opposite: a high degree of self-satisfied, even proud identification with so-called European values.[15] Whether these values are actually European or national, local, sectional, ideological, religious, and so forth, remains highly debatable. What is remarkable, though, is that in poll after poll we can see—throughout the nineties and today—the slow, gradual, but steady rise of a divide that pollsters label as "cultural" or "civilizational." In France as in Germany, in Italy as in the Scandinavian countries—to a noticeable extent even in Britain—European citizens at large, as well as professional, intellectual, and political elites, claim a sort of moral superiority of Europe over the United States.

At issue in this divide are not the overtly political values: democracy, free markets, and individual freedom are and remain key aspects of America that are deemed not only positive, but indeed emblematic of the common ground the two societies occupy and share. In particular, Americans and Europeans seem to agree that "people are better off in a free market economy," a statement supported by 60 percent to 70 percent of all those polled in North America as well as in western Europe, without conspicuous national differences. Similar or even larger majorities—particularly noticeable in younger generations—believe that globalization is a good thing and it is not the malignant engine of the more widely held causes of concerns (jobs, divide between rich and poor). Even on the environment the American and European public do not show large divergences, with substantial majorities claiming that conservation should be pursued even if it gets in the way of economic growth.

North Americans and Europeans also seem to share a certain distrust of multinationals (which receive their worst worldwide ratings in the two societies that have given life to most of them and that certainly enjoy most of their economic benefits!). And they are still relatively united in a surprisingly diffuse contempt for, and sometimes fear of, the threat that consumerism and commercialism represent for their cultures. Similarities prevail also in the degree to which most Americans and West Europeans—and especially the elderly—believe that their "way of life needs to be protected against foreign influence." Americans seem to consider it a generic statement that can coexist with positive attitudes on ethnic minorities and immigration, while West Europeans connect such fear to widely held negative opinions on migrants and ethnic groups.[16]

But serious differences do emerge when people are questioned on the role of government, on relationships between collective solidarity and individual responsibility, and on moral and religious values. Here, European opinions not only diverge from American ones, but appear to emphasize a stark contrast between two societal models. In particular, what springs out is the perception of a more "humane," cohesive, communitarian, and morally commendable European society. America is openly criticized (even by a considerable share of those who support its global role as strategic leader) as a society that neglects social issues, that does not care about the poor, the elderly or the sick, that does not provide appropriate welfare, education, and health care to its citizens, that does not protect the environment, that premises its law and order policies on principles that many Europeans deem morally questionable if not shameful, as in the case of the death penalty.[17]

Throughout Europe (and Canada) large majorities believe that governments have the responsibility to see to it that "no one is in need." Such a proposition is supported only by one-third of Americans, while 58 percent of them attribute more importance to the "freedom to pursue individual goals without government interference." What's more interesting, these contrasting majorities have both grown larger over the last decade, indicating a deepening divergence between the United States and other Western societies. A similar trend is reflected in opinions about "success." An expanding majority of Europeans believe that success derives largely from external forces that individuals cannot control, while more than 60 percent of Americans (and Canadians) reply that an individual's success in life is an outcome largely of his or her own making.

Europeans and Americans are at odds—though to a lesser extent—also on the value they attribute to the traditional family composed of a male breadwinner and a housewife. Only tiny minorities of West Europeans are truly fond of it, while a substantial minority of Americans (37 percent) praises its alleged virtues. And if more than 70 percent of West Europeans believe that homosexuality "should be accepted by society," such an opinion is held by a bare majority of 51 percent of Americans. In these international comparisons, United States' opinions appear far closer to those of Latin Americans than Europeans. And this is especially evident on the issue of religion. When questioned on the possibility for an individual to be moral even aside from religious principles, large majorities of West Europeans (and Canadians) agree, while 58 percent of Americans believe that it is "necessary to believe in God to be moral."[18]

Many of these differences are not particularly new, and every single one might not be terribly relevant per se. But the increasing divergence that they portray points to a widening fissure in the perception (as well as reality) of what used to be considered an undifferentiated "West." Besides, the public awareness of, and mass-media noise about, such a divergence is visibly growing on both sides of the ocean, and gets congealed in stereotypical axioms that reinforce the trend.

This emphasis on societal differences—which can easily be perceived as moral or "civilizational"—does not fluctuate and seems indeed to take deeper roots, to gather strength over time, with only a feeble correlation to the varying chronicle of political events. Not all surveys are broken down by age, but there are good indications that such a view of Europe as a less harsh and more "humane" society is particularly widespread in the younger cohorts. Indeed there are signs that point to a disproportionate diffusion of such a specific Europe versus America attitude among younger Europeans. A French poll in December 2001, for instance, registered a damning denunciation of the perceived inequality of American society by the younger cohort, while older citizens were far less concerned about it.[19] A most recent comparative poll shows that young people in the largest countries of Western Europe (Great Britain, France, and Germany) have more negative views of America than do people in other age groups.[20]

This low-key but firm, solid sense of "civilizational" superiority appears more widespread on the left of the political spectrum but is by no means limited to it. It is shared by most of the Catholic world (progressive as well as conservative) and by many conservative nationalists, not only in France. It does not seem to be ideologically based, and therefore we should not categorize it—and somehow dismiss it—as one more manifestation of the attitude that accompanied Europe's convulsions throughout the twentieth century: the recurrent dread of American modernity by threatened intellectual elites. Because what now appears absent, or much less relevant, is the doom-and-gloom, declinist prophecy that animated European intellectual lamentations about America in the interwar and postwar decades.

The voice of present-day Europe that resonates from these polls and surveys, not to speak of the media, does not whine. It does not mourn a superior, glorious but fated past. Europe no longer feels at risk of being swallowed up and obliterated by a rising materialist giant. It rather appears as the self-assured, confident, almost smug carrier of a softer, more balanced approach to economic and technological change, the standard-bearer—in Brussels-speak—of a more sustainable future rather than the dejected epitome of a world that was believed to be sadly disappearing.

The most illuminating parameter of such a new attitude is to be found in the wide, deep gap that nowadays separates Americans from Europeans on what had traditionally been, for millions and millions of people, *the* comparative issue across the Atlantic; whether people who move to the United States actually enjoy a better life. Americans overwhelmingly believe this to be the case—88 percent of them say that people who move to the United States from other countries have a better life. By contrast, just 14 percent of Germans, 24 percent of French, and 41 percent of British think that people who left their countries and moved to the United States have achieved a better life.[21] The promised land clearly holds as an American narrative, but West Europeans no longer buy into it.

The West Is No Longer a Singular Noun

What matters here is not the degree of accuracy of this rosy European view. One can see it as a realistic assessment or as pure wishful-thinking. In my opinion it combines both these elements. Rather, what needs to be emphasized is the relative novelty—at least in historical terms—of such an attitude, its pervasiveness, and, above all, its durability over and beyond contingent political events that influence other type of judgments about the United States.

The conclusion that can be drawn is that we are rapidly moving away from some of the social and cultural patterns that prevailed for most of the Cold War decades. The power gap between the United States and Europe used to be justified, or at least rationalized, in historical and strategic terms. Europeans had to make up for the disastrous effects of two world wars, and they needed American protection from the neighboring Soviet threat. But no less important was the social background against which that gap was evaluated, and the image of the future that went with it.

For most of the Cold War period the dominant view—that we all shared a set of values, institutions, and procedures—descended from cultural representations of "the West" and its history. But the strength of such a view, its pervasiveness and resilience, had also a lot do with its firm grounding in dynamics that we used to take for granted, but are actually no longer with us.

To begin with, from the 1950s to the 1980s there was actual convergence. Western Europe was catching up with America in GDP levels, per capita income, standards and type of consumption, technological prowess, and several other indicators. Accordingly, a common and single "West" was also the obvious, almost undisputed view of the future, as our economies and societies were coming together in the undistinguishable makeup of what we used to call the "industrialized nations."

Second, the approach to such assumed convergence was driven and to a large extent shaped—as we have seen—by innovative social actors. As the younger generations that were born and raised in the postwar era came to dominate the consumption of mass culture and increasingly to shape Europe's public culture, the boundaries of European distinctiveness were pushed further and further back. A few Europeans surely bemoaned such a fate, but their "anti-Americanism" was increasingly marginalized by the much more numerous and robust supporters of American-inspired modernizing trends. By the 1980s traditional anti-Americanism could be plausibly dismissed as a relic of the past,[22] and public culture often celebrated the advent of a homogenized transatlantic society.

Then, somewhere in the mid-1990s, many of these trends, attitudes, and fads began to veer and sometimes backtrack. The generation that was coming of age in a globalized world no longer needed the United States as a beacon or symbolic aim. America was gradually becoming more and more different, particularly along the secular-versus-religious axis. And convergence gave way to actual divergence. A new technology gap began to appear and widen. Rates of economic growth diverged. Perhaps more crucially, cultural adaptation to the globalized imperatives of flexibility, innovation, mobility, and migration acquired different meanings (and took a different pace) on the two sides of the Atlantic. Even the aging of our "mature" societies grew dissimilar, and projected rather different futures for a truly aging Europe and a relatively youthful America. A few indicators—like the frequency of American TV programs—now point even to a rollback of America's cultural presence in Europe.[23]

For a few years, such a divergence did not seem to entail a deliberate, conscious distancing. But the tensions brought by different policy responses to the terrorist challenge, and the different assessments of the post–September 11 environment, did the trick. All of a sudden, different views about foreign policy priorities, antiterrorist strategies, and rules of international behavior precipitated not only a political clash but a truly public outbreak of different collective perceptions about one's own society and its transatlantic counterpart. A visible resurgence of European anti-Americanism was this time matched by the flaring-up of a more circumscribed but muscular anti-Europeanism in the United States.[24]

Throughout 2003, poll after poll registered not only a dramatic worsening of European opinions on U.S. foreign policy but a swell of negative views on a range of real or alleged American "responsibilities." The Eurobarometer surveys reveal that large majorities of West Europeans deem America a poor, or negative, force for world peace, for the fight against poverty, and for environmental protection. Almost 75 percent of European Union citizens believe that the United States exercises too much influence on globalization, and express distrust towards the U.S. government on global issues. Europe, on the other hand, is seen by more than 60 percent as having a positive role for world peace.[25]

Similar attitudes emerge from comparative multination polls. The transatlantic clash on Iraq brought a large majority of Europeans to believe that Europe should take a more independent approach to foreign and security policy, should assume a superpower role comparable to America's (even though the Europeans' perceptions of international threats appear far less global than America's), and should actively contrast the U.S. propensity to bypass international organizations. Aside from specific policy issues—where disagreement is obvious but also tightly focused (invasion of Iraq, support of Israeli policies, economic pressures on Arab countries and Palestinians)—what emerges as an aftermath of the war in Iraq is the historical shift from the traditionally favorable to an unfavorable overall opinion of the United States for a majority of Europeans. As Richard Bernstein effectively (if somewhat crudely) summed it up, "the view of the United States as a bully has entered the popular culture"[26] and has become commonplace.

In particular, what the Iraqi war and its aftermath crystallized in European minds is a perception of U.S. strategies and motivations as alien, destabilizing, and potentially hurtful for Europe. In the major multinational poll, taken one year after the invasion of Iraq, overwhelming majorities in every country surveyed (except the United States) are convinced that "the United States acts internationally without taking account of the interests of other nations," and specifically of their own. In Europe, this opinion is held by majorities ranging from 84 percent in France to 61 percent in Britain. Europeans also seem to agree that "the war in Iraq hurt, rather than helped, the war on terrorism," and here again they appear attuned to the opinions that prevail in countries as different as Turkey and Russia, while Americans once again appear isolated in holding the opposite view.[27]

In France and Germany these contrasts are especially stark. Most West Europeans believe that "the United States is overreacting to the threat of terrorism," but in the two countries that most directly opposed the Iraqi war there are majorities or vast pluralities (49 percent in Germany) who agree with the view (most typical in Muslim countries) that "America is exaggerating the terrorist threat." Thus, the explanation favored by vast majorities in both countries is that "the U.S. is conducting the war on terrorism in order to control Mideast oil and dominate the world." As a result, support for the very notion of a war on terrorism—at least as it was articulated by the Bush administration and propagated by many American media—has shrunk to half (in Germany) or less than half (in France) of the public. Consequently, eight in ten of the French citizens surveyed, and seven in ten Germans, now declare that "because of the war they have less confidence that the U.S. is intent on promoting democracy around the world."[28] There are at the moment no directly comparable data for Italy and Spain, or the northern European countries, but every other indicator points towards a similar picture. Data on eastern Europe is even more sporadic. If overall opinions on the United States are more favorable—especially in Poland—trust in U.S. foreign policy is very low, and only tiny minorities declare that U.S. policies help, or just take account of, their country's interests.[29]

It is hard to escape the conclusion that the war in Iraq has eroded—perhaps even demolished—the main pillars of the transatlantic trust that defined the post–World War II era: the perception that U.S. international attitudes were, on balance, helpful for democracy and prosperity; and the notion that European interests had a place in Washington's deliberations. The only significant factor that appears to act as a countervailing force to this wider-and-deeper-the-Atlantic mood is the clear distinction that all European publics draw between the U.S. as a nation (and particularly a government) and the American people. Opinions on Americans remain decidedly favorable not only in Great Britain but also in Germany, in Russia, and even in France, where 55 percent of those polled expressed a positive view of Americans. It has to be noticed, however, that the number of those who hold such positive views, although reassuringly high, has declined rather significantly from the far higher averages of the years before the Iraq war.[30]

In the New Landscape of Estrangement

Sudden, deep crises like the one that ruptured the transatlantic community in early 2003 are precipitated by contingent events and particular policy choices. There is no need here to dwell on the specific agency, and relative weight, of Bush's decision for war or Chirac's opposition to it at the United Nations Security Council. What is clear is that most West Europeans perceived the abrupt change of style and substance brought by the Bush administration as the primary source of the crisis. In the circumscribed world of statesmen and diplomats, such breaks can be overcome by a mix of soothing gestures and judicious policy solutions. At times, though, such crises bring to the surface long-term trends that had gone undetected for some time, put a spotlight on them, and magnify their effects. In the most serious cases, they kick off paradigm shifts that acquire a momentum of their own in their aftermath. If polls and other such indicators are even minimally reliable, we seem to be in the middle of such a paradigm shift for many, perhaps most, Europeans.

A growing perception of societal and cultural differences, with strong ethical underpinnings, is eroding the sense of transatlantic commonality that prevailed in the Cold War era. What most Americans see after September 11 is an international arena where it is imperative to wage and win a war, while most Europeans appear convinced that the task is to prevent one. In European eyes, many of the measures the U.S. government deems necessary to fight such a war appear as an unprecedented American effort "to set global norms all by itself," and to claim exception from the agreed international rules and conventions that buttressed and legitimized the Cold War alliance. As a consequence, the image of the benign, consensual U.S. hegemony that most West Europeans valued for over fifty years is being replaced by the perception of a much more traditional, overbearing imperial power.[31]

What are we going to find, what can we expect in this new landscape of estrangement? One historical conclusion can already be drawn. If we look at what used to be an American "consensual hegemony"[32] in Europe as a chemical compound, I have tried to argue that some of its components are withering away or losing their potency; a few others are gradually counterbalanced by diverging and possibly contrasting trends; above all, the glue, the web that linked them all together in an effective, influential concoction is unraveling. Some of those elements will long remain influential. Cultural landscapes do not change overnight. We are not witnessing a sudden crash. It is rather a complex, continuous metamorphosis, a shifting of emphases and relevancies that gained pace over the last decade and accelerated abruptly in 2003. Ever since the 1940s, observers and scholars of transatlantic relationships have measured the ebb and flow of American hegemony, gauging its internal changes, regularly (and often obsessively) checking its pulse and temperature. But we rarely, if ever, imagined that it would not be with us tomorrow. Now, for the first time since World War II, that possibility is there, is real. It is not yet a foretold conclusion, but it looks like the most likely outcome.

We can then consider the possible impact of all this at the policy level. The common interests that the United States and Europe share are so large and significant that policy solutions to the present rift should be found, in due time. Americans and Europeans in no way threaten each other's major interests. They still share a common body of values, habits, and principles that distinguishes them from other societies. Their economies are not only more intertwined than ever, but constantly growing into the more deeply interdependent sections of the global economy.[33] The question then is whether the depth of economic, political, cultural, and historical ties can prevent further deterioration.

Diplomacy can heal and mend, and it is trying to do so. But any new transatlantic bargain will be different in several respects. The strategic landscape that bound us together has vanished not just in reality (that happened more than a decade ago) but, at long last, in perceptions as well. Compared to the Cold War era, Europe is now far less important for the United States, and the United States is less necessary for the Europeans. Thus, their unequal but mutual dependence is going to be far less binding. Their strategic interests might often converge, and occasionally even coincide, but they will be different; above all, they will be defined and assessed differently.

In particular, the public meaning and reading of those interests will no longer be a (largely) joint one, as European and American societies follow divergent trends and contemplate their future with different spectacles. Europe's distancing from America need not be cataclysmic or irreversible, but the foreign policy issues they face cannot be dealt with, or even properly assessed, without due attention to the impact and import of such distancing.

For most Europeans perceptions of policy issues appear increasingly framed in ethical terms that entail an ambitious urge to redefine the continent's identity and self-perception. Thus, a large section of the public—probably the majority—will attribute a distinct, often decisive value to Europe's ability to take an "independent" stance. The need to pursue an effective, incisive foreign policy could very well take a backseat to the expression of Europe's autonomy. In particular, a manifestation of autonomy from the United States, of diversity from Washington's desires, will often become the main parameter upon which the European Union's—or each national government's—actions will be evaluated by their own voters. To no small extent this is quite visible in a public debate centered on the degree of differentiation and distancing from the United States much more than on Europe's specific interests, goals, and possibilities, particularly on Iraq and the Middle East in general.

Surveys make clear that most West Europeans want the EU to plot a more independent course in security and diplomatic affairs. This feeling, and the demand it puts upon governments, has grown markedly since 2003, even in Britain. Many go beyond such a stance and declare that "it would be a good thing if the European Union becomes as powerful as the United States." One might not be surprised that 90 percent of the French entertain such an aspiration, but the fact that it is also embraced by 70 percent of Germans and about 50 percent of Britons conveys the depth of the change that has reshaped the landscape of Europe's public opinion. It is also clear, however, that this ambition reflects less a strategic view, or a determined drive for power, than a nebulous desire for Europe's symbolic aggrandizement, and more specifically for a reduction of America's preeminence. When questioned on the degree of safety the world would enjoy "if another country rivaled the power of the U.S." most Europeans are quite skeptical, and only in France a majority (54 percent) believes that a full-fledged bipolarism would entail more safety.[34]

This urge for a higher degree of detachment from Washington can propel national governments and the EU itself onto a more effective effort to devise new European foreign and security policies. Critics may very well point out that this has long been an unfulfilled fancy entertained by ineffectual, daydreaming Euro-enthusiasts. Even those few Europeans who fantasize about counterbalancing the United States, or the many who simply want to acquire more international clout, are notoriously and consistently wary of the costs involved, and are not prepared to pay for them. Critics may also point out institutional obstacles. The construction of a unified Europe, especially in the field of foreign and security policy, is slow and stuttering, often goes in reverse, and has repeatedly proven incapable of rising to the challenges that history puts in its way.

And yet, the process of European autonomization from the former Atlantic framework—however sluggish and inadequate it might appear to Euro-enthusiasts—is nonetheless inching forward. It proceeds along a road that might run parallel with America for some time, perhaps even a long time on several issues of common interest, but it is bound ultimately to diverge rather than converge, as a European political and military identity of some sort grows (however haltingly) more defined.

More importantly, what had previously kept Europeans from seriously venturing onto a more independent course were not simply inbuilt institutional obstacles or plain stinginess, but the apparent lack of its necessity. Even at the time of the 1990s wars in the ex-Yugoslavia, when a common European course of action was often praised as a most desirable option, it did not appear truly indispensable to large sections of public opinion. It is the shock of the American decision to invade Iraq that seems to have changed this, and altered what most people see as the basic priorities.

The clearest symptom of such a change comes from the dynamics of electoral politics. Starting in 2002 the transatlantic world, while absorbed in bitter but inconclusive debates on anti-Americanism, has actually been confronted with a historic novelty that cuts through intellectual disputes. Criticizing America and dissociating from it became a vote-catching resource, and it occasionally worked wonders. During the Cold War calls for autonomy from America had routinely been voiced by opposition forces in many West European countries. They might momentarily mobilize specific groups of voters, but they never managed to unite large coalitions, and were never truly successful. As an electoral resource they were a useless, losing proposition. In Germany they were an absolute taboo. Only France—where a varying but explicit degree of "anti-Americanism" tinted the public discourse of the Left as well as the Gaullist Right—stood out as an exception.

Now, however, sharp criticism of the United States—and the symbolic affirmation of autonomy it entails—helped German chancellor Gerhard Schroeder win national elections in 2002, had a significant role in the Spanish elections of 2003, and is playing an influential role in the politics of Italy and Britain. Rather than a virtuous circle between an "Atlanticist" stance and the strengthening of domestic coalitions and parliamentary majorities—the typical dynamic that defined western Europe's political regimes from 1947 to the 1990s—we might now be witnessing an inverse trend. The pursuit (or at least the proclamation) of autonomy from the United States is probably going to become one of the important, ascendant paradigms in several nations, and so is the rallying cry against "Anglo-American," free-market interpretations of globalization. The French exception will not turn overnight into the European norm, but the electoral appeal of "anti-American" positions, whether garbed in nationalist or Europeanist clothes, is here to stay and will intermittently affect Europe's electoral cycle and political discourse.

The problem is, of course, that this European urge to become—or at least to feel—more independent from America is not in itself a sufficient condition for an autonomous and effective foreign policy. It might prod governments in that direction, but it cannot dissolve the cultural, economic, and institutional impediments that have so far prevented the emergence of the European Union as a full-fledged global power. Therefore, the European public might very well have set its eyes on an unattainable goal. If a sufficient number of political forces find it expedient to stir up these sentiments, or if another American venture exposes once again the practical irrelevance of multilateral rules and of Europe's attitudes, the stage is set for a politics of resentment. A few seeds are already visible. The public reception of several recent U.S. foreign policy decisions—from the rejection of the Kyoto accord to the invasion of Iraq—was often marked by the belief that Washington's ultimate, disguised aim was the weakening of Europe. It does not really matter that this is not the central axis of U.S. policies in the "war on terror" but simply a by-product (although gleefully celebrated by Donald Rumsfeld and many neoconservatives). Even if exaggerated or unfounded, such recriminations are a very popular way to excuse Europe's own marginality, and they can fuel a paranoid, Eurocentric way of thinking that might flare up once again and deepen the transatlantic gap.

The danger, in short, is not an abrupt rise of sustained Euro-American rivalry, but a possible short-circuit. If public ambitions towards an independent European role on the global stage get repeatedly frustrated, if Washington's policies appear once again to assert U.S. unilateral dominance, and if such policies are read in Europe as aimed against Europe itself, European opinions could easily turn towards a volatile mix of fervent anti-Americanism and a shortsighted, strident isolationism fueled by impotent bitterness. Protectionist and xenophobic attitudes are fairly widespread in many countries and are increasingly surfacing in policy debates. The longer Europe appears as a (potential) solution that does not come to fruition, somehow a broken promise, the more likely it becomes that Europeans will revert to national and nationalist-minded solutions that will elevate globalization, foreign immigrants, multinationals and American policies into convenient scapegoats.

All this is not unavoidable, nor is it the most likely outcome. After all, the unipolarity of U.S. supremacy does not necessarily need to be managed by unilateral decrees. The fears and misgivings of Europeans do not have to be inflated by shortsighted electoral ambitions. It is ultimately up to European and American elites to avoid such an ugly turn, but the paradigm shift that most Europeans are experiencing makes any prospect of a new Euro-American accord a much more frail, transient, and vulnerable proposition. There might be many instances of transatlantic cooperation, but there is no longer an Atlantic or Euro-American community.

Notes

1. Woodrow Wilson, *An Address to the Senate*, January 22, 1917, in Arthur Link, ed., *The Papers of Woodrow Wilson* (Princeton: Princeton University Press, 1966–), 40:535–37.

2. See *The Economist*, April 24, 1999, 32.

3. Due to my specific and limited expertise, as well as the necessity to keep a close focus, throughout this essay the term *Europe* will be used as a shorthand for what used to be called Western Europe, and particularly for the larger countries in it.

4. For two examples see respectively Stanley Hoffmann, "The High and the Mighty: Bush's National-Security Strategy and the New American Hubris," *American Prospect*, January 13, 2003; and Robert Kagan, *Of Paradise and Power: America and Europe in the New World Order* (New York: Knopf, 2002).

5. See Michael Cox, "Gli europei vengono da Venere e gli americani da Marte? Le relazioni transatlantiche dall'11 settembre all'Iraq," in Giuseppe Vacca, ed., *Il dilemma euroatlantico* (Bari: Dedalo, 2004), 31–62.

6. For brevity's sake, I will leave aside the equally intriguing but less studied theme of anti-Europeanism in contemporary America.

7. See the overview and discussion by David Ellwood, *The Twilight of American Cultural Hegemony: A Historical Perspective on Western Europe's Distancing From America*, in Heide Fehrenbach and Uta G. Poiger, eds., *Transactions, Transgressions, Transformations: American Culture in Western Europe and Japan* (New York: Berghahn, 2000), 26–44.

8. Pew Research Center, Pew Global Attitudes Project, survey of December 2001, at http://www.people-press.org.

9. See, for instance, the study by Paul Hollander, *Anti-Americanism: Critiques at Home and Abroad, 1965–1990* (Oxford: Oxford University Press, 1992), or the opinions of such columnists as Charles Krauthammer and William Safire.

10. See, for instance, Jean-Francois Revel, *Anti-Americanism* (San Francisco: Encounter, 2004).

11. *Le Monde*, January 6, 2002.

12. *La Repubblica*, October 19, 2001.

13. Mary Nolan, "Anti-Americanism and Anti-Europeanism," in Lloyd Gardner and Marilyn Young, eds., *The New American Empire: A 21st-Century Teach-In on U.S. Foreign Policy* (New York: New Press, 2005), 113–32.

14. See David Ellwood and Rob Kroes, eds., *Hollywood in Europe: Experiences of a Cultural Hegemony* (Amsterdam: VU University Press, 1994); Heide Fehrenbach and Uta G. Poiger, eds., *The American Cultural Impact on Germany, France, Italy, and Japan, 1945–1995* (Providence, R.I.: Berghahn, 1997); Rob Kroes,

ed., *Cultural Transmissions and Receptions: American Mass Culture in Europe* (Amsterdam: VU University Press, 1993); Rob Kroes, *If You've Seen One, You've Seen the Mall: Europeans and American Mass Culture* (Urbana: University of Illinois Press, 1996); Richard Pells, *Not Like Us: How European Have Loved, Hated, and Transformed American Culture since World War II* (New York: Basic Books, 1997); Federico Romero, "Americanization and National Identity: The Case of Postwar Italy," in *Europe, Its Borders and the Others,* ed. Luciano Tosi (Naples: Edizioni Scientifiche Italiane, 2000), 263–77; Mel van Elteren, *Imagining America: Dutch Youth and Its Sense of Place* (Tilburg: Tilburg University Press, 1994); Reinhold Wagnleitner, *Coca-Colonization and the Cold War: The Cultural Mission of the United States in Austria after the Second World War* (Chapel Hill: University of North Carolina Press, 1994); Reinhold Wagnleitner and Elaine Tyler May, eds., *"Here, There, and Everywhere": The Foreign Policy of American Popular Culture* (Hanover, N.H.: University Press of New England, 2000).

15. European Commission, *How European See Themselves,* Brussels, 2001, at http://europa.eu.int/comm/publications/booklets/eu_documentation/05/txt_en.pdf.

16. See Pew Global Attitudes Project, *Views of a Changing World,* June 2003, at http://people-press.org/reports/pdf/185.pdf, and also the commentary at http://people-press.org/commentary/display.php3?AnalysisID=86. Similar data and results emerge from the *Globalisation. Flash Eurobarometer* survey, November 2003, at http://europa.eu.int/comm/public_opinion/flash/FL151b GlobalisationREPORT.pdf.

17. See Pew Research Center. *Multinational Poll in France, Germany, Great Britain, and Italy,* August 15, 2001, at http://www.people-press.org.

18. See Pew Global Attitudes Project, *Views of a Changing World.*

19. *Le Nouvel Observateur,* December 18, 2001.

20. See Pew Global Attitudes Project, *A Year after Iraq War: Mistrust of America in Europe Ever Higher, Muslim Anger Persists,* March 16, 2004, at http://people-press.org/reports/print.php3?PageID=796

21. Pew Global Attitudes Project, *Year after Iraq War.*

22. See, for instance, Denis Lacorne, Jacques Rupnik, and Marie-France Toinet, eds., *The Rise and Fall of Anti-Americanism: A Century of French Perceptions* (London: Macmillan, 1990), especially "Introduction: France Bewitched by America," by Lacorne and Rupnik, 1–31.

23. See the survey "A Nation Apart," in *The Economist,* November 8, 2003. For the data on TV programming, *The Economist,* April 5, 2003.

24. Among the many instant analyses of this phenomenon see, in particular, Timothy Garton Ash, "Anti-Europeanism in America," *New York Review of Books,* February 13, 2003.

25. *Eurobarometer 60. Public Opinion in the European Union*, Autumn 2003, at http://europa.eu.int/comm/public_opinion/archives/eb/eb60/eb60_rapport_standard_en.pdf; and *Globalisation. Flash Eurobarometer*.

26. See Pew Global Attitudes Project, *Views of a Changing World; Worldviews 2002. American and European Public Opinion and Foreign Policy*, at http://www.worldviews.org/detailreports/compreport.pdf; *Transatlantic Trends 2003*, at http://www.transatlantictrends.org/; and Richard Bernstein, "Foreign Views of U.S. Darken Since Sept. 11," *New York Times*, September 11, 2003.

27. See Pew Global Attitudes Project, *Year after Iraq War*.

28. Pew Global Attitudes Project, *Year after Iraq War*.

29. Pew Global Attitudes Project, *American Character Gets Mixed Results. U.S. Image Up Slightly, but Still Negative*, June 2005, at www.pewglobal.org; also *Transatlantic Trends Overview 2005*, at www.transatlantictrends.org.

30. Pew Global Attitudes Project, *American Character*.

31. Geir Lundestad, *The United States and Western Europe since 1945: From "Empire" by Invitation to Transatlantic Drift* (Oxford: Oxford University Press, 2003), 281–84.

32. Charles. S. Maier, "The Politics of Productivity: Foundations of American International Economic Policy after World War II," *International Organization* 31, no. 4 (1977): 630.

33. Joseph P. Quinlan, in "Drifting Apart or Growing Together? The Primacy of the Transatlantic Economy," 2003, available at in http://transatlantic.sais-jhu.edu/PDF/Quinlan%20Text%20FINAL%20March%202003.pdf, derives, from an interesting analysis of foreign direct investment flows, the following conclusions: "Globalization is happening faster and reaching deeper between Europe and America than between any other two continents. . . . The years since the fall of the Berlin Wall have witnessed one of the greatest periods of transatlantic economic integration in history. Our mutual stake in each other's prosperity has grown dramatically since the end of the Cold War."

34. See Pew Global Attitudes Project, *Year after Iraq War*.

INDEX

❑